Thomas Aquinas

On Law, Morality, and Politics

Second Edition

Thomas Aquinas

On Law, Morality, and Politics

Second Edition

Translated by
RICHARD J. REGAN

Edited, with Introduction, Notes, and Glossary, by
WILLIAM P. BAUMGARTH AND RICHARD J. REGAN

Hackett Publishing Company, Inc.
Indianapolis/Cambridge

Printed in the United States of America

18 17 16 15   3 4 5 6 7

For further information, please address:

Hackett Publishing Company, Inc.
P.O. Box 44937
Indianapolis, IN 46244-0937
www.hackettpublishing.com

Cover design by Listenberger Design & Associates

Library of Congress Cataloging-in-Publication Data
Thomas, Aquinas, Saint, 1225?–1274
    [Summa theologica. English. Selections.]
    On law, morality, and politics / Thomas Aquinas; translated by Richard J.
Regan; edited, with introduction, notes, and glossary by William P. Baumgarth
and Richard J. Regan.—2nd ed.
        p. cm.
    Includes bibliographical references and index.
    ISBN 0-87220-664-5 (cloth)—ISBN 0-87220-663-7 (paper)
        1. Natural law. 2. Law and ethics. 3. Law and politics. I. Regan, Richard J.
II. Baumgarth, William P. III. Title.

K447.T45 A2 2002
340'.11—dc21

                                                                    2002032739

ISBN-13: 978-0-87220-664-9 (cloth)
ISBN-13: 978-0-87220-663-2 (pbk.)

Contents

v

Preface

The writings of Thomas Aquinas on morals and politics deserve wide circulation for a host of reasons. No student of political thought can be considered well-grounded in the Western tradition if the contribution of the Middle Ages to that tradition is ignored. All too often, courses in political philosophy skip rapidly from the ancients to the moderns with very little comment on the medieval period. Aquinas, of course, is not the only or even, perhaps, the most characteristic theorist of that era in the Christian West. But his ideas ought to be more familiar than those of others because we inherit from him a notion of natural law. A full, inexpensive anthology of the parts of the *Summa Theologica* dealing with the natural law will enable the student to judge firsthand the vitality of that inheritance. In our selections, we reproduce the bulk of Aquinas' analysis of law, omitting only those sections that deal with particulars of the Old and New Laws. In addition, the relationship of religion and morals to public policy is one of perennial significance. We have, therefore, included in this volume selections giving Aquinas' views on the subject as well as his treatment of conscience, justice, property, war, rebellion, and statecraft.

We present the complete argument of Aquinas on the items selected from the *Summa*, generally following the order of the *Summa* itself. We have supplemented selections from the *Summa* with a few selections from other works by him.

Translators should be faithful to the text and express the meaning of the text in felicitous English. The two objectives are often difficult to reconcile. Fidelity to the text has been our priority, but we are confident that the reader will also find the translation clear and idiomatic. The translation of some key words varies with the context and/or involves interpretation. For example, we have variously translated *ratio*, the generic Latin word for "reason," as "argument," "aspect," "consideration," "nature," "plan," "reason," and "reasoning," as appropriate in different contexts. Notes in several places indicate why we chose a particular English word as appropriate.

We wish to thank the anonymous reader who painstakingly reviewed the manuscript and made many necessary corrections and useful suggestions. We thank the University of Scranton Press for permission to adopt and adapt material in chapter one from *The Human Constitution and Virtue: Way to Happiness.*

Note on the Text

The translation of selections of the *Summa* is from the 1952 Marietti recension of the Leonine text. The translation of selections of the *Commentary on the Sentences* of Peter Lombard is from the 1856–1857 Parma edition. The translation of selections of the work *On Kingship* is from the 1979 Leonine text. In citing books and passages in the Bible, we have followed the Revised Standard Version, but we have translated Aquinas' biblical quotations as he phrases them, not as they appear in the Latin Vulgate. We have cited Plato according to the Stephanus divisions, and Aristotle according to the Bekker divisions. For patristic citations or quotations, we have referred the reader to the Migne edition.

WILLIAM P. BAUMGARTH
RICHARD J. REGAN
BRONX, NEW YORK

Introduction

Thomas Aquinas flourished in the second and third quarters of the 13th century of our era (A.D. 1224/1225–1274). A Dominican friar, he lectured at the University of Paris and taught Dominican students at Naples. Some of his writings take the form of commentaries, and we have included several selections from his *Commentary on the Sentences* of Peter Lombard. Other writings express more directly his views on certain topics, and we have included several chapters from one of these, the treatise *On Kingship*. In this genre is the *Summa Theologica*, a summary of theology he wrote toward the end of his life to introduce beginners to the study of the disciple. Selections from the *Summa* constitute the bulk of the texts in this volume.

The *Summa Theologica* is divided into four parts. Part I deals with God, creatures, and human nature. Part I–II deals with the human end, human acts in general, virtue in general, and law. Part II–II deals with specific moral virtues and specific human acts. Part III, which Aquinas did not live to complete, deals with Christ's redemptive sacrifice and the role of the sacraments in communicating its merits to the faithful.

Each part of the *Summa* consists of a number of general topics called questions, most of which are subdivided into particular inquiries called articles. For example, ST I–II, Q. 90 examines the definition of law, and A. 1 of the question defends the position that law is essentially an ordinance of reason. The articles begin with a series of objections, some of which incorporate Aquinas' own previously expressed positions into arguments against the positions he is defending in the articles. He then states and defends his own position in the particular inquiry. He concludes with replies to the objections. As Joseph Pieper has observed,[1] the structure of the articles is somewhat similar to the Socratic method employed in Platonic dialogues, but unlike the reader of Platonic dialogues, the reader of the *Summa* knows exactly what position Aquinas holds.

In the course of summarizing Christian theology, Aquinas explicitly deals with many topics of philosophical interest and advances explicitly philosophical arguments, that is, arguments based on reason rather than on Scripture or church authority. This anthology aims to present such arguments on topics related to legal, moral, and political philosophy.

---

[1]Joseph Pieper, *Guide to Thomas Aquinas* (New York: Pantheon, 1962), p. 47.

The Intellectual Context

The chief institution in which Aquinas studied and taught was the University of Paris. Beginning at Bologna in the 11th century of our era, universities rose in western Europe to provide scholarly and professional education beyond that provided by cathedral and monastic schools.[2] The University of Paris, which developed from the cathedral school of Notre Dame in the last quarter of the 12th century, was, like other universities, a corporation of students and masters free to govern itself.

The University of Paris had four faculties: arts, medicine, law, and theology. Aquinas taught in the theology faculty but also had to contest certain positions held by members of the arts faculty. The arts faculty taught arts of writing and speech (grammar, logic, and rhetoric), mathematical arts (arithmetic, geometry, astronomy, and harmony), and Aristotelian scientific and philosophical arts (principally physics, psychology, ethics, and metaphysics). The theology faculty was the most distinguished in medieval Christendom and boasted such masters as Alexander of Hales (A.D. 1170/1185–1245), Albert the Great (A.D. 1200?–1280), Bonaventure (A.D. 1217?–1274), and Aquinas himself. The lecture format typically consisted of a master's commentary on the *Sentences* of Peter Lombard (A.D. 1100?–1160), but the public disputation provided the discipline's cutting edge. The *Summa* adopted the basic question-and-answer format of the public disputation.

The chief intellectual event of the 12th and 13th centuries of our era was the reintroduction of the texts of the major works of Aristotle into western Europe.[3] Aside from logic and rhetoric, Aristotle's works had been lost to the West since the collapse of the Roman empire, although early medieval thinkers knew citations of the works by Latin authors. In the 12th century, James of Venice translated the *Physics*, the *De anima*, and the *Metaphysics* of Aristotle into Latin. In the 13th century, Robert Gosseteste produced the first complete translation of the *Nichomachean Ethics*, and William of Moerbeke revised the translations of James and newly translated other works of Aristotle. In short, by the last quarter of the 13th century, the basic corpus of Aristotle's philosophical work was

[2]On medieval universities generally, see Hilda De Ridder-Symoens, ed., *A History of the University in Europe*, vol. 1: *Universities in the Middle Ages* (Cambridge: Cambridge University Press, 1991).

[3]For an older but useful survey of the reception of Aristotle until 1277 A.D., see Fernand van Steenberghen, *Aristotle in the West: The Origins of Latin Averroism*, trans. L. Johnson (Louvain: E. Nauwalaerts, 1955). For a recent survey and annotated bibliography, see Mark D. Jordan, "Aristotelianism, Medieval," *Routledge Encyclopedia of Philosophy*, gen. ed. Edward Craig (London: Routledge, 1998).

readily available to Latin-literate scholars of the universities of western Europe. The Arabic works of Averroes (A.D. 1126–1198) had also been translated into Latin by 1240 A.D.[4]

Reconciling Aristotle with the tenets of the Christian faith posed serious problems.[5] Aristotle held that the world was uncreated, and he could be read to hold the common Greek view that the world always existed and could not have not existed, but the Christian church taught that God freely created the world and that the world had a beginning and could have not existed. Aristotle's Prime Mover was a self-absorbed intelligence who had no providential design for the world or its human inhabitants, but the Christian God was an intelligence who providentially created the world and each human being. Aristotle never clearly affirmed the personal immortality of the individual human soul, and he considered proper human behavior exclusively as a prerequisite for happiness in this life, but the Christian unequivocally affirmed the personal immortality of the individual human soul and unequivocally conditioned blessedness in the next life on proper human behavior in this one.

The nearly simultaneous introduction of Averroes as the most authoritative interpreter of Aristotle compounded these problems.[6] Where Aristotle could be interpreted to suppose rather than to affirm that the world was eternal and necessary,[7] Averroes explicitly affirmed that the world was such. Where Aristotle could be interpreted to hold that the individual human soul was intellectual and so immortal,[8] Averroes categorically denied that the individual human soul was intellectual by its own power and held that it perished with the dissolution of the human composite. And Averroes asserted not only that philosophical and religious faith were different ways of knowing but also that the way of reason, that

---

[4]Van Steenberghen, *op. cit.*; Jordan, *art. cit.*

[5]On Aristotle generally, see J. L. Ackrill, *Aristotle the Philosopher* (Oxford: Oxford University Press, 1981), and J. Barnes, *Aristotle* (Oxford: Oxford University Press, 1982).

[6]On Averroes generally, see M.-R. Heyoun and A. de Libera, *Averroes et l'averroisme* (Paris: Presses Universitaires, 1991), and O. Leaman, *Averroes and His Philosophy*, 2d ed. (Richmond, Eng.: Curzon, 1997). On Averroes and the intellect, see H. A. Davidson, *Alfarabi, Avicenna, and Averroes on Intellect* (New York: Oxford University Press, 1992).

[7]Aquinas so interpreted Aristotle. ST I, Q. 46, A. 1.

[8]Aquinas, partially on the basis of a faulty Latin translation, so interpreted Aristotle (*Commentary on the De anima* of Aristotle, Lecture 10, nn. 742–5). Aristotle himself seems to hold that the human soul as such perishes with the dissolution of the composite. He explicitly holds that the active intellect, and only the

is, the way of philosophy, is superior to the way of faith, that is, the way of theology. (Needless to add, the latter position in particular aroused opposition from contemporary Muslim theologians.)

Some masters of the arts faculty of the University of Paris enthusiastically embraced a radical Aristotelianism on the world and the human soul similar to that of Averroes. Prominent among these masters were Siger of Brabant (A.D. 1240?–1281/1284) and John of Jandun (A.D. 1286?–1328). Since radical Aristotelian views about the world and the human soul were clearly in conflict with central tenets of Christian belief, masters who taught such views openly risked condemnation by the church. Whether for this practical reason or for theoretical reasons, radical Aristotelians like Siger and John seemed to resort to what orthodox adversaries called a theory of double truth. Such a theory would involve maintaining that a proposition can be true from the perspective of reason and philosophy and simultaneously false from the perspective of faith and theology.

Augustine of Hippo (A.D. 354–430) was the foremost Western patristic theologian, and the theology faculty of the University of Paris regarded his explanation and exposition of Christian doctrine as authoritative and quasi-normative. Augustine's theology reflects the dominant Neoplatonist philosophical tradition of his time.[9] Some aspects of the Neoplatonist tradition were unacceptable to Christian thinkers. The Neoplatonist theory of emanation, the theory that the material world necessarily originated by a series of hierarchically descending radiations from an infinite source, for example, is clearly contrary to the Judeo-Christian theory of creation. But there were other elements of Neoplatonism that were attractive to Christian thinkers. The infinite perfection of the One of Neoplatonism is compatible with the infinite perfection of the Christian God. The ideal forms of Neoplatonism, if interpreted as ideas in God's mind regarding the natures of the things he created, ground the intelligibility of the world and his providence. And the Neoplatonist emphasis on the superiority of spirit over matter resonated with Christian doctrine.

---

active intellect, is immortal (*De anima* III, 5. 430a17–25), but he is ambiguous about whether that intellect is a faculty of each human being or a separate substance operative in human beings only during their lifetime. If he means the former, which is unlikely, the individual human soul as such would presumably not be immortal, although part of it would be. If he means the latter, which is likely, there would evidently be no immortality of any part of the individual human soul.

[9]On Augustine generally, see Henry Chadwick, *Augustine* (New York: Oxford University Press, 1986). On Neoplatonism in the Latin tradition, see S. Gersh, *Middleplatonism and Neoplatonism: The Latin Tradition* (Notre Dame, Ind.: University of Notre Dame Press, 1986).

On the other hand, the Aristotelian approach to philosophy was attractive from many perspectives. Aristotle's explanation of intellection, rooted in sense perception and not merely occasioned by it, seemed to correspond more closely to human experience. Where Neoplatonists regarded material things as ephemeral and unintelligible apart from the ideal forms of which they were obscure reflections, Aristotle regarded material things as unqualifiedly real and intelligible by reason of their own forms. Aristotle was thereby able to study material things, including the human composite of matter and spirit, in terms of their four causes (efficient, final, formal, and material) and foster physical sciences, albeit not physical sciences in the modern sense. Where Neoplatonists argued to the existence of the One from intramental data, Aristotle argued to the existence of the Prime Mover from extramental data (motion and change). Some of the arts faculty of the University of Paris embraced the Aristotelian philosophical perspective without reservation, and Aquinas adopted it with caution.

The Aristotelian Background

Aristotle's epistemology is realist: external reality is the measure of consciousness, and consciousness is the window on external reality. Human beings with their senses perceive an extramental material world and the things in it, and human beings with their intellects understand the nature, that is, the essential structure, of different kinds of material things, including their own. And human beings in the course of their intellectual activity know themselves as the source of their internal activities and external human actions.

We tend to identify intellectual activity with the process of reasoning, that is, the process of drawing inferences from observed facts and general principles. This reasoning can be theoretical or practical. In empirical sciences, scientists, among other things, form theories to explain observed events, deduce from the theory consequences that can be observed, and then test to see whether the deduced consequences occur. If the consequences do occur, the theory is supported but not conclusively verified; if the consequences do not occur, the theory is demonstrably false. In mathematics, mathematicians employ pure deduction to draw conclusions from postulated premises. In everyday affairs, human beings employ both inductive and deductive reasoning to reach conclusions about everything from tomorrow's likely weather to the best route to use during rush-hour traffic.

But Aristotle identifies another kind of intellectual activity, the activity by which we understand the nature or essential structure of things, including our own nature, and he is chiefly concerned with this activity

Understanding the nature of things is at the heart of Aristotle's philosophy generally, and understanding human nature is at the heart of his ethical theory specifically.

The central theme of Aristotle's metaphysics is that the natures of things determine their type of activity, and, conversely, that their specific type of activity indicates the things' natures. Plants, horses, and human beings have different ends and act in specifically different ways to achieve their ends. In Aristotle's view, the essences or natures of things, their specific ends, and the ordering of activities to ends are intelligible to human beings.

Aristotle recognizes rationality in all its dimensions, that is, both activities of reason itself (intellectual virtues) and activities in accord with right reason (moral virtues), as the characteristic that specifically distinguishes the activity of human beings from that of other animals. (See Glossary, s.v. *Intellectual Virtues, Moral Virtues.*) Human beings, of course, have animal appetites that they act to satisfy: they eat to satisfy hunger, they seek to avoid pain, and they engage in sexual activity. But as long as they act consciously, the animal activities are not merely animal but also subject to judgments of reason. That is to say, human beings have to make judgments about the relation of animal activities to the human end; they have to decide when and how much is humanly proper to eat, how to avoid and alleviate pain in humanly proper ways, and when and with whom it is humanly proper for them to have sex. They perceive food and sex as good for them, but they also, on reflection, understand that food and sex are not always good for them as individual human beings or as members of human society. And so human beings are presented with choices in their conscious activities. Human beings can understand their essential constitution and much about the world in terms of cause and effect (e.g., that eating and drinking too much will make them sick, and that indiscriminate sex will cause harm to others). And human beings by their free acts determine how they are to live in the world. Moreover, Aristotle insists that human intelligence and freedom enable human beings to develop friendships and to love other human beings.

Aristotle identifies happiness as the ultimate goal of human life and understands happiness as the objective fulfillment and perfection of human nature, not a subjective state of euphoria. And since human nature is specifically rational, human beings, in order to be happy, should engage in activities of reason itself and other activities according to right reason.[10] By repeatedly good acts, human beings develop good habits of behavior, moral virtues such as justice, moderation, and courage.

---

[10]Human beings should also engage in activities of reason itself according to right reason (i.e., neither too little nor too much).

The intellectual virtue of practical wisdom (prudence) determines the appropriate means to achieve moral virtues and so governs them. (See Glossary, s.v. *Practical Wisdom*.) Selections in this anthology chiefly involve the moral virtue of justice and the intellectual virtue of practical wisdom, especially the practical wisdom in governance. (See Glossary, s.v. *Kingly Wisdom, Political Wisdom*.)

Aristotle situates the individual's quest for virtue quintessentially within a structured society with other human beings. For him and ancient Greeks generally, only those who were more than human (pure spirits) or less than human (brute animals) could be fulfilled apart from the *polis* (the Greek city-state), and Aristotle accordingly devoted an entire work, the *Politics*, to the right ordering of the *polis*, which would develop intellectually and morally virtuous citizens. Human beings are by their nature inclined to live cooperatively in a community with other human beings, and they should do so if they wish to be happy.

The first level of human society is the family. Because human beings by their nature incline to mate and procreate, they form nuclear families, and nuclear families form extended families of blood relatives and in-laws. Out of these extended families come clans and tribes. But neither families nor small groups of families can adequately provide for their physical security or their economic sufficiency. Moreover and especially, they cannot adequately provide a broad base for the development of intellectual and moral virtues or for the cultivation of personal friendships. Only a larger, politically organized society can adequately do so.

The Thomist Perspective

Aristotle proposed the limited, albeit daunting, goal of theoretical wisdom as the most important ingredient of human happiness. (See Glossary, s.v. *Theoretical Wisdom*.) Aquinas agrees with Aristotle that theoretical wisdom is a major ingredient of happiness in this life, and that human beings, in order to be happy in this life, need a suitably sound body, external goods, and the company of friends. But Aquinas insists that the happiness attainable in this life is incomplete and imperfect, a pale reflection of the perfect happiness of beholding God's essence, and that no material or created spiritual thing, including human friendship, is essential to such perfect happiness.[11]

Both Aristotle and Aquinas recognize that human happiness in this life requires right reason to direct external action and govern internal

---

[11]Aquinas treats of happiness in ST I–II, QQ. 2–4.

emotions, as well as a rightly ordered will regarding the requisite ends of human actions and emotions. But Aquinas goes beyond Aristotle to argue that rectitude of the will entails loving as good whatever God loves, and that there is no complete rectitude of the will without conformity to God's will and his commands.[12] Reason and revelation communicate God's commands, and so human beings should conform their wills to the divine commands of both. Although it may be true, as Aquinas thought and most Christians then thought and now think, that there can be no real conflict between right reason and Christian duty, there remain questions about whether particular moral judgments of reason are right, whether Christian faith imposes particular religious duties, and how to reconcile apparent conflicts.

The goodness of the will depends exclusively on the will's object, and so it depends on reason, which presents the object to the will as in accord or discord with reason. Since the light of human reason participates in the eternal law, the goodness or malice of the will depends even more on that law. Every will acting contrary to reason, even erroneous reason, is evil, but some acts of the will in accord with erroneous reason may be evil, since human beings may be directly or indirectly (through avoidable ignorance) responsible for the fact that their reason judges erroneously.[13]

The most striking contrast between Aquinas' treatment of human acts and Aristotle's is the attention that Aquinas pays to the moral goodness and malice of individual human acts. Aristotle was largely concerned about the moral character of human acts in connection with the development of moral virtue, that is, with the consequences of morally good and bad acts for acquiring morally good or bad habits.[14] But Aquinas, although similarly concerned about the development of morally good habits, is also and primarily concerned about the moral character of individual human acts for attaining heavenly blessedness or incurring eternal damnation. That is to say, he is concerned about the moral character of human acts not only in relation to dictates of right reason and to the acquisition of virtue in this life, but also and primarily in relation to dictates of God's law and to the acquisition of the beatific vision in the next life.

For Aristotle, a virtuous life constitutes its own reward, and a vicious life constitutes its own punishment. For Aquinas, a virtuous life in this world does not confer complete happiness on human beings, and a vicious

---

[12]ST I–II, Q. 19, A. 9.   [13]ST I–II, Q. 19, AA. 1–6.

[14]But Aristotle holds certain actions, such as murder, adultery, and theft, and certain emotions, such as spite and envy, to be always shameful, that is, morally wrong. *Nichomachean Ethics* II, 6 (1107a9–27).

life does not sufficiently punish human beings with unhappiness. Moreover, not only are morally bad acts bad for their perpetrators, in Aquinas' view, but they are also and primarily offenses against God and for that reason are justly punished by him. Accordingly, the morality of every human involving serious matter is of supreme importance for human beings. For example, murder is not only contrary to the humanity of the murderer and an offense against the victim but also a serious offense against God, who justly inflicts the punishment of hell on unrepentant murderers. Conversely, just acts are not only acts that are just to others and virtuous but also acts that God's grace can render salvific, that is, worthy of heavenly reward.

Aquinas holds that some external acts are intrinsically evil.[15] Some acts are evil because their objects are evil. For example, an innocent human being does not deserve to die, and so no one should deliberately kill such a person.[16] Other acts are evil because they frustrate the intrinsic purposes of the acts. For example, lying, narrowly defined, is always wrong because it frustrates the intrinsic purpose of communicative speech,[17] and some sexual behavior is always wrong because it is contrary to the intrinsic purpose of sex.[18] Such a position on the intrinsic evil of some acts rests on the unarticulated premise that no larger purpose, however good, can render the evil acts good, and the position differs at least from Aristotle's general concern.

In his treatment of moral virtues, Aquinas follows Aristotle in many respects. As with Aristotle, the key virtue in moral matters is intellectual. Practical wisdom, that is, practical reason, directs the moral virtues by prescribing their ends (e.g., to act justly, moderately, and courageously) and by choosing the means to achieve those ends. And Aquinas, like Aristotle, recognizes that human beings acquire moral virtues by repeatedly acting virtuously. But Aquinas does not rest there. To live a consistently virtuous life, human beings after the fall of Adam need added help. And so, to strengthen the radically weakened power of human beings after the fall, God infuses supernatural moral virtues and the theological virtue of charity, which informs every moral virtue, whether naturally acquired or supernaturally infused, in those he justifies. (See Glossary, s.v. *Habit, Virtue.*)

Neither Aristotle nor Aquinas is optimistic about the possibility or likelihood of most human beings by their own power living a virtuous life. Natural aptitude, of course, will decidedly limit the possibility of most human beings acquiring scientific knowledge or theoretical wisdom, and

---

[15]ST I–II, Q. 18, A. 2.   [16]ST I–II, Q. 64, A. 6.   [17]ST II–II, Q. 110, A. 1.
[18]ST II–II, Q. 154, especially A. 11.

the dominance of inordinate desires will limit the possibility of most human beings acquiring moral virtues. Both Aristotle and Aquinas think that a rightly organized community could considerably rectify the individual's moral situation, although moral evil and its consequences can never be eliminated. They look to enlightened political leaders, that is, those with a specific practical wisdom, political prudence, to guide the community by framing laws that encourage virtue and discourage vice. Political prudence, as practical reason, should do so only in reasonable ways, sometimes punishing vice, sometimes rewarding virtue, and sometimes refraining from doing either. Coercion is appropriate only to repress vices harmful to society, and it is most appropriate to repress the vices most harmful to society (e.g., murder and robbery).[19]

But Aquinas looks primarily to the church to inculcate moral virtues in the faithful. The church accomplishes this, in part, by promising heavenly blessedness to the virtuous and by threatening sinners with the punishment of hell. This poses a problem. If both church and state are assigned authoritative roles, conflict is likely and almost inevitable unless the respective roles are clearly distinguished. In this context, it is important to realize how much Aquinas' concept of the role of religion in organized society differs from that of Aristotle. For Aristotle and the Greeks generally, religion was a necessary part of civic life that required of citizens only ritual observance. For Aquinas, the Christian religion calls the faithful to a comprehensive way of life, and the Christian church inculcates a comprehensive moral code of conduct.

Aquinas distinguishes the two roles. He calls the earthly society secular, its end the secular common good, and its structure of authority the secular power. And he calls the ecclesial society spiritual, its end the spiritual common good, and its structure of authority the spiritual power. In his view, the pope is the supreme ruler of the secular societies of medieval Christendom and of the church but ordinarily exercises secular power only in the Papal States.[20] Secular rulers exercise secular power elsewhere, and they should exercise that power to assist the spiritual power of the church,[21] even to the point of putting persistent public heretics to death.[22] They should also defer to the spiritual power of the church in cases of conflict regarding religion and morals.[23]

Aquinas' subordination of secular society to the church is incompatible with the democratic principle of personal religious freedom. The secular-

---

[19]ST I–II, Q. 96, A. 2.   [20]CS II, dist. 44, explanation of the text, *ad* 4.

[21]CS IV, dist. 37, explanation of the text, comment.

[22]ST II–II, Q. 11, A. 3.   [23]See nn. 20 and 21, supra.

spiritual terminology may have contributed to the inadequate distinction of the two societies, since secular things can involve spiritual things, and spiritual things can involve secular things. Liberal thinkers made a conceptually sharper and more functionally useful distinction. They distinguished the secular order from the *sacral* order, not the spiritual, and they explicitly denied to the state any competence in sacral matters as such, and to the church any competence in secular matters as such. This distinction is now normative in the Western world.

God's act of creation is the foundation of Aquinas' theory of moral obligation as legal obligation. By that very act, God ordains created things for their specific goals, and specific goals for an architectonic goal, and he manifests his ordinance in the natures he creates. Aquinas can properly refer to God's act of creation as law because God ordains the activities of creatures, and as eternal because his act is identical with himself.

Human beings have no choice regarding their specific goal or the rectitude of means to that goal, but they are endowed with reason and so understand that they should act in ways conducive to their specific goal. In doing so, they participate freely in the eternal law and share with their own reason and will in God's plan for themselves as individuals and as a community. And so Aquinas can properly refer to this human participation in the eternal law as natural law. Contrary to the Kantian critique of natural-law theory, Aquinas, by assigning a participatory role to human beings in legislating the eternal law for and to themselves, recognizes the necessity of personal autonomy for authentic moral decisions.

Aquinas was a Christian theologian. He considered creation, and so natural law, as one aspect of God's salvific plan for humankind. Whereas Aristotle rested content with human goodness in a self-sufficient *polis*, Aquinas was concerned as well with Christian holiness and with obedience to God's commands as part of God's salvific will. It is in this regard that the natural law has a supernatural dimension: observance of the natural law can be a grace-enriched act, and failure to observe the natural law is a sinful act. In Aquinas' view, divine revelation plays a supportive role in recognizing demands of the natural law, and divine grace plays an indispensable role in its consistent and substantial observance. Moreover, love of God is the guiding source of the morally virtuous activity of the faithful.

For both Aristotle and Aquinas, human beings need to form a body politic in order to promote their proper human development, that is, to develop themselves intellectually and morally as well as materially. But Aquinas links human law essentially to the natural law: human law is either a conclusion based on the natural law (e.g., do not steal) or a further specification of natural law (e.g., drive on the right side of the road).[24] This linkage is absolutely essential if human law is to qualify as law at all, that is, to be morally obligatory, and if human law departs from the natural law in any way, it is no law at all, that is, not morally obligatory.[25] Aquinas, however, admits that citizens may be morally obliged to obey some unjust laws, if those laws are not contrary to divine law, for the sake of the common good, namely, to avoid civil unrest and the breakdown of legal observance.[26]

Conclusion

The issues of political philosophy considered by Aquinas—the nature of the political order, the power of reason, the function of law, the meaning of justice, the relation of human acts to God's designs—reflect the concerns of the society and theology of his time. With the Western rediscovery of Aristotle in the late 12th and early 13th centuries of our era, Christian philosophers and theologians were forced to rethink the rational underpinnings of their faith. To understand Aquinas, one needs to know his philosophical and theological milieu.

But Aquinas' views on law, morality, and politics remain relevant today. The norm of morality, the function of law, the meaning of justice, and the purposes of organized society are perennial concerns. For contemporary students of moral and political theory, as for those of the past, Aquinas' views can provide insight into central problems of ethical and political life.

---

[24]ST I–II, Q. 95, A. 2.   [25]Ibid. and ST I–II, Q. 96, A. 4.
[26]ST I–II, Q. 96, A. 4.

Biblical Abbreviations

Col.	Colossians	Kgs.	Kings
Cor.	Corinthians	Lev.	Leviticus
Dan.	Daniel	Lk.	Luke
Dt.	Deuteronomy	Mc.	Maccabees
Eccl.	Ecclesiastes	Mt.	Matthew
Eph.	Ephesians	Num.	Numbers
Est.	Esther	Pet.	Peter
Ex.	Exodus	Prov.	Proverbs
Ez.	Ezekiel	Ps.	Psalms
Gal.	Galatians	Rom.	Romans
Gen.	Genesis	Sam.	Samuel
Heb.	Hebrews	Sir.	Sirach
Hos.	Hosea	Th.	Thessalonians
Is.	Isaiah	Tim.	Timothy
Jer.	Jeremiah	Tit.	Titus
Jgs.	Judges	Wis.	Wisdom
Jn.	John	Zech.	Zechariah
Jos.	Joshua		

Alternate Abbreviations

A., AA.	article, articles	Obj. (obj.)	objection
ad	response to objection	PG	J. P. Migne, *Patrologia Graeca*
c.	chapter	PL	J. P. Migne, *Patrologia Latina*
CS	Thomas Aquinas, *Commentary on the Sentences* of Peter Lombard	Q.(q.), QQ.	question, questions
		ST	Thomas Aquinas, *Summa Theologica*
dist.	distinction	tr.	treatise
Lat.	Latin	v.	verse
n.	number		

Works Cited by Aquinas

Alexander of Hales
Summary of Theology

Ambrose, St.
On Abraham
On Duties
On Faith
On Paradise
Sermons

Anselm, St.
On Truth

Aristotle
Categories
Ethics (Nicomachean)
Metaphysics
Physics
Politics
Rhetoric

Augustine
Against Adimantus, Disciple of Mani
On Catechizing the Uneducated
On the Morals of the Church
The City of God
Commentary on the Book of Genesis
Commentary on Genesis, against the Manicheans
Commentary on the Gospel of John
Confessions
Eighty-Three Questions
Enchiridion
Against Faustus
On Free Choice
On Heresies
Letters

On the Lord's Sermon on the Mount
Against Lying
On the Marital Good
Narrations on the Psalms
On the Nature of Good
On Order
Questions on the Heptateuch
Response to the Letter of Parmenian
Sermons
Sermons to the People
On the Spirit and Letter of the Law
On the Trinity
On True Religion
Against the Two Letters of Pelagius

Basil, St.
Homily on the Beginning of the Book of Proverbs
On the Six Days of Creation

Bernard of Clairvaux, St.
On Contemplation

Boethius
On the Consolation of Philosophy
On Groups of Seven

Bonaventure, St.
Commentary on the Sentences of Peter Lombard

Caesar, Julius
Gallic Wars

Cassiodorus
Expositions on the Psalms

Cato, Denis
Concise Opinions and Distichs on Morals

Chrysostom, St. John
  Homilies on the Gospel of Matthew

Cicero, Marcus Tullius
  On Duties
  On Friendship
  Rhetoric

Damascene, St. John
  On Orthodox Faith

Denis the Pseudo-Areopagite
  On the Divine Names

Glossae interlineares

Glossae ordinariae

Gratian
  Decretum

Gregory the Great, Pope St.
  Morals

Gregory IX, Pope
  Decretals

Hilary, St.
  On the Trinity

Hugh of St. Victor
  On the Sacraments

Isidore, St.
  Etymologies
  Synonyms

Authors Cited by Aquinas

Alexander of Hales (A.D. 1170?–1245)

Ambrose, St. (A.D. 340?–397)

Anselm, St. (A.D. 1033–1109)

Aristotle, "the Philosopher" (384–327 B.C.)

Augustine, St. (A.D. 354–430)

Basil, St. (A.D. 329?–379)

Bernard of Clairvaux, St. (A.D. 1090–1153)

Boethius (A.D. 480?–524?)

Bonaventure, St. (A.D. 1217?–1274)

Caesar, Julius (100–44 B.C.)

Cassiodorus (A.D. 490?–583)

Cato, Denis (fourth century A.D.)

Chrysostom, St. John (A.D. 345?–407)

Cicero, Marcus Tullius (106–43 B.C.)

Damascene, St. John (A.D. 700?–754?)

Denis the Pseudo-Areopagite (early sixth century A.D.)

Gratian (first half of 12th century A.D.)

Gregory the Great, Pope St. (A.D. 540?–604)

Gregory IX, Pope (A.D. 1170?–1241)

Hilary, St. (A.D. 315?–368?)

Hugh of St. Victor (A.D. 1096?–1141)

Isidore, St. (A.D. 560?–636)

Jerome, St. (A.D. 347?–419/420)

Justinian, "the Jurist" (A.D. 483–565)

Lombard, Peter (A.D. 1100?–1160)

Nicholas I, Pope (A.D. 819?–867)

Origen (A.D. 185?–254?)

Paul, St., "the Apostle" (first century A.D.)

Plato (428?–348/347 B.C.)

Seneca, Lucius Annaeus (4? B.C.–A.D. 65)

Valerius Maximus (early first century A.D.)

Vegetius, Flavius (fourth century A.D.)

eternal law - the plan of government within God,
all other governments are subsequent to it
natural law - how rational individuals share in the
eternal plan
human law - we advance from natural law to
particular matters

Conscience

In the view of Thomas and other medieval theologians, human beings through the use of reason can know what they should or should not do. They called this moral consciousness conscience. In ST I, Q. 79, on the intellectual powers of the soul, he distinguishes conscience from synderesis, the habitual knowledge of first moral principles (A. 12), and moral consciousness about prospective action from psychological consciousness and moral consciousness about past actions (A. 13).

In ST I–II, Q. 19, on good and evil acts of the will, Thomas explains why one is obliged not to act contrary to erroneous conscience (A. 5) but may not be excused if one acts in accord with erroneous conscience (A. 6).

ST I
Question 79
On the Intellectual Powers of the Soul

[This question is divided into thirteen articles, two of which are included here.]

TWELFTH ARTICLE
Is *Synderesis* a Special Power of the Soul?

We thus proceed to the twelfth article. It seems that *synderesis* is a special intellectual power, for the following reasons:

Obj. 1. Things that fall within one and the same classification seem to belong to one and the same genus. But a gloss of Jerome on Ez. 1:6 contradistinguishes *synderesis* from the irascible, concupiscible, and rational powers,[1] which are particular powers. Therefore, *synderesis* is a particular power.

Obj. 2. Contraries belong to the same genus. But *synderesis* and sense appetites seem to be contraries, since *synderesis* always tends toward good, and sense appetites always tend toward evil. (And it is by reason of the latter tendency that the serpent symbolizes sense appetites, as Augustine makes clear in his work *On the Trinity*.[2]) Therefore, it seems that *synderesis* is a power, just as sense appetites are powers.

---

[1]*Commentary on the Book of Ezekiel*, on 1:6 (PL 25:22).
[2]*On the Trinity* XII, 12 and 13 (PL 42:1007, 1009).

Obj. 3. Augustine says in his work *On Free Choice* that the natural power of judgment has certain "rules and sources of virtue that are both true and invariable,"[3] and we call these rules and sources of virtue *synderesis*. Therefore, since the invariable rules by means of which we judge belong to reason regarding its higher part, as Augustine says in his work *On the Trinity*,[4] it seems that synderesis is the same as reason. And so it is a power.

On the contrary, "rational powers are disposed toward contraries," as the Philosopher says.[5] But *synderesis* is not disposed toward contraries; rather, synderesis tends only to what is good. Therefore, *synderesis* is not a power. For if *synderesis* were to be a power, it would necessarily be a rational power, since it does not exist in irrational animals.

I answer that synderesis is a characteristic disposition rather than a power, notwithstanding the fact that some thinkers held *synderesis* to be a power higher than reason,[6] and other thinkers said that *synderesis* is reason itself, not as the power of reason but as human nature.[7]

And to prove this, we need to consider that, as I have said before,[8] human reasoning, since it is a movement, progresses from an understanding of some things, namely, things known by nature without inquiry by reason, as from a fixed source. And human reasoning also terminates in understanding, since it is by naturally self-evident principles that we judge about the things we discover in the process of reasoning. Moreover, practical reason evidently reasons about practical matters just as theoretical reason reasons about theoretical matters. Therefore, as nature needs to implant in us the first principles concerning theoretical matters, so also does nature need to implant in us the first principles concerning practical matters.

But the first principles about theoretical matters, principles implanted in us by nature, do not belong to any special power but to a special characteristic disposition, which we call "the understanding of principles," as the *Ethics* makes clear.[9] And so the principles about practical matters, principles implanted in us by nature, likewise do not belong to a special power but to a characteristic disposition from nature, and we call this disposition *synderesis*. And so also we say that *synderesis* incites to good and complains about evil, since we progress by first principles to discovery and judge about the things we have discovered. Therefore, *synderesis* is clearly a characteristic disposition from nature, not a power.

---

[3]*On Free Choice* II, 10 (PL 32:1256).   [4]*On the Trinity* XII, 2 (PL 42:999).

[5]*Metaphysics* IX, 2 (1046b4–7).   [6]E.g., William of Auxerre, *Golden Summary* II, tr. 2, c. 1.   [7]E.g., Alexander of Hales, *Summary of Theology* I–II, n. 418.

[8]ST I, Q. 79, A. 8.   [9]Aristotle, *Ethics* VI, 6 (1140b31–1141a8).

*Reply Obj.*1. We note Jerome's classification with respect to different acts, not different powers. And different acts can belong to the same power.

Reply Obj. 2. Similarly, we note the contrariety of sense appetites and *synderesis* by the contrariety of acts, not the contrariety of different species belonging to the same genus.

Reply Obj. 3. Such invariable considerations are the first principles about practical matters, and there can be no error about the principles. And we attribute such considerations to reason as the power and to *synderesis* as the characteristic disposition. And so also do we judge by nature by both, namely, by reason and *synderesis*.

THIRTEENTH ARTICLE
Is Conscience a Power?

We thus proceed to the thirteenth article.

It seems that conscience is a power, for the following reasons:

Obj. 1. Origen says that conscience is "the correcting spirit and companion teacher of the soul whereby the soul is dissociated from evil and clings to good."[10] But spirit designates a power of the soul. And this power is either the very power of the mind, as Eph. 4:23 says: "Be renewed in the spirit of your minds," or the very power of imagination, which is also why we call the sight of imagination "spiritual," as Augustine makes clear in his *Commentary on the Book of Genesis.*[11] Therefore, conscience is a power.

Obj. 2. Only powers of the soul are subjects of sin. But conscience is a subject of sin, since Tit. 1:15 says of certain individuals that "their minds and consciences are defiled." Therefore, it seems that conscience is a power.

Obj. 3. Conscience needs to be either an act or a characteristic disposition or a power. But conscience is not an act, since conscience would thereby not always abide in human beings. Nor is conscience a characteristic disposition, for conscience would thereby be many things rather than one thing, since many cognitive characteristic dispositions guide us in practical matters. Therefore, conscience is a power.

On the contrary, conscience can be laid aside, but a power cannot be. Therefore, conscience is not a power.

I answer that conscience, properly speaking, is an act, not a power. And this is evident both from the meaning of the word and from the things that we in our ordinary way of speaking attribute to conscience. For conscience, according to the proper meaning of the word, signifies

[10]*Commentary on the Letter to the Romans* II, on 2:15 (PG 14:893).

[11]*Commentary on the Book of Genesis* XII, 7 and 24 (PL 34:459, 475).

the relation of knowledge to something else, since we define *con-science* as knowledge with something else. But acts connect knowledge to things. And so it is clear from the meaning of the word that conscience is an act.

And the same conclusion is evident from the things that we attribute to conscience. For we say that conscience bears witness, morally obliges or stirs to action, and accuses or disquiets or reproves. And all of these things result from connecting some knowledge of ours to what we do. And this connection arises in three ways. It arises in one way as we recognize that we have or have not done something, as Eccl. 7:23 says: "Your conscience knows" that you have "very often" spoken evil "of others." And we accordingly say that conscience bears witness. In a second way, we connect our knowledge to something as we by our conscience judge that we should or should not do something. And we accordingly say that conscience incites to action or morally obliges. In a third way, we connect our knowledge to something as we by our conscience judge that we have or have not done something worthily. And we accordingly say that conscience excuses, or accuses and disquiets. But all three of these ways clearly result from the actual connection of knowledge to what we do. And so, properly speaking, conscience designates an act.

Nevertheless, because characteristic dispositions are the sources of acts, we sometimes apply the word *conscience* to the initial characteristic dispositions from nature, namely, *synderesis*. For example, Jerome in a gloss on Ez. 1:6 calls conscience *synderesis*,[12] and Basil calls it "the natural power of judgment,"[13] and Damascene calls it "the law of our intellect." For we customarily designate causes and effects by one another.[14]

Reply Obj. 1. Because conscience is an utterance of the mind, we call conscience spirit insofar as we equate spirit and mind.

Reply Obj. 2. We do not say that conscience has defilement as a subject, but we say that conscience has defilement as something known belongs to knowledge, namely, as one knows that one is defiled.

Reply Obj. 3. Although acts in themselves do not always abide, they nonetheless abide in their causes, which are powers and characteristic dispositions. But all the characteristic dispositions that shape conscience, however many, still have their efficacy from one that is primary, namely, the characteristic disposition of first principles. And we call this characteristic disposition *synderesis*. And so we sometimes in a special way call this characteristic disposition conscience, as I have said before.[15]

---

[12]See n. 1, supra.

[13]*Homily on the Beginning of the Book of Proverbs* (PG 31:405).

[14]*On Orthodox Faith* IV, 22 (PG 94:1200).   [15]In the body of the article.

ST I–II
Question 19
On the Goodness and Malice of Interior Acts of the Will

[This question is divided into ten articles, two of which are included here.]

FIFTH ARTICLE
Is the Will Evil if It Wills Contrary to Erroneous Reason?

We thus proceed to the fifth article. It seems that the will is not evil if it wills contrary to erroneous reason, for the following reasons:

Obj. 1. Reason is the rule of the human will insofar as reason derives from the eternal law, as I have said.[1] But erroneous reason does not derive from the eternal law. Therefore, erroneous reason is not the rule of the human will. Therefore, the will is not evil if it wills contrary to erroneous reason.

Obj. 2. The command of a subordinate official does not oblige a subject if the command happens to be contrary to the command of a higher authority, as Augustine says.[2] For example, a subject is not obliged to obey if a provincial governor should command something that the emperor prohibits. But erroneous reason at times presents to the will something contrary to the command of a higher authority, namely, God, whose power is supreme. Therefore, the judgment of erroneous reason does not oblige persons to obey. Therefore, the will is not evil if it wills contrary to erroneous reason.

Obj. 3. We trace every bad will to a species of malice. But we cannot trace a will that wills contrary to erroneous reason to a species of evil. For example, if reason erroneously tells a person to fornicate, we cannot trace the person's willing not to do so to any species of evil. Therefore, the will is not evil if it wills contrary to erroneous reason.

On the contrary, conscience simply applies one's knowledge to actions, as I have said before.[3] And knowledge belongs to the power of reason. Therefore, the will that wills contrary to erroneous reason wills contrary to conscience. But every such willing is evil, for Rom. 14:23 says: "Everything not of faith," that is, everything contrary to conscience, "is sin." Therefore, the will is evil if it wills contrary to erroneous reason.

I answer that to ask whether the will is evil when it acts contrary to erroneous reason is the same as to ask whether erroneous conscience

---

[1]ST I–II, Q. 19, A. 4.   [2]*Sermons to the People*, sermon 62, c. 8 (PL 38:421).
[3]ST I, Q. 79, A. 13.

obliges persons to obey. This is so because conscience is in a way a judgment of reason, since conscience applies one's knowledge to actions, as I have said in the First Part.[4]

And on this matter, some thinkers have distinguished three kinds of acts: some acts are indeed good by their nature, some acts morally indifferent, and some acts evil by their nature.[5] Therefore, they say that there is no error in reason or conscience if reason or conscience should tell a person to do something that is good by its nature. Similarly, there is no error if reason or conscience should tell a person not to do something that is evil by its nature, for the same power of reason commands persons to do good and forbids them to do evil. But if reason or conscience should tell a person that human beings are obliged by precept to do something intrinsically evil, or that human beings are prohibited from doing something intrinsically good, the person's reason or conscience will be in error. And reason or conscience will likewise be in error if it should tell someone that something as such morally indifferent (e.g., picking up straw from the ground) is forbidden or commanded.

Therefore, they say that reason or conscience, when it errs about morally indifferent things, whether by command or injunction, obliges one to obey, so that the will will be evil if it wills contrary to erroneous reason, and there will be sin. On the other hand, reason or conscience, when it errs by commanding something intrinsically evil, or when it errs by forbidding something intrinsically good and necessary for salvation, does not oblige persons to obey. And so the will in such cases is not evil if it wills contrary to erroneous reason or conscience.

But such an explanation is unsound. For the will that wills contrary to erroneous reason or conscience in morally indifferent matters, is somehow evil because of the will's object, on which the will's goodness or malice depends. And this is not because of the object's own nature but because reason happens to understand the object as an evil to be committed or shunned. And the will's object is what reason presents to the will, as I have said.[6] Therefore, by tending toward something that reason proposes as evil, the will takes on the character of evil. And this happens both in the case of morally indifferent things and in the case of things intrinsically good or evil. For not only can morally indifferent things happen to take on the character of good or evil, but good things can likewise take on

---

[4]Ibid.   [5]St. Bonaventure, *Commentary on the Sentences* II, dist. 39, a. 1, q. 3; Alexander of Hales, *Summary of Theology* II–II, n. 388.
[6]ST I–II, Q. 18, A. 3.

the character of evil, or evil things the character of good, because reason so understands them.

For example, abstaining from fornication is good, although the will tends toward this good only insofar as reason so presents it. Therefore, if erroneous reason presents such abstinence as evil, the will tends toward it as evil. And so the will will be evil because it wills something evil, indeed not something intrinsically evil but something that happens to be evil because reason so understands it. And similarly, belief in Christ is intrinsically good and necessary for salvation, but the will tends toward that good only insofar as reason so presents it. And so the will tends toward belief in Christ as evil if reason so presents it, not because such belief is intrinsically evil, but because it happens to be evil due to the way reason understands it.

And so the Philosopher says in the Ethics that "an intemperate person is, strictly speaking, one who does not follow right reason, but those who do not follow erroneous reason are also incidentally intemperate."[7] And so we need to say without qualification that every will that wills contrary to reason, whether reason be correct or erroneous, is always evil.

Reply Obj. 1. Although the judgments of erroneous reason are not derived from God, erroneous reason nonetheless presents its judgments as true and so derived from God, who is the source of all truth.

Reply Obj. 2. The statement of Augustine is appropriate when we know that a subordinate official commands something contrary to the command of a higher authority. But if a subject were to believe that the emperor commands what the provincial governor commands, the subject would scorn the emperor's command if the subject scorned the provincial governor's command. And similarly, human beings would not be obliged to follow reason if they were to know that human reason commanded something contrary to God's command, although reason would not then be completely in error. But if reason presents something to the will as God's command, to scorn the dictate of reason would then be the same as to scorn God's command.

Reply Obj. 3. Whenever reason understands something to be evil, reason understands it under some aspect of evil, for example, evil because contrary to God's command, or because of scandal, or for some such reason. And then we trace such a bad will to such a species of evil.

---

[7] *Ethics* VII, 9 (1151a29–b4).

SIXTH ARTICLE
Is the Will Good if It Wills in Accord with Erroneous Reason?

We thus proceed to the sixth article. It seems that the will is good if it wills in accord with erroneous reason, for the following reasons:

Obj. 1. As a will that wills contrary to reason tends toward what reason judges to be evil, so a will that wills in accord with reason tends toward what reason judges to be good. But the will is evil if it wills contrary to reason, even erroneous reason. Therefore, the will is good if it wills in accord with reason, even erroneous reason.

Obj. 2. A will is always good if it is in accord with God's commands and the eternal law. But the understanding of reason, even erroneous reason, presents the eternal law and God's commands to us. Therefore, the will is good even if it wills in accord with erroneous reason.

Obj. 3. The will is evil when it wills contrary to erroneous reason. Therefore, if the will be also evil when it wills in accord with erroneous reason, it seems that the will is evil whenever the person willing reasons erroneously. And so such human beings will be caught in a dilemma and necessarily sin, and this is inappropriate. Therefore, the will is good when it wills in accord with erroneous reason.

On the contrary, the will of those who killed the Apostles was evil. And yet the will of those killers was in accord with erroneous reason, as Jn. 16:2 says: "The hour is coming, and then all those who kill you will think that they are offering service to God." Therefore, the will can be evil when it wills in accord with erroneous reason.

I answer that, as the previous question is the same as to ask whether an erroneous conscience obliges persons, so the present question is the same as to ask whether an erroneous conscience excuses persons. But the present question depends on what I previously said about ignorance. For I have previously said that ignorance sometimes causes and sometimes does not cause things to be involuntary.[8] And acts have moral good and evil insofar as they are voluntary, as is evident from what I have previously explained.[9] Therefore, the ignorance that causes things to be involuntary evidently takes away the character of moral good and evil, while the ignorance that does not cause things to be involuntary evidently does not take away that character. I have also said before that the ignorance that is in any way voluntary, whether directly or indirectly, does not cause things to be involuntary.[10] And I call that ignorance directly voluntary toward which acts of the will tend. And I call that ignorance indirectly voluntary that is

---

[8]ST I–II, Q. 6, A. 8.   [9]ST I–II, Q. 19, A. 2.   [10]ST I–II, Q. 6, A. 8.

due to negligence, in that persons do not will to know what they are obliged to know, as I have said before.[11]

Therefore, if reason or conscience should err voluntarily, whether directly or due to negligence (in that persons err about things they are obliged to know), then such an error of reason or conscience does not excuse from evil the will that wills in accord with the reason or conscience erring in this way. But if the error that causes something to be involuntary comes from ignorance of a particular circumstance without any negligence on the person's part, then such an error of reason or conscience excuses the person. And so the person's will is not evil when it wills in accord with erroneous reason. For example, if erroneous reason should tell a man that he ought to have intercourse with someone else's wife, the will in accord with such an erroneous reason is evil, since the error springs from ignorance of God's law, which he is obliged to know. But if his reason should err in thinking that the woman lying with him is his wife, and he should will to have intercourse with her when she seeks from him the right of a wife to intercourse with her husband, his will is excused and so is not evil. This is because the error springs from ignorance of the circumstance. And such ignorance excuses the person and causes the evil deed to be involuntary.

Reply Obj. 1. As Denis says in his work *On the Divine Names*,[12] "an uncorrupted cause causes good, and single defects cause evil." And so for us to call evil things toward which the will inclines, it suffices either that the things be evil by their nature, or that we understand them to be evil. But for the things to be good, they need to be good in both ways.

Reply Obj. 2. The eternal law cannot err, but human reason can. And so the will is not always correct when it wills in accord with human reason, nor is such a will always in accord with the eternal law.

Reply Obj. 3. As unsuitable consequences necessarily result from unsuitable antecedents in the case of syllogistic arguments, so unsuitable consequences necessarily result from unsuitable suppositions in the case of moral matters. For example, supposing that persons seek vainglory, they will sin whether they on that account do or omit to do what they are obliged to do. And yet they are not caught in a dilemma, since they can abandon their evil intention. And similarly, supposing an error of reason or conscience that springs from inexcusable ignorance, evil in the will necessarily results. And yet persons so erring are not caught in a dilemma, since they can draw away from their error, because their ignorance is voluntary and can be overcome.

---

[11]Ibid. [12]*On the Divine Names* 4 (PG 3:729).

2

Law

In ST I–II, Q. 90, Thomas defines law: law is an ordinance of reason for the common good by one competent to make it, and promulgated. In Q. 91, he distinguishes four kinds of law: eternal, natural, human, and divine. The effect of law is to make human beings good (Q. 92). The eternal law is God's plan of creation, which directs the actions of creatures to their appointed ends (Q. 93). The natural law is God's plan for human beings as communicated to them by reason, and the law includes primary and secondary precepts (Q. 94). Human laws are ordinances of rulers for their subjects, beneficial to human beings, and derived from the natural law in two ways (Q. 95). Only just human laws impose moral obligation on subjects, and the laws need not prohibit all vices (Q. 96). Customs help to interpret human laws, and the laws should be revised cautiously (Q. 97). There was one divine law of the Old Testament, and there is now a divine law of the New Testament (Q. 91, A. 5).

Q. 100 examines the relationship of the moral precepts of the Old Law, especially the Ten Commandments, to the natural law, in the course of which Thomas makes an important distinction between proximate and remote secondary precepts of the natural law (A. 3).

In Q. 105, A. 1, Thomas describes different forms of government and defends the "mixed" regime under Moses and the Judges as the best. For more on the topic of human governance, see Chapter 8.

ST I–II,
Question 90
On the Essence of Law

FIRST ARTICLE
Does Law Belong to Reason?

We thus proceed to the first inquiry. It seems that law does not belong to reason, for the following reasons:

Obj. 1. The Apostle in Rom. 7:23 says: "I perceive another law in my bodily members," etc. But nothing belonging to reason belongs to bodily members, since reason does not use bodily organs. Therefore, law does not belong to reason.

Obj. 2. Only power, habits, and acts belong to reason. But law is not the very power of reason. Likewise, law is not a habit of reason, since habits of reason are intellectual virtues, about which I have spoken before.[1] Nor is law an act of reason, since law would cease when the lawmaker ceased to reason (e.g., when he is sleeping). Therefore, law does not belong to reason.

Obj. 3. Law induces those subject to the law to act rightly. But inducing to act rightly belongs in the strict sense to the will, as is evident from what I have said before.[2] Therefore, law belongs to the will rather than to reason, as the Jurist also says: "The pleasure of the ruler has the force of law."[3]

On the contrary, it belongs to law to command and forbid. But to command belongs to reason, as I have maintained before.[4] Therefore, law belongs to reason.

I answer that law is a rule and measure of acts that induces persons to act or refrain from acting. For *law* [Lat.: *lex*] is derived from *binding* [Lat.: *ligare*] because law obliges persons to act. And the rule and measure of human acts is reason, which is the primary source of human acts, as is evident from what I have said before.[5] For it belongs to reason to order us to our end, which is the primary source regarding our prospective action, as the Philosopher says.[6] And the source in any kind of thing is the measure and rule of that kind of thing (e.g., units in numbers and first movements in movements). And so we conclude that law belongs to reason.

Reply Obj. 1. We say that law, since it is a rule or measure, belongs to something in two ways. It belongs in one way as to what measures and rules. And law in this way belongs only to reason, since measuring and ruling belong to reason. Law belongs to something in a second way as to what is ruled and measured. And then law applies to everything that a law induces to something, so that we can call every inclination resulting from a law law by participation, as it were, not essentially. And we in this way call the very inclination of bodily members to concupiscence the law of the bodily members.

Reply Obj. 2. Regarding external acts, we can consider the activity and the product of the activity (e.g., building and the work built). Just so, regarding acts of reason, we can consider the very acts of reason (i.e., acts of understanding and reasoning) and the things produced by such acts. And regarding theoretical reason, definitions are indeed the first product. Propositions are the second product. And syllogisms and arguments the third product. And practical reason also uses a kind of syllogism regarding prospective actions, as I have maintained before,[7] and as the

---

[1]ST I–II, Q. 57.   [2]ST I II, Q. 9, A. 1.   [3]*Digest* I, title 4, law 1.
[4]ST I–II, Q. 17, A. 1.   [5]ST I–II, Q. 1, A. 1, *ad* 3   [6]*Physics* II, 9 (200a22–4).
[7]ST I–II: Q. 13, A. 3; Q. 76, A. 1; Q. 77, A. 2, *ad* 4.

Philosopher teaches in the *Ethics*.[8] Therefore, there are things in practical reason that are related to actions as propositions in theoretical reason are related to conclusions. And such universal propositions of practical reason related to actions have the nature[9] of law. And reason indeed sometimes actually considers and sometimes only habitually retains these propositions.

Reply Obj. 3. Reason has from the will the power to induce activity, as I have said before,[10] since reason commands means because one wills one's end. But an act of reason needs to rule the will regarding the means commanded in order that the willing have the nature of law. And we in this way understand that the will of a ruler has the force of law. Otherwise, the willing of the ruler would be injustice rather than law.

SECOND ARTICLE
Is Law Always Ordered to the Common Good?

We thus proceed to the second article. It seems that law is not ordered to the common good as its end, for the following reasons:

Obj. 1. It belongs to law to command and forbid. But precepts are ordered to particular goods. Therefore, the end of law is not always the common good.

Obj. 2. Law directs the actions of human beings. But human acts regard particulars. Therefore, law is likewise ordered to particular goods.

Obj. 3. Isidore says in his *Etymologies*: "If law is based on reason, everything founded on reason will be law."[11] But both things ordered to the common good and things ordered to private good are based on reason. Therefore, law is ordered both to the common good and to the private good of individuals.

On the contrary, Isidore says in his *Etymologies* that laws are "enacted for no private convenience but for the common benefit of citizens."[12]

I answer that, as I have said,[13] law belongs to the source of human acts, since law is their rule and measure. And as reason is the source of human acts, so also is there in reason itself something that is the source of all other kinds of acts. And so law needs chiefly and especially to belong to this source.

---

[8]Ethics VII, 3 (1147a24–31).

[9]*Ratio* in this and like contexts (e.g., ST I–II, Q. 94, AA. 2 and 4) signifies the character or essential element of some class of thing, the objective content of the idea of the class. We use the word "nature" here and elsewhere to convey this sense where appropriate.

[10]ST I–II, Q. 17, A. 1.   [11]*Etymologies* II, 10 (PL 82:130); V, 3 (PL 82:199).

[12]Ibid., V, 21 (Pl 82:203).   [13]ST I–II, Q. 90, A. 1.

And the first source in practical matters, with which practical reason is concerned, is the ultimate end. But the ultimate end of human life is happiness or blessedness, as I have maintained before.[14] And so law especially needs to regard the order of things to blessedness.

Moreover, law in the strict sense needs to concern the order of things to happiness in general, since every part is related to a whole as something imperfect to something perfect. And so also the Philosopher, regarding the cited definition of law,[15] speaks of both happiness and political community. For he says in the *Ethics* that "we call those laws just that constitute and preserve happiness and its particulars by citizens' sharing in a political community."[16] For the political community is the perfect community, as he says in the *Politics*.[17]

And regarding any kind of thing, the one we call most such is the source of the others, and we call the others such by their relation to that one. For example, fire, which is hottest, causes heat in composite material substances, which we call hot insofar as they share in fire. And so, since we chiefly call something law because it orders things to the common good, every other precept regarding particular acts has the nature of law only because it orders things to the common good. And so every law is ordered to the common good.

Reply Obj. 1. Precepts signify the application of laws to things regulated by the laws. And the order of things to the common good, which belongs to law, can be applied to particular ends. And so there can be precepts even regarding particular matters.

Reply Obj. 2. Actions indeed concern particular matters, but such particulars can be related to the common good by sharing in the final cause, insofar as we call the common good the common end, not by sharing in a genus or species.

Reply Obj. 3. As theoretical reason firmly establishes nothing except by tracing things back to first indemonstrable principles, so practical reason firmly establishes nothing except by ordering things to our ultimate end, that is, our common good. And what reason so establishes has the nature of law.

THIRD ARTICLE
Is Any Person's Reason Competent to Make Law?

We thus proceed to the third article. It seems that any person's reason is competent to make law, for the following reasons:

---

[14]*ST* I–II: Q. 2, A. 7; Q. 3, A. 1; Q. 69, A. 1.   [15]In the section *On the contrary*.
[16]*Ethics* V, 1 (1129b17–9).   [17]*Politics* I, 1 (1252a5–7).

Obj. 1. The Apostle says in Rom. 2:14 that "when the Gentiles, who do not have the law, by nature do the things the law prescribes, they make law for themselves." But we say the same about everybody. Therefore, anyone can make law for oneself.

Obj. 2. As the Philosopher says in the *Ethics*,[18] "lawmakers aim to induce human beings to virtue." But any human being can lead others to virtue. Therefore, the reason of any human being is competent to make law.

Obj. 3. As the ruler of a political community governs that community, so the head of a household governs his household. But the ruler of a political community can make laws regarding the political community. Therefore, any head of a household can make laws regarding his household.

On the contrary, Isidore says in his *Etymologies*,[19] and the *Decretum*[20] maintains: "Law is an ordinance of the people whereby elders and commoners together prescribe things." Therefore, not every person's reason is competent to make law.

I answer that law in the strict sense primarily and chiefly regards the order of things to the common good. But ordering things to the common good belongs either to the whole people[21] or to persons acting in the name of the whole people. And so lawmaking belongs either to the whole people or to a public personage who has the care of the whole people. For also in all other matters, ordering things to ends belongs to those to whom the ends belong.

Reply Obj. 1. As I have said before,[22] law belongs both to those who rule and, by participation, to those who are ruled. And it is in the latter way that everyone makes law for oneself, as one participates in the ordinances of the ruler. And so also the Apostle adds in Rom. 2:15: "And they manifest the law's operation written in their hearts."

Reply Obj. 2. Private persons cannot effectively induce others to virtue. For private persons can only offer advice and have no coercive power if their advice should not be accepted. And law should have coercive power in order to induce others effectively to virtue, as the Philosopher says in the *Ethics*.[23] But the people or a public personage has such coercive power

---

[18]*Ethics* II, 1 (1103b3–4).   [19]*Etymologies* V, 10 (PL 82:200).

[20]Gratian, *Decretum* I, dist. 2, c. 1.

[21]The Latin word *multitudo* literally signifies ordinary people, the many as opposed to the few (usually the rulers). But Thomas here uses the word in the same sense as the Latin word *populus*, the people as a political unit. The modifying adjective "whole" makes this usage clear. Cf. ST I–II, Q. 97, A. 3, *ad* 3, where he uses *multitudo* and *populus* interchangeably.

[22]ST I–II, Q. 90, A. 1, *ad* 1.   [23]*Ethics* X, 9 (1180a20).

and the right to inflict punishment, as I shall explain later.[24] And so it belongs only to the people or a public personage to make law.

Reply Obj. 3. As human beings are parts of a household, so households are parts of a political community, as the *Politics* says.[25] And so, as the good of a human being is not the ultimate end of that individual but ordered to the common good, so also the good of a household is ordered to the good of a political community, which is a perfect community. And so those who govern households can indeed make precepts and rules, but such precepts and rules do not have the nature of law in the strict sense. *nature of law is for polity*

FOURTH ARTICLE
Is Promulgation an Essential Component of Law?

announcing the law

We thus proceed to the fourth article. It seems that promulgation is not an essential component of law, for the following reasons:

Obj. 1. The natural law most has the nature of law. But the natural law does not need to be promulgated. Therefore, promulgation is not an essential component of law.

Obj. 2. Obligation to do or not to do things belongs in the strict sense to law. But both those to whom laws have been promulgated and those to whom laws have not are obliged to obey laws. Therefore, promulgation is not an essential component of law.

Obj. 3. The obligation to obey laws also extends to the future, since "laws impose obligation regarding future affairs," as the *Code* says.[26] But laws are promulgated to those present at their promulgation. Therefore, promulgation is not an essential component of law.

On the contrary, the *Decretum* says that "laws are established when they are promulgated."[27]

I answer that laws are imposed on others as rules and measures, as I have said.[28] But rules and measures are imposed by being applied to those ruled and measured. And so laws, in order to oblige persons, as is proper to law, need to be applied to those who are to be ruled by the laws. But the promulgation leading them to knowledge achieves such application. And *OFC?* so promulgation is necessary for laws to be in force.

And so we can compose the definition of law from the four characteristics I have mentioned: law is an order of reason for the common good by one who has the care of the community, and promulgated.

---

[24] ST I–II, Q. 92, A. 2, *ad* 3; II–II, Q. 64, A. 3.

[25] Aristotle, *Politics* I, 1 (1252a5–7).   [26] Justinian, *Code* I, title 14, law 7.

[27] Gratian, *Decretum* I, dist. 4, c. 3.   [28] ST I–II, Q. 90, A. 1.

Reply Obj. 1. The natural law is promulgated by God when he implants it in the minds of human beings so that they know it by nature.

Reply Obj. 2. Those to whom a law is not promulgated are obliged to observe it insofar as others make it known to them, or it can become known to them after it has been promulgated.

Reply Obj. 3. The present promulgation of a law reaches into the future through the durability of written words, which in a way are always promulgating it. And so Isidore says in his *Etymologies* that "we derive *law* [Lat.: *lex*] from *reading* [Lat.: *legere*], since law is written."[29]

Question 91
On Different Kinds of Law

FIRST ARTICLE
Is There an Eternal Law?

We thus proceed to the first inquiry. It seems that there is no eternal law, for the following reasons:

Obj. 1. Every law is imposed on particular persons. But there was no one from eternity on whom law could be imposed, since only God was from eternity. Therefore, no law is eternal.

Obj. 2. Promulgation is an essential component of law. But there could be no promulgation from eternity, since there was no one from eternity to whom a law would be promulgated. Therefore, no law can be eternal.

Obj. 3. Law signifies the direction to an end. But nothing ordered to an end is eternal, since only the ultimate end is eternal. Therefore, no law is eternal.

On the contrary, Augustine says in his work *On Free Choice*: "No one with intelligence can perceive the law called supreme reason not to be immutable and eternal."[1]

I answer that, as I have said before,[2] law is simply a dictate of practical reason by a ruler who governs a perfect community. But supposing that God's providence rules the world, as I maintained in the First Part,[3] his reason evidently governs the entire community of the universe. And so the plan of governance of the world existing in God as the ruler of the universe has the nature of law. And since God's reason conceives eternally, as Prov. 8:23 says, not temporally, we need to say that such law is eternal.

---

[29]*Etymologies* II, 10 (PL 82:130); V, 3 (PL 82:199).

[1]*On Free Choice* I, 6, n. 15 (PL 32:1229).   [2]ST I–II, Q. 90: A. 1, *ad* 2; AA. 3–4.
[3]ST I, Q. 22, AA. 1, 2.

Reply Obj. 1. Things that do not exist in themselves exist with God insofar as he foreknows and foreordains them, as Rom. 4:17 says: "And he calls nonexisting things into existence." Therefore, the eternal conception of God's law has the nature of an eternal law insofar as he orders that law to the governance of the world he foreknows.

Reply Obj. 2. Word and inscription promulgate law. And God promulgates his eternal law in both ways, since the Word of God and the inscription of the predestined in the Book of Life[4] are eternal. But as regards the creatures who hear or read God's law, the promulgation cannot be eternal.

Reply Obj. 3. Law signifies actively ordering things to an end, namely, that law order things to an end. And law does not signify being passively ordered to an end, that is, that law itself need be ordered to another end, except incidentally in the case of human rulers, whose end is extrinsic to themselves. And then the rulers' laws also need to be ordered to that extrinsic end. But the end of God's governance is God himself,[5] and his law is indistinguishable from himself. And so the eternal law is not ordered to another end.

SECOND ARTICLE
Is There a Natural Law in Us?

We thus proceed to the second article. It seems that there is no natural law in us, for the following reasons:

Obj. 1. The eternal law sufficiently governs human beings. For Augustine says in his work *On Free Choice* that "the eternal law is that whereby it is right that all things be most orderly."[6] But nature does not abound in superfluities, nor is it wanting in necessities. Therefore, there is no natural law for human beings.

Obj. 2. Law orders human beings to their end regarding their actions, as I have maintained before.[7] But nature does not order human actions to their end, as happens in the case of irrational creatures, which act for their ends only by natural appetites. Rather, human beings act for their end by the use of their reason and will. Therefore, there is no natural law for human beings.

Obj. 3. The freer one is, the less one is subject to law. But human beings are freer than all other animals because human beings, unlike other animals, have free choice. Therefore, since other animals are not subject to a natural law, neither are human beings.

---

[4]Cf. ST I, Q. 24, A. 1. [5]Cf. ST I: Q. 22, A. 1; Q. 103, A. 2.
[6]*On Free Choice* I, 6, n. 15 (PL 32:1229). [7]ST I-II, Q. 90, A. 2.

On the contrary, a gloss on Rom. 2:14, "When the Gentiles, who do not have the law, do by nature things prescribed by the law," etc., says: "Although they do not have the written law, they have a natural law, whereby each of them understands and is conscious of good and evil."[8]

I answer that, as I have said before,[9] law, since it is a rule or measure, can belong to things in two ways: in one way to those who rule and measure; in a second way to those ruled and measured, since things are ruled or measured insofar as they partake of the rule or measure. But the eternal law rules and measures everything subject to God's providence, as is evident from what I have said before.[10] And so everything evidently shares in some way in the eternal law, namely, insofar as all things have inclinations to their own acts and ends from its imprint on them. But the rational creature is subject to God's providence in a more excellent way than other things, since such a creature also shares in God's providence in providing for itself and others. And so it shares in the eternal plan whereby it has its natural inclination to its requisite activity and end. And we call such participation in the eternal law by rational creatures the natural law. And so Ps. 4:6, after saying, "Offer just sacrifices," asks: "Who shows us just things?" and replies: "The light of your countenance, O Lord, has been inscribed on us." The Psalmist thus signifies that the light of natural reason whereby we discern good and evil is simply the imprint of God's light in us. And so it is clear that the natural law is simply rational creatures' sharing in the eternal law.

Reply Obj. 1. The argument of this objection would be valid if the natural law were to be something different from the eternal law. But the natural law shares in the eternal law, as I have said.[11]

Reply Obj. 2. Every activity of reason and the will in us is derived from what exists by nature, as I have maintained before,[12] since every process of reasoning is derived from first principles known by nature, and every desire of means is derived from the natural desire for our ultimate end. And so also the natural law needs first to direct our acts to their end.

Reply Obj. 3. Even irrational animals, like rational creatures, share in the eternal law in their own way. But because rational creatures share in the eternal law by using their intellect and reason, we call their participation in the eternal law law in the strict sense, since law belongs to reason, as I have said before.[13] And irrational creatures do not share in the eternal law by the use of reason. And so we can call the latter participation law only by analogy.

---

[8]*Glossa ordinaria,* on Rom. 2:14 (PL 114:476); Peter Lombard, *Glossa,* on Rom. 2:14 (PL 191:1345).   [9]ST I–II, Q. 90, A. 1, *ad* 1.   [10]ST I–II, Q. 91, A. 1.   [11]In the body of the article.   [12]ST I II, Q. 10, A. 1.   [13]ST I–II, Q. 90, A. 1.

THIRD ARTICLE
Are There Human Laws?

We thus proceed to the third inquiry. It seems that there are no human laws, for the following reason:

Obj. 1. The natural law shares in the eternal law, as I have said.[14] But the eternal law "renders all things most orderly," as Augustine says in his work *On Free Choice*.[15] Therefore, the natural law suffices for ordering all human affairs. Therefore, there is no need for human laws.

Obj. 2. Law has the nature of a measure, as I have said.[16] But human reason is not the measure of things. Rather, the converse is true, as the *Metaphysics* says.[17] Therefore, human reason can produce no law.

Obj. 3. A measure should be most certain, as the *Metaphysics* says.[18] But dictates of human reason about things to be done are uncertain, as Wis. 9:14 says: "The thoughts of mortal human beings are fraught with fear, and our foresight uncertain." Therefore, human reason cannot produce laws.

On the contrary, Augustine in his work *On Free Choice* posits two kinds of law, one kind eternal, and the other temporal, which he calls human.[19]

I answer that law is a dictate of practical reason, as I have said before.[20] But there are similar processes of practical and theoretical reason, since both proceed from principles to conclusions, as I have maintained before.[21] Therefore, we should say that we advance in theoretical reason from indemonstrable first principles, naturally known, to the conclusions of different sciences, conclusions not implanted in us by nature but discovered by exercising reason. Just so, human reason needs to advance from the precepts of the natural law, as general and indemonstrable first principles, to matters that are to be more particularly regulated. And we call such regulations devised by human reason human laws, provided that the other conditions belonging to the nature of law are observed, as I have said before.[22] And so also Cicero says in his *Rhetoric*: "Human law originally sprang from nature. Then things became customs because of their rational benefit. Then fear and reverence for law validated things that both sprang from nature and were approved by custom."[23]

Reply Obj. 1. Human reason cannot partake of the complete dictates of God's reason but partakes of them in its own way and incompletely. And

---

[14]ST I–II, Q. 91, A. 2.   [15]*On Free Choice* I, 6, n. 15 (PL 32:1229).

[16]ST I–II, Q. 90, A. 1.   [17]Aristotle, *Metaphysics* X, 1 (1053a31–b3).

[18]Ibid.   [19]*On Free Choice* I, 6 and 15 (PL 32:1229, 1238).

[20]ST I–II, Q. 90, A. 1, *ad* 2.   [21]Ibid.   [22]ST I–II, Q. 9, AA. 2, 3, 4.

[23]*Rhetoric* II, 53.

so regarding theoretical reason, we by our natural participation in God's wisdom know general principles but do not specifically know every truth, as God's wisdom does. Just so regarding practical reason, human beings by nature partake of the eternal law as to general principles but not as to particular specifications of particular matters, although such specifications belong to the eternal law. And so human reason needs to proceed further to determine the particular prescriptions of human law.

Reply Obj. 2. Human reason as such is not the rule of things, but the first principles implanted by nature in human reason are the general rules or measures of everything related to human conduct. And natural reason is the rule and measure of such things, although not of things from nature.

Reply Obj. 3. Practical reason regards practical matters, which are particular and contingent, and does not regard necessary things, as theoretical reason does. And so human laws cannot have the absolute certainty of demonstrated scientific conclusions. Nor need every measure be unerring and certain in every respect. Rather, every measure needs to be such only to the extent possible in its kind of thing.

FOURTH ARTICLE
Did Human Beings Need a Divine Law?

We thus proceed to the fourth inquiry. It seems that human beings did not need any divine law, for the following reasons:

Obj. 1. The natural law is our sharing in the eternal law, as I have said.[24] But eternal law is divine law, as I have said.[25] Therefore, we do not need another divine law besides the natural law and the human laws derived from natural law.

Obj. 2. Sir. 15:14 says that "God left human beings in the hands of their own deliberation." But deliberation is an act of reason, as I have maintained before.[26] Therefore, God left human beings to the governance of their own reason. But the dictates of human reason are human laws, as I have said.[27] Therefore, human beings do not need to be governed by another, divine law.

Obj. 3. Human nature is more self-sufficient than irrational creatures. But irrational creatures have no divine law besides the inclinations that nature implants in them. Therefore, much less should rational creatures have a divine law besides the natural law.

On the contrary, David petitioned God to lay out the law before him, saying in Ps. 119:33: "Teach me the law, O Lord, in the way of your statutes."

---

[24]ST I–II, Q. 91, A. 2.   [25]ST I–II, Q. 91, A. 1.   [26]ST I–II, Q. 14, A. 1.
[27]ST I–II, Q. 91, A. 3.

I answer that in addition to the natural law and human laws, divine law was necessary to give direction to human life. And there are four reasons for this:

First, indeed, law directs our acts in relation to our ultimate end. And human beings, if they were indeed ordered only to an end that did not surpass the proportion of their natural ability, would not, regarding reason, need to have any direction superior to the natural law and human laws derived from the natural law. But because human beings are ordered to the end of eternal blessedness, which surpasses their proportional natural human capacity, as I have maintained before,[28] God needed to lay down a law superior to the natural law and human laws to direct human beings to their end.

Second, because of the uncertainty of human judgment, especially regarding contingent and particular matters, different persons may judge differently about various human actions, and so even different and contrary laws result. Therefore, in order that human beings can know beyond any doubt what they should do or should not do, a divinely revealed law, regarding which error is impossible, was needed to direct human beings in their actions.

Third, human beings can make laws regarding things they are able to judge. But human beings can judge only sensibly perceptible external acts, not hidden internal movements. And yet human beings need to live righteously regarding both kinds of acts in order to attain complete virtue. And so human laws could not prohibit or adequately order internal acts, and divine law needed to supplement human laws.

Fourth, human laws cannot punish or prohibit all evil deeds, as Augustine says in his work *On Free Choice*.[29] This is because in seeking to eliminate all evils, one would thereby also take away many goods and not benefit the common good necessary for human companionship. Therefore, in order that every evil be forbidden and punished, there needed to be a divine law forbidding all sins.

And Ps. 19:7 touches on these four reasons when it says: "The law of the Lord is pure," that is, permitting no sinful wickedness; "converting souls," since it directs both external and internal acts; "the Lord's faithful witness" because of its certain truth and rectitude; "offering wisdom to the little ones," since it orders human beings to a supernatural and divine end.

Reply Obj. 1. The natural law partakes of the eternal law in proportion to the capacity of human nature. But human beings need to be directed in

---

[28]ST I–II, Q. 5, A. 5.   [29]*On Free Choice* I, 5 (PL 32:1228).

[handwritten: divine eternal human]

a higher way to their ultimate supernatural end. And so God gives an additional law that partakes of the eternal law in a higher way.

Reply Obj. 2. Deliberation is an inquiry, and so deliberation needs to advance from some principles. And it does not suffice that it advance from first principles implanted by nature, that is, precepts of the natural law, for the aforementioned reasons.[30] Rather, other principles, namely, precepts of divine law, need to be supplied.

[handwritten: first principles]

Reply Obj. 3. Irrational creatures are not ordered to higher ends than those proportioned to their natural powers. And so the argument of the objection is inapplicable.

[handwritten: humans have a higher purpose]

FIFTH ARTICLE
Is There Only One Divine Law?

We thus proceed to the fifth article. It seems that there is only one divine law, for the following reasons:

Obj. 1. There is one set of laws of one king in one kingdom. But the whole human race is related to God as one king, as Ps. 47:7 says: "God is king of all the earth." Therefore, there is only one divine law.

Obj. 2. Every law is ordered to the end the lawmaker intends regarding those subject to the law. But God intends one and the same thing regarding all human beings, as 1 Tim. 2:4 says: "He wills all human beings to be saved and to come to the knowledge of the truth." Therefore, there is only one divine law.

Obj. 3. The divine law seems to approximate the eternal law, which is one, more than the natural law does, as the revelation of grace is higher than the knowledge of nature. But there is one natural law for all human beings. Therefore, much more is there one divine law for them.

On the contrary, the Apostle says in Heb. 7:12: "Since the priesthood has been transferred, the law needed to be changed." But the priesthood is twofold, namely, the priesthood of Leviticus and the priesthood of Christ, as Heb. 7:11 says. Therefore, there are two divine laws, namely, the Old Law and the New Law.

I answer that division causes number, as I said in the First Part.[31] And we distinguish things in two ways: in one way as things are altogether specifically different (e.g., horses and oxen); in a second way as the complete and the incomplete in the same species (e.g., adults and children). And it is in the latter way that we distinguish divine law into the Old and the New Law. And so the Apostle in Gal. 3:24–5 compares the condition

---

[30]In the body of the article.   [31]ST I, Q. 30, A. 3.

of the Old Law to that of a child subject to a tutor, and the condition of the New Law to an adult no longer subject to a tutor.

And we note the perfection and imperfection of the two Laws by three things belonging to the divine law, as I have said before.[32] For in the first place, it belongs to any law to be directed to the common good as its end, as I have said before.[33] And this common good can be of two kinds. It may be a sensibly perceptible and earthly good, and the Old Law was directly ordered to such a good. And so the people were invited at the very institution of the Old Law to occupy the earthly kingdom of the Canaanites.[34] Or the common good may be an intelligible and heavenly good, and the New Law orders human beings to such a good. And so Christ at the very outset of his preaching invited human beings to the kingdom of heaven, saying: "Repent, for the kingdom of heaven is at hand."[35] And so Augustine says in his work *Against Faustus* that "the Old Testament contains promises of temporal things and so is called old, but the promise of eternal life belongs to the New Testament."[36]

Second, it belongs to the divine law to direct human acts regarding the order of righteousness. And the New Law surpasses the Old Law in this respect by ordering internal spiritual acts, as Mt. 5:20 says: "Unless your righteousness exceeds that of the Scribes and Pharisees, you will not enter the kingdom of heaven." And so there is the saying that "the Old Law stays our hand, the New Law stays our spirit."[37]

Third, it belongs to the divine law to induce human beings to observe the commandments. And the Old Law indeed accomplished this by fear of punishments, while the New Law accomplishes this by love, which the grace of Christ, foreshadowed in the Old Law and conferred in the New Law, pours into our hearts. And so Augustine says in his work *Against Adimantus, Disciple of Mani* that "there is a little difference between the Law and the Gospel, namely, the difference between fear and love."[38]

Reply Obj. 1. As the head of a household issues different commands to children and adults, so also the one king, God, in his one kingdom gave one law to human beings still imperfect and another more perfect law to those already led by the former law to a greater capacity for divine things.

---

[32]ST I–II: Q. 90, A. 2; Q. 90, A. 3, *ad* 2; Q. 91, A. 4.   [33]ST I–II, Q. 90, A. 2.
[34]Ex. 3:8–17.   [35]Mt. 4:17.   [36]*Against Faustus* IV, 2 (PL 42:217–8).
[37]Cf. Peter Lombard, *Sentences* III, dist. 40, c. 1.
[38]*Against Adimantus, Disciple of Mani* 17 (PL 42:159). The "little difference" alludes to the fact that the Latin word for fear (*timor*) has one more letter than the Latin word for love (*amor*).

needed word of law to prepare Christ [handwritten margin note]

Reply Obj. 2. Only Christ could save human beings, as Acts 4:12 says: "There is no other name given to human beings wherein we should be saved." And so a law completely leading all human beings to salvation could be given only after the coming of Christ. But a law containing rudiments of salvific righteousness needed to be given beforehand to the people from whom Christ was to be born, in order to prepare them to receive him.

Reply Obj. 3. The natural law directs human beings by certain general precepts in relation to which both the perfect and the imperfect are the same, and so the natural law is one and the same for everyone. But divine law also directs human beings regarding particular matters, for which the perfect and the imperfect are not similarly disposed. And so there needed to be two divine laws, as I have already said.[39]

SIXTH ARTICLE
Is There a Law of Concupiscence?

We thus proceed to the sixth article. It seems that there is no law of concupiscence, for the following reasons:

Obj. 1. Isidore says in his *Etymologies* that "law is based on reason."[40] But concupiscence is not based on reason. Rather, concupiscence deviates from reason. Therefore, concupiscence does not have the nature of law.

Obj. 2. Every law obliges, so that we call those who do not observe it transgressors. But concupiscence does not render persons transgressors because they do not follow its inclinations. Rather, concupiscence renders persons transgressors if they do. Therefore, concupiscence does not have the nature of law.

Obj. 3. Law is ordered to the common good, as I have maintained before.[41] But concupiscence does not incline us to the common good. Rather, concupiscence inclines us to private good. Therefore, concupiscence does not have the nature of law.

On the contrary, the Apostle says in Rom. 7:23: "I perceive another law in my bodily members repugnant to the law of my mind."

I answer that law belongs essentially to those who rule and measure and, by participation, to the ruled and measured, as I have said before.[42] And so we call every inducement or order in things subject to law law by participation, as is evident from what I have said before.[43] But in things subject to law, there can be inducements from the lawmaker in two ways. There are inducements in one way insofar as lawmakers directly induce

---

[39]In the body of the article.   [40]*Etymologies* V, 3 (PL 82:199).
[41]ST I–II, Q. 90, A. 2.   [42]ST I–II: Q. 91, A. 2; Q. 90, A. 1, *ad* 1.   [43]Ibid.

their subjects to things and, sometimes, different subjects to different actions. And we can accordingly speak of one law for soldiers and another law for merchants. There are inducements in a second way insofar as lawmakers indirectly induce their subjects to things, namely, insofar as lawmakers by depriving subjects of some office transfer them to another position in society and to another law, as it were. For example, if a soldier should be discharged from the army, he will be transferred to the law governing farmers or merchants.

Therefore, God, the lawmaker, subjects different creatures to different inducements, so that what is in one way law for one kind of creature, is in another way contrary to law for another kind of creature. This is as if I should say that ferocity is in one way the law for dogs but in another way contrary to the law for sheep or other meek animals. Therefore, it is the law for human beings, which is allotted by God's order according to their condition, that they act according to reason. And this law was indeed so effective in our first condition that nothing outside reason or contrary to reason could come upon Adam surreptitiously. But when Adam withdrew from God, he fell subject to the impulses of his sense appetites. And this also happens in particular to each human being the more the individual has withdrawn from reason, so that the individual in a way resembles beasts, who are carried away by the impulses of their sense appetites. Just so, Ps. 49:20 says: "Human beings, although they were in a condition of honor, did not understand; they have been paired with mindless beasts and became like them."

Therefore, in other animals, the very inclinations of sense appetites, which we call concupiscence, indeed directly have the nature of law in an absolute sense, although in the way we can speak of law in such things. And in human beings, such inclinations of sense appetites do not have the nature of law. Rather, they are deviations from the law of reason. But since divine justice stripped human beings of original justice and the full force of reason, the very impulses of sense appetites that impel human beings have the nature of law, since such impulses are a punishment and the result of divine law depriving human beings of their dignity.

Reply Obj. 1. The argument of this objection is valid regarding concupiscence considered as such, as it inclines us to evil. For concupiscence does not have the nature of law in this way, as I have said,[44] but has the nature of law insofar as it results from the justice of divine law. This is as if we were to say that the law allows nobles to be put to servile work because of their misdeeds.

---

[44]In the body of the article.

Reply Obj. 2. The argument of this objection is valid regarding law as a rule or measure. For those deviating from the law are thus constituted transgressors of the law. But concupiscence is not a law in this sense. Rather, concupiscence is a law by a participation, as I have said before.[45]

Reply Obj. 3. The argument of this objection is valid about concupiscence as to its own inclinations but not as to its origin. And yet if we were to consider the inclinations of sense appetites as they exist in other animals, then the inclinations are ordered to the common good, that is, the preservation of nature specifically and individually. And this is also true regarding human beings insofar as their sense appetites are subject to reason. But we are talking about concupiscence insofar as it departs from the order of reason.

Question 92
On the Effects of Law

FIRST ARTICLE
Is the Effect of Law to Make Human Beings Good?

We thus proceed to the first inquiry. It seems that it does not belong to law to make human beings good, for the following reasons:

Obj. 1. Virtue makes human beings good, since "virtue makes those possessing it good," as the *Ethics* says.[1] But human beings have virtue only from God, since he "produces virtue in us apart from our efforts,"[2] as I have said before regarding the definition of virtue.[3] Therefore, it does not belong to law to make human beings good.

Obj. 2. Law benefits human beings only if they obey law. But goodness causes human beings to obey law. Therefore, human beings first need goodness in order to obey law. Therefore, law does not make them good.

Obj. 3. Law is ordered to the common good, as I have said.[4] But some ill disposed regarding their own good are well disposed regarding what belongs to the common good. Therefore, it does not belong to law to make human beings good.

Obj. 4. Some laws are tyrannical, as the Philosopher says in the *Politics*.[5] But a tyrant strives for his own good, not the good of his subjects. Therefore, it does not belong to law to make human beings good.

---

[45]Ibid.

[1]Aristotle, *Ethics* II, 6 (1106a15–6).

[2]Cf. Peter Lombard, *Sentences* II, dist. 27, c. 5.   [3]ST I–II, Q. 55, A. 4.

[4]ST I–II, Q. 90, A. 2.   [5]*Politics* III, 6 (1282b12).

On the contrary, the Philosopher says in the *Ethics* that it is "the will of every lawmaker to make human beings good."[6]

I answer that, as I have said before,[7] law is simply a ruler's dictate of reason that governs his subjects. And the virtue of every subject is to be duly subject to the ruler. Just so, we perceive that the virtue of the irascible and concupiscible powers consists of being duly obedient to reason. And accordingly, "the virtue of every subject consists of being duly subject to the ruler," as the Philosopher says in the *Politics*.[8] And every law is ordained to be obeyed by those subject to it. And so it evidently belongs to law to induce subjects to their requisite virtue. Therefore, since virtue makes those possessing it good, the proper effect of law is consequently to make its subjects good, either absolutely or in some respect. For if the aim of the lawmaker strives for real good, that is, the common good regulated by divine justice, law consequently makes human beings absolutely good. But if the aim of lawmakers is set upon what is not absolutely good but what is useful or desirable for themselves or contrary to divine justice, then law makes human beings relatively, not absolutely, good, namely, in relation to such a regime. So also does good belong to things in themselves evil. For example, we speak of a good robber, since he acts suitably to accomplish his end.

Reply Obj. 1. There are two kinds of virtue, namely, acquired virtues and infused virtues, as is evident from what I have said before.[9] And habitual action contributes something to both but in different ways. For habitual action causes acquired virtue, disposes persons to receive infused virtue, and preserves and augments infused virtues already possessed. And because laws are laid down to direct human actions, law makes human beings good as much as their actions conduce to virtue. And so also the Philosopher says in the *Politics* that "lawmakers make subjects good by habituating them to good deeds."[10]

Reply Obj. 2. People do not always obey law out of the perfect goodness of virtue. Rather, they sometimes indeed obey law out of fear of punishment and sometimes only out of dictates of reason, which cause virtue, as I have maintained before.[11]

Reply Obj. 3. We weigh the goodness of any part in relation to the whole to which it belongs. And so also Augustine says in his *Confessions* that "every part is base that is in discord with the whole to which it belongs."[12] Therefore, since every human being is part of a political

---

[6]*Ethics* II, 1 (1103b3–4).   [7]ST I–II, Q. 90: A. 1, *ad* 2; AA. 3, 4.

[8]*Politics* I, 5 (1260a20–4).   [9]ST I–II, Q. 63, A. 2.

[10]Actually, *Ethics* II, 1 (1103b3–4).   [11]ST I–II, Q. 63, A. 1.

[12]*Confessions* III, 8 (PL 32:689).

community, no human being can be good unless rightly related to the common good. Nor can a whole be rightly constituted except by parts rightly related to it. And so the common good of a political community can be rightly disposed only if its citizens, at least those to whom its ruling belongs, are virtuous. But it suffices as regards the good of the community that other citizens be virtuous enough to obey the commands of the law. And so the Philosopher says in the *Politics* that "the virtue of a ruler and that of a good man are the same, but the virtue of any ordinary citizen and that of a good man are not."[13]

Reply Obj. 4. A tyrannical law, since it is not in accord with reason, is not a law, absolutely speaking. Rather, it is a perversion of law. And yet such a law strives to make citizens good inasmuch as it partakes of the nature of law. For it only partakes of the nature of law insofar as it is a ruler's dictate for his subjects and strives to make them duly obedient, that is, to make them good in relation to such a regime, not absolutely good.

SECOND ARTICLE
Do We Suitably Designate Legal Acts?

We thus proceed to the second article. It seems that we do not suitably designate legal acts to consist of "commanding, forbidding, permitting, and punishing,"[14] for the following reasons:

Obj. 1. "Every law is a general precept," as the Jurist says.[15] But giving a command is the same as laying down a precept. Therefore, the other three things are superfluous.

Obj. 2. The effect of law is to induce subjects to good, as I have said before.[16] But counsel concerns a higher good than precept concerns. Therefore, counsel belongs more to law than precept does.

Obj. 3. As punishment spurs human beings to good deeds, so also do rewards. Therefore, as we reckon punishment an effect of law, so also should we reckon reward.

Obj. 4. A lawmaker aims to make human beings good, as I have said before.[17] But those who obey law only out of fear of punishment are not good, since "although some do good out of servile fear, which is fear of punishment, they do not do it rightly," as Augustine says.[18] Therefore, it does not seem to belong to law to punish.

On the contrary, Isidore says in his *Etymologies:* "Every law either permits something (e.g., that a brave man may ask for a reward) or prohibits

---

[13]*Politics* III, 2 (1277a20–3).   [14]Justinian, *Digest* I, title 3, law 7.
[15]Ibid., I, title 3, law 1.   [16]ST I–II, Q. 92, A. 1.   [17]Ibid.
[18]*Against the Two Letters of Pelagius* II, 9, n. 21 (PL 44:586).

something (e.g., that no one is permitted to seek marriage with a consecrated virgin) or punishes something (e.g., that murderers be beheaded)."[19]

I answer that as statements are dictates of reason by declaring things, so also laws are dictates of reason by commanding things. But it belongs to reason to lead us from some things to other things. And so, as reason in the case of demonstrative sciences leads us to assent to conclusions from certain first principles, so also reason leads us to assent to legal precepts from knowledge of certain things.

And legal precepts concern human actions, which law directs, as I have said before.[20] And there are three kinds of human acts. For as I have said before,[21] some human acts are good by their nature, that is, virtuous. And laws are supposed to prescribe or command such acts, since "laws command every kind of virtuous act," as the *Ethics* says.[22] And some human acts are evil by their nature, that is, vicious. And laws are supposed to forbid such acts. And some human acts are morally indifferent by reason of their kind. And laws are supposed to permit such acts. And we can call all slightly good or slightly evil human acts morally indifferent.

But fear of punishment is what law makes use of to induce obedience, and we in this respect posit punishment as an effect of law.

Reply Obj. 1. As desisting from evil partakes of the nature of good, so also prohibitions partake of the nature of precept. And so, understanding precept broadly, we call every law a precept.

Reply Obj. 2. Counseling is not a peculiar function of law. Rather, counseling falls also within the competence of private persons, who are without competence to establish law. And so also the Apostle, in proposing to give a counsel, says in 1 Cor. 7:12: "I, not the Lord, make this statement." And so we do not posit counseling among the effects of law.

Reply Obj. 3. Anyone is competent to bestow rewards, but only administrators of law, under the authority of which punishments are inflicted, are competent to punish. And so we posit only punishments, not rewards, as legal acts.

Reply Obj. 4. By beginning to become habituated to avoid evil deeds and to do good deeds out of fear of punishment, persons are sometimes brought to behave in such a way with pleasure and of their own will. And so law even by inflicting punishments induces human beings to be good.

---

[19]*Etymologies* V, 19 (PL 82:202).
[20]ST I–II: Q. 90, AA. 1, 2; Q. 91, A. 4.
[21]ST I–II, Q. 18, A. 8.
[22]Aristotle, *Ethics* V, 1 (1129b19–23).

Question 93
On the Eternal Law

FIRST ARTICLE
Is the Eternal Law a Supreme Plan[1] in God?

We thus proceed to the first article. It seems that the eternal law is not a supreme plan in God, for the following reasons:

Obj. 1. There is only one eternal law. But there are many natures of things in the mind of God, for Augustine says in his work *Eighty-Three Questions* that "God made each thing with its own nature[2]."[3] Therefore, the eternal law is not the same as the plan in his mind.

Obj. 2. It belongs to the nature of law that it be promulgated in words, as I have said before.[4] But regarding divine things, we speak of the Word as person, as I maintained in the First Part,[5] but we speak of the divine plan as belonging to God essentially. Therefore, the eternal law is not the same as the divine plan.

Obj. 3. Augustine says in his work *On True Religion*: "We perceive that there is a law superior to our minds, a law we call truth."[6] But the law superior to our minds is the eternal law. Therefore, truth is the eternal law. But the nature of truth is not the same as the nature of a plan. Therefore, the eternal law is not the same as a supreme plan.

On the contrary, Augustine says in his work *On Free Choice* that "the eternal law is the supreme plan that we should always obey."[7]

I answer that as there preexists in every craftsman a plan for the things produced by his skill, so also there needs to exist in every ruler an orderly plan for the things his subjects ought to do. And as we call the plan for the things that a craft produces, the craft or ideal type of the things crafted, so also the plan of a ruler for his subjects' actions has the nature of law, provided that the other conditions that I cited before regarding the nature of law[8] are observed. And God in his wisdom creates all things and is related to them like a craftsman to the products of his craft, as I have

---

[1] In ST I, Q. 15, A. 2, Thomas uses *ratio* to signify God's "idea" of the order of the whole universe. This "idea" in connection with creation evidently constitutes a plan, and we translate *ratio* in this context accordingly.

[2] Each kind of thing has a proper nature or essence. Both Augustine and Thomas use *ratio* to signify the natures or essences of things as "ideas" in God's mind. Cf. ST I, Q. 15, A. 2. Also see Glossary, s.v. *Essence*.

[3] *Eighty-Three Questions*, q. 46, n. 2 (PL 40:30).   [4] ST I–II: Q. 90, A. 4; Q. 91, A. 1, *ad* 2.   [5] ST I, Q. 34, A. 1.   [6] *On True Religion* 30 (PL 34:147).

[7] *On Free Choice* I, 6, n. 15 (PL 32:1229).   [8] ST I–II, Q. 90.

maintained in the First Part.[9] God also governs all the actions and movements in particular kinds of creatures, as I have likewise maintained in the
First Part.[10] And so, as the plan of divine wisdom has the nature of a craft
or type or idea because all things are created through it, so the plan of
divine wisdom causing the movement of all things to their requisite ends
has the nature of law. And so the eternal law is simply the plan of divine
wisdom that directs all the actions and movements of created things.

Reply Obj. 1. Augustine is speaking in the cited text about ideal
natures, which concern the requisite natures of particular things. And so
these types have some diversity and plurality regarding their different
relations to things, as I have maintained in the First Part.[11] But we speak
of law directing actions in relation to the common good, as I have said
before.[12] And we consider things in themselves diverse as one insofar as
they are ordered to the common good. And so there is one eternal law,
which is this orderly plan.

Reply Obj. 2. We can consider two things regarding any word, namely,
the word itself and what the word expresses. For example, spoken words
are utterances from the mouths of human beings, and these words express
what the words signify. And mental words, which are simply the mental
concepts whereby human beings express mentally the things about which
they are thinking, have the same nature. Therefore, regarding divine
things, we speak of the Word itself, which the Father's understanding
conceives, as the Second Person of the Trinity, and this Word expresses
everything in the Father's knowledge, whether things proper to God's
essence or things proper to each Person or things created by God, as
Augustine makes evident in his work *On the Trinity.*[13] And among other
things so expressed, the Word itself also expresses the eternal law itself.
But it does not follow that we speak of the eternal law as the Second
Person of the Trinity, although we appropriate the eternal law to the Son
because of the appropriateness of the divine plan for the Word.

Reply Obj. 3. The nature of the divine intellect is otherwise related to
things than the nature of the human mind is. For things are the measure
of the human mind, that is to say, we call human concepts true because
they are in accord with things, not because of the concepts themselves,
since "opinions are true or false because things are or are not such."[14] But
the divine intellect is the measure of things, since everything has as much
truth as it is modeled on the divine intellect, as I have maintained in the

---

[9]*ST* I, Q. 14, A. 8.   [10]*ST* I, Q. 103, A. 5.   [11]*ST* I, Q. 15, A. 2.
[12]*ST* I–II, Q. 90, A. 2.   [13]*On the Trinity* XV, 14 (PL 42:1076).
[14]Aristotle, *Categories* 4 (2a7–8).

First Part.[15] And so the divine intellect is true in itself. And so its nature is truth itself.

SECOND ARTICLE
Do All Know the Eternal Law?

We thus proceed to the second article. It seems that not everybody knows the eternal law, for the following reasons:

Obj. 1. The Apostle says in 1 Cor. 2:11: "Only the Spirit of God knows the things proper to God." But the eternal law is a plan in God's mind. Therefore, no one but God knows the eternal law.

Obj. 2. Augustine says in his work *On Free Choice*: "The eternal law is that by which it is right that all things be most orderly."[16] But not everybody knows how all things are most orderly. Therefore, not everybody knows the eternal law.

Obj. 3. Augustine says in his work *On True Religion* that "human beings cannot judge regarding the eternal law."[17] But "everyone judges rightly about things one knows," as the *Ethics* says.[18] Therefore, we do not know the eternal law.

On the contrary, Augustine says in his work *On Free Choice* that "knowledge of the eternal law is imprinted on us."[19]

I answer that we can know things in two ways: in one way in themselves; in a second way in their effects, which are like the things. For example, those who are not looking at the sun know it in the effects of its rays. Therefore, we should say no one except the blessed, who see God by his essence, can know the eternal law as it is in itself. But every rational creature knows it in some of its radiating effects, whether greater or lesser effects. For every knowledge of truth is a radiation and participation of eternal law, which is incommunicable truth, as Augustine says in his work *On True Religion*.[20] For everybody knows truth to some extent, at least regarding the general principles of the natural law. But some share more and some less in knowing truth regarding other things. And so also they know more or less of the eternal law.

Reply Obj. 1. We indeed cannot know things proper to God in themselves, but such things are evident to us in their effects, as Rom. 1:20 says: "We perceive the invisible things of God when they are understood through the things he created."

Reply Obj. 2. Although everyone knows the eternal law according to

---

[15]ST I, Q. 16, A. 1.   [16]*On Free Choice* I, 6, n. 15 (PL 32:1229).

[17]*On True Religion* 31 (PL 34:148).   [18]Aristotle, *Ethics* I, 3 (1094b27–1095a2).

[19]*On Free Choice* I, 6, n. 15 (PL 32:1229).   [20]*On True Religion* 31 (PL 34:147).

one's capacity, in the aforementioned way, no one can know it comprehensively, since its effects cannot completely reveal it. And so it is not necessary that those who know the eternal law in the aforementioned way know the whole order of things, whereby all things are most orderly.

Reply Obj. 3. Judging about things can be understood in two ways. Judging about things can be understood in one way as a cognitive power judges regarding its own object, as Job 12:11 says: "Do not ears discern words, and diners' taste buds discern taste?" And the Philosopher in this way of judging says that "everyone judges rightly things that one knows," namely, in judging whether a proposition is true. We can understand judging in a second way as superiors judge about subordinates by practical judgments, namely, whether subordinates should or should not be such and such. And no one can judge about the eternal law in that way.

THIRD ARTICLE
Is Every Law Derived from the Eternal Law?

We thus proceed to the third inquiry. It seems that not every law is derived from the eternal law, for the following reasons:

Obj. 1. There is a law of concupiscence, as I have said before.[21] But that law is not derived from divine law, that is, eternal law, since wisdom of the flesh, which the Apostle in Rom. 8:7 says "cannot be subject to the law of God," belongs to the law of concupiscence. Therefore, not every law comes from the eternal law.

Obj. 2. Nothing evil can come from the eternal law, since "eternal law is that whereby it is right that all things be most orderly,"[22] as I have said before.[23] But some laws are evil, as Is.10:1 says: "Woe to those who make wicked laws." Therefore, not every law comes from the eternal law.

Obj. 3. Augustine says in his work *On Free Choice* that "laws prescribed for ruling a people rightly permit many things that divine providence punishes."[24] But the plan of divine providence is the eternal law, as I have said.[25] Therefore, not every right law comes from the eternal law.

On the contrary, divine wisdom in Prov. 8:15 says: "Kings rule by me, and lawmakers discern what is just." But the plan of divine wisdom is the eternal law, as I have said before.[26] Therefore, all laws derive from the eternal law.

I answer that law signifies a plan directing acts to an end, as I have said

---

[21]ST I–II, Q. 91, A. 6.   [22]Augustine, *On Free Choice* I, 6, n. 15 (PL 32:1229).
[23]ST I–II, Q. 93, A. 2, obj. 2.   [24]*On Free Choice* I, 5, n. 13 (PL 32:1228).
[25]ST I–II, Q. 93, A. 1.   [26]Ibid.

before.[27] But in the case of all interrelated causes, the power of a secondary cause needs to be derived from the power of the primary cause, since a secondary cause causes only insofar as the primary cause moves the secondary cause. And so also we perceive the same regarding all who govern, that the chief ruler communicates his plan of government to secondary administrators. For example, a king communicates his plan for the affairs of a political community by issuing commands to subordinate administrators. And also in the case of things requiring the skill of craftsmen, a master builder communicates his plan for the activities requiring those skills to subordinate craftsmen, who carry out the manual work involved. Therefore, since the eternal law is the plan of government in the supreme ruler, all plans of government in subordinate rulers need to be derived from the eternal law. But such plans of subordinate government consist of all the other laws besides the eternal law. And so all laws are derived from the eternal law insofar as they partake of right reason. And so Augustine says in his work *On Free Choice* that "nothing is just or lawful in earthly laws that human beings have not derived for themselves from the eternal law."[28]

Reply Obj. 1. Concupiscence has the nature of law regarding human beings insofar as it is a punishment resulting from divine justice, and it is in this respect evidently derived from eternal law. But insofar as it inclines human beings to sin, it is contrary to God's law and does not have the nature of law, as is clear from what I have said before.[29]

Reply Obj. 2. Human law has the nature of law insofar as it is in accord with right reason, and then it is evidently derived from eternal law. But we call human law evil insofar as it withdraws from reason. And then it has the nature of brute force rather than of law. And yet insofar as some likeness of law is preserved in an evil law because one empowered to make law ordained it, it is also in this respect derived from the eternal law. For "every ruling power is from the Lord God," as Rom. 13:1 says.

Reply Obj. 3. We speak of human law permitting some things because it is unable to direct them, not because it approves them. But divine law directs many things that human law cannot, since more things are subject to higher causes than to lower causes. And so the fact that human law is not imposed regarding things that it cannot direct derives from the order of eternal law. But it would be otherwise if human law were to approve things that eternal law condemns. And so we conclude that human law cannot completely attain the eternal law, not that human law is not derived from eternal law.

---

[27]ST I–II, Q. 90, AA. 1, 2.   [28]*On Free Choice* I, 6, n. 15 (PL 32:1229).
[29]ST I–II, Q. 91, A. 6.

FOURTH ARTICLE
Are Necessary and Eternal Things Subject to the Eternal Law?

We thus proceed to the fourth inquiry. It seems that necessary and eternal things are subject to the eternal law, for the following reasons:

Obj. 1. Everything reasonable is subject to reason. But the divine will is reasonable, since it is just. Therefore, it is subject to reason. But the eternal law is the divine plan. Therefore, God's will is subject to the eternal law. But God's will is eternal. Therefore, eternal and necessary things are subject to the eternal law.

Obj. 2. Everything subject to a king is subject to the king's law. But the Son "will be subject to the God and Father, since the Son will hand over the kingdom to the Father," as 1 Cor. 15:24, 28 says. Therefore, the Son, who is eternal, is subject to the eternal law.

Obj. 3. The eternal law is the plan of divine providence. But there are many necessary things subject to divine providence (e.g., the permanence of spiritual substances and heavenly bodies). Therefore, even necessary things are subject to the eternal law.

On the contrary, necessary things cannot be disposed otherwise than they are, and so they do not need any restraint. But laws are imposed on human beings to restrain them from evil, as is evident from what I have said before.[30] Therefore, necessary things are not subject to the law.

I answer that the eternal law is the plan of divine governance, as I have said before.[31] Therefore, everything subject to divine governance is also subject to the eternal law, but things not subject to divine governance are not subject to the eternal law. And we can consider the distinction between the two kinds of things in regard to matters that concern us. For example, things that human beings can do are subject to human governance, but things that belong to the nature of human beings (e.g., that human beings have souls or hands or feet) are not subject to human governance. Therefore, everything belonging to created things, whether contingent or necessary, belongs to the eternal law, but things belonging to the divine nature or essence are in reality the eternal law itself and not subject to the eternal law.

Reply Obj. 1. We can speak about God's will in two ways. We can speak about his will in one way regarding the will itself, and then his will, since it is his very essence, is the same as the eternal law and not subject to divine governance or the eternal law. We can speak of God's will in a second way as to the things God wills regarding creatures, things indeed subject to the eternal law, since the plan for them belongs to his wisdom.

---

[30]ST I–II, Q. 92, A. 2.   [31]ST I–II, Q. 93, A. 1.

And we call God's will reasonable because of these things. Otherwise, considering his will itself, we should call it the very plan.

Reply Obj. 2. God does not make the Son of God but by nature begets him. And so the Son is not subject to divine providence or the eternal law. Rather, he is the eternal law by appropriation, as Augustine makes clear in his work *On True Religion.*[32] And we say that he is subject to the Father by reason of his human nature, and we say that the Father is greater than he in the same regard.[33]

Reply Obj. 3. We grant the argument of this objection, since it deals validly with created necessary things.

Reply Obj. 4.[34] As the Philosopher says in the *Metaphysics,*[35] the necessity of some necessary things is caused, and then they have from something else the fact that they cannot be otherwise than they are. And this is a most effective restraint, since we speak of restrained things being restrained insofar as they cannot do otherwise than they are disposed to do.

FIFTH ARTICLE
Are Contingent Natural Things Subject to the Eternal Law?

We thus proceed to the fifth article. It seems that contingent natural things are not subject to the eternal law, for the following reasons:

Obj. 1. Promulgation belongs to the nature of law, as I have said before.[36] But promulgation can be made only to rational creatures, to whom things can be declared. Therefore, only rational creatures are subject to the eternal law. Therefore, contingent natural things are not.

Obj. 2. "Things that obey reason partake of reason in some respect," as the *Ethics* says.[37] But the eternal law is a supreme plan, as I have said before.[38] Therefore, contingent natural things, since they are completely irrational and do not in any way partake of reason, do not seem to be subject to the eternal law.

Obj. 3. The eternal law is most efficacious. But deficiencies occur in contingent natural things. Therefore, such things are not subject to the eternal law.

On the contrary, Prov. 8:29 says: "When he [God] set bounds to the sea and imposed a law on its waters not to transgress their limits."

I answer that we should speak about the law of human beings and the eternal law, the law of God, in different ways. For the law of human beings

---

[32]*On True Religion* 31 (PL 34:147).   [33]Jn. 14:28.

[34]This reply qualifies the argument in the section *On the contrary*.

[35]*Metaphysics* V, 5 (1015b10–5).   [36]ST I–II, Q. 90, A. 4.

[37]Aristotle, *Ethics* I, 13 (1102b25–28).   [38]ST I–II, Q. 93, A. 1.

governs only rational creatures subject to human beings. And the reason for this is that law directs actions proper to those subject to another's governance. And so, strictly speaking, one does not impose a law on one's own actions. But all the things done regarding the use of irrational things subject to human beings are done by the actions of the very human beings causing the things done. For irrational creatures so used are acted upon by other things and do not act upon themselves, as I have maintained before.[39] And so human beings cannot impose law on irrational things, however much the latter are subject to the former. But human beings can impose law on rational beings subject to them, insofar as human beings by precepts or declarations communicate to their subjects rules to govern the subjects' actions.

And as human beings by their declarations imprint an inner source of action on other human beings subject to them, so also God imprints on all the things of nature the sources of their own activities. And so we say in this respect that God commands the whole of nature, as Ps. 148:6 says: "He established an ordinance, and it will not pass away." And all movements and actions of the whole of nature are also in this respect subject to the eternal law. And so irrational creatures, as directed by divine providence, not by understanding God's commands, are subject to the eternal law in a different way than rational creatures are.

Reply Obj. 1. The imprint of inner sources of activity is to natural things as promulgation of law is to human beings, since the promulgation of law imprints on human beings a source that directs their actions, as I have said.[40]

Reply Obj. 2. Irrational creatures do not partake of human reason, nor do they obey it, but they partake of God's reason by obeying it. For the power of God's reason extends to more things than the power of human reason does. And as members of the human body are moved at the command of human reason but do not partake of reason, since they do have any cognition subordinated to reason, so also God causes the movements of irrational creatures, which are not on that account rational.

Reply Obj. 3. Deficiencies that occur in things of nature, although outside the order of particular causes, are not outside the order of universal causes, and especially of the first cause, that is, God, whose providence nothing can escape, as I have said in the First Part.[41] And because the eternal law is the plan of divine providence, as I have said,[42] so deficiencies of things of nature are subject to the eternal law.

---

[39]ST I–II, Q. 1, A. 2. [40]In the body of the article.
[41]ST I, Q. 22, A. 2. [42]ST I–II, Q. 93, A. 1.

Are All Human Affairs Subject to the Eternal Law?

We thus proceed to the sixth article. It seems that not all human affairs are subject to the eternal law, for the following reasons:

Obj. 1. The Apostle says in Gal. 5:18: "If the Spirit guides you, you are not under the law." But righteous human beings, who are children of God by adoption, are led by the Spirit of God, as Rom. 8:14 says: "Those led by the Spirit of God are children of God." Therefore, not every human being is under the eternal law.

Obj. 2. The Apostle says in Rom. 8:17: "The wisdom of the flesh is the enemy of God, since that wisdom is not subject to the law of God." But there are many human beings in whom wisdom of the flesh dominates. Therefore, not all human beings are subject to the eternal law, that is, the law of God.

Obj. 3. Augustine says in his work *On Free Choice* that "the eternal law is the means whereby the wicked merit unhappiness, and the virtuous a blessed life."[43] But human beings already blessed or already damned are not in a condition to merit. Therefore, such human beings are not subject to the eternal law.

On the contrary, Augustine says in *The City of God*: "Nothing is in any way withdrawn from the laws of the most high creator and lawgiver, who administers the peace of the universe."[44]

I answer that there are two ways in which things are subject to the eternal law, as is evident from what I have said before:[45] one way as things partake of the eternal law in a conscious way; a second way by acting and being acted upon as things partake of the eternal law by reason of causes acting on them. And irrational creatures are subject to the eternal law in the second way, as I have said.[46] But because rational natures, along with what is common to all creatures, have something proper to them as rational, they are consequently subject to the eternal law in both ways. This is because they know the eternal law in some regard, as I have said,[47] and each rational creature has an inclination from nature toward things consonant with the eternal law. For "we are by nature equipped to possess virtues," as the *Ethics* says.[48]

But both ways are indeed incomplete and in some regard destroyed in the wicked, in whom both the natural inclination to virtue is perverted by vicious habits, and the natural knowledge of goodness is darkened by

---

[43]*On Free Choice* I, 6, n. 15 (PL 32:1229).

[44]*The City of God* XIX, 12 (PL 41:640).   [45]ST I–II, Q. 93, A. 5

[46]Ibid.   [47]ST I–II, Q. 93, A. 2.   [48]Aristotle, *Ethics* II, 1 (1103a25–6).

emotions and sinful habits. And both ways are more complete in the virtuous, since knowledge of faith and of wisdom is added to their natural knowledge of goodness, and the inner causal activity of grace and virtue is added to their natural inclination toward goodness.

Therefore, the virtuous are completely subject to the eternal law, as they always act in accord with it. And the wicked are indeed incompletely subject to the eternal law regarding their own actions, as they incompletely recognize and incompletely incline to goodness. But what their actions lack is proportionately supplemented by what they undergo, namely, as they suffer what the eternal law dictates for them insofar as they fail to do what befits the eternal law. And so Augustine says in his work *On Free Choice*: "I think that the righteous act subject to the eternal law."[49] And he says in his work *On Catechizing the Uneducated* that "God knows how to supply the inferior parts of his creation with the most suitable laws, by the just wretchedness of souls that abandon him."[50]

Reply Obj. 1. We can understand the words of the Apostle in two ways. We can understand them in one way as we understand to be under the law those who are subject to the obligations of the law against their will, as if pinned down by a weight. And so a gloss on the cited text says that "those are under the law who abstain from evil deeds out of fear of the punishment that the law threatens, not out of the love of justice."[51] And in this sense, spiritual human beings are not under the law, since they willingly fulfill the obligations of the law by the charity that the Holy Spirit pours into their hearts.

We can understand the words of the Apostle in a second way as we say that the deeds of human beings led by the Holy Spirit are deeds of the Spirit rather than deeds of the human beings. And so since the Holy Spirit, like the Son, is not subject to the law, as I have said before,[52] such deeds, as they belong to the Holy Spirit, are as a result not under the law. And the Apostle attests to this, saying in 2 Cor. 3:17: "Where there is the Spirit of the Lord, there is freedom."

Reply Obj. 2. Wisdom of the flesh cannot be subject to the law of God regarding resulting actions, since that wisdom inclines human beings to actions contrary to his law. But it can be subject to the law of God regarding what human beings undergo as a result, since it deserves to suffer punishment by the law of divine justice.

---

[49] *On Free Choice* I, 15, n. 31 (PL 32:1238).
[50] *On Catechizing the Uneducated* 18 (PL 40:333).
[51] *Glossa ordinaria*, on Gal. 5:18 (PL 114:584); Peter Lombard, *Glossa*, on Gal. 5:18 (PL 192:158–9).   [52] ST I–II, Q. 93, A. 4, *ad* 2.

Nonetheless, wisdom of the flesh does not so dominate in any human being that the whole goodness of nature is destroyed. And so human beings retain an inclination to do the things that belong to the eternal law. For I have maintained before that sin does not take away the whole goodness of nature.[53]

Reply Obj. 3. The same cause preserves things when they reach their end and inclines them to it. For example, the weight of heavy things causes them to rest in lower places and to be moved there. And so we should say that, as the eternal law causes persons to merit blessedness or wretchedness, so the same law causes them to be preserved in blessedness or wretchedness. And both the blessed and the damned are in this way subject to the eternal law.

Question 94
On the Natural Law

FIRST ARTICLE
Is the Natural Law a Habit?

We thus proceed to the first article. It seems that the natural law is a habit, for the following reasons:

Obj. 1. "Three things belong to the soul: powers, habits, and emotions," as the Philosopher says in the *Ethics.*[1] But the natural law is neither a power of the soul nor an emotion. Therefore, the natural law is a habit.

Obj. 2. Basil says that conscience, that is, *synderesis*, is "the law of our intellect,"[2] and we can only understand such regarding the natural law. But *synderesis* is a habit, as I maintained in the First Part.[3] Therefore, the natural law is a habit.

Obj. 3. The natural law always abides in human beings, as I shall make clear later.[4] But human beings' reason, to which that law belongs, is not always thinking about the natural law. Therefore, the natural law is a habit, not an act.

On the contrary, Augustine says in his work *On the Marital Good* that "habits are the means whereby we do things when we need to."[5] But the natural law is not such, since that law belongs to infants and the damned, who cannot act by reason of its presence. Therefore, the natural law is not a habit.

---

[53]ST I–II, Q. 85, A. 2.

[1]*Ethics* II, 5 (1105b20–1).

[2]*On the Six Days of Creation*, homily 7, n. 5 (PG 29:157).   [3]ST I, Q. 79, A. 12.

[4]ST I–II, Q. 94, A. 6.   [5]*On the Marital Good* 21 (PL 40:390).

I answer that we can speak about habits in two ways. We speak of them in one way in the strict sense and essentially, and then the natural law is not a habit. For I have said before that the natural law is constituted by reason,[6] just as propositions are works of reason. And what one does and the means whereby one does it are not the same. For example, one makes a fitting speech by means of the habit of grammar. Therefore, since habits are the means whereby one does things, the natural law cannot be a habit in the strict sense and essentially.

We can speak of habits in a second way as what we possess by reason of habits. For example, we call faith what we have by reason of the habit of faith. And so, as reason sometimes actually considers precepts of the natural law and sometimes only habitually possesses them, we can in the latter way say that the natural law is a habit. Just so, the indemonstrable first principles in theoretical matters are principles belonging to the habit of first principles, not the habit.

Reply Obj. 1. The Philosopher in the cited text is attempting to discover the genus of virtues. And since virtues are evidently sources of activity, he posits only things that are sources of human activity, namely, powers, habits, and emotions.[7] But other things belong to the soul besides the latter three. For example, certain acts belong to the soul: willing to those willing, and things known to those knowing. And the natural properties of the soul, such as immortality and the like, belong to the soul.

Reply Obj. 2. Basil calls *synderesis* the law of our intellect insofar as it is the habit that contains the precepts of the natural law, that is, the first principles of human actions.

Reply Obj. 3. The argument of this objection reaches the conclusion that we possess the natural law in a habitual way, and we concede this.

Qualification of the argument in the section On the contrary. Sometimes, due to an impediment, one cannot make use of what one possesses habitually. For example, human beings cannot make use of habitual knowledge when they are asleep. And likewise, children cannot make use of habitual understanding of first principles, or even of the natural law, which they possess habitually, due to their immature age.

---

[6]ST I–II, Q. 90, A. 1, *ad* 2.

[7]We have here and in like contexts translated *passio* as "emotion." There is, however, a nuance to *passio* that "emotion" does not convey. *Passio* in general means being acted upon, that is, *undergoing* emotion. Substituting "passion," which would etymologically preserve the nuance, might suggest to English readers that the word means violent or sexual emotion. In any case, the nuance does not seem relevant to these contexts.

SECOND ARTICLE
Does the Natural Law Include Several Precepts or Only One?

We thus proceed to the second inquiry. It seems that that the natural law includes only one precept, not several, for the following reasons:

Obj. 1. Law belongs to the genus of precept, as I have maintained before.[8] Therefore, if there were to be many precepts of the natural law, it would follow logically that there would also be many natural laws.

Obj. 2. The natural law results from the nature of human beings. But human nature as a whole is one, although multiple regarding its parts. Therefore, either there is only one precept of the natural law because of the unity of the whole, or there are many precepts because of the many parts of human nature. And so even things that regard inclinations of con- cupiscible power will need to belong to the natural law.

Obj. 3. Law belongs to reason, as I have said before.[9] But there is only one power of reason in human beings. Therefore, there is only one pre- cept of the natural law.

On the contrary, the precepts of the natural law in human beings are related to action as the first principles in scientific matters are related to theoretical knowledge. But there are several indemonstrable first princi- ples of theoretical knowledge. Therefore, there are also several precepts of the natural law.

I answer that, as I have said before,[10] the precepts of the natural law are related to practical reason as the first principles of scientific demonstra- tions are related to theoretical reason. For both the precepts of the natu- ral law and the first principles of scientific demonstrations are self-evident principles. And we speak of things being self-evident in two ways: in one way as such; in a second way in relation to ourselves. We indeed speak of self-evident propositions as such when their predicates belong to the nature of their subjects, although such propositions may not be self-evident to those who do not know the definition of the subjects. For example, the proposition "Human beings are rational" is by its nature self-evident, since to speak of something human is to speak of something rational, although the proposition is not self-evident to one who does not know what a human being is. And so, as Boethius says in his work *On Groups of Seven,*[11] there are axioms or universally self-evident proposi- tions, and propositions whose terms all persons know (e.g., "Every whole is greater than one of its parts" and "Things equal to the same thing are

---

[8]ST I–II, Q. 92, A. 2.   [9]ST I–II, Q. 90, A. 1.   [10]ST I–II, Q. 91, A. 3.

[11]*On Groups of Seven* (PL 64:1311). This work is otherwise known as *How Substances as Existing Things Are Good.*

themselves equal") are such. But some propositions are self-evident only to the wise, who understand what the proposition's terms signify. For example, for those who understand that angels are not material substances, it is self-evident that angels are not circumscriptively in a place, something not evident to the uneducated, who do not understand the nature of angels.

And there is a priority regarding the things that fall within the understanding of all persons. For what first falls within our understanding is being, the understanding of which is included in everything that one understands. And so the first indemonstrable principle is that one cannot at the same time affirm and deny the same thing. And this principle is based on the nature of being and nonbeing, and all other principles are based on it, as the *Metaphysics* says.[12] And as being is the first thing that without qualification falls within understanding, so good is the first thing that falls within the understanding of practical reason. And practical reason is ordered to action, since every efficient cause acts for the sake of an end, which has the nature of good. And so the first principle in practical reason is one based on the nature of good, namely, that good is what all things seek. Therefore, the first precept of the natural law is that we should do and seek good, and shun evil. And all the other precepts of the natural law are based on that precept, namely, that all the things that practical reason by nature understands to be human goods or evils belong to precepts of the natural law as things to be done or shunned.

And since good has the nature of end, and evil the nature of the contrary, reason by nature understands to be good all the things for which human beings have a natural inclination, and so to be things to be actively sought, and understands contrary things as evil and to be shunned. Therefore, the order of our natural inclinations ordains the precepts of the natural law.

First, for example, human beings have an inclination for good by the nature they share with all substances, namely, as every substance by nature seeks to preserve itself. And regarding this inclination, means that preserve our human life and prevent the contrary belong to the natural law.

Second, human beings have more particular inclinations by the nature they share with other animals. And so the *Digest* says that things "that nature has taught all animals," such as the sexual union of male and female, and the upbringing of children, and the like, belong to the natural law.[13]

Third, human beings have inclinations for good by their rational nature, which is proper to them. For example, human beings by nature

---

[12]Aristotle, *Metaphysics* III, 3 (1005b29–34).

[13]Justinian, *Digest* I, title 1, law 1.

have inclinations to know truths about God and to live in society with other human beings. And so things that relate to such inclinations belong to the natural law (e.g., that human beings shun ignorance, that they not offend those with whom they ought to live sociably, and other such things regarding those inclinations).

Reply Obj. 1. All the precepts of the natural law, insofar as they relate to one first precept, have the nature of one natural law.

Reply Obj. 2. All the inclinations of any part of human nature (e.g., the concupiscible and irascible powers), insofar as reason rules them, belong to the natural law and are traced to one first precept, as I have said.[14] And so there are many precepts of the natural law as such, but they share a common foundation.

Reply Obj. 3. Reason, although as such one power, ordains everything that concerns human beings. And so the law of reason includes everything that reason can rule.

THIRD ARTICLE
Do All Virtuous Acts Belong to the Natural Law?

We thus proceed to the third inquiry. It seems that not all virtuous acts belong to the natural law, for the following reasons:

Obj. 1. It belongs to the nature of law that law be ordered to the common good, as I have said before.[15] But some virtuous acts are ordered to the private good of an individual, as is particularly evident in the case of acts of the virtue of moderation. Therefore, not all virtuous acts are subject to the natural law.

Obj. 2. All sins are contrary to certain virtuous acts. Therefore, if all virtuous acts belong to the natural law, it seems that all sins are consequently contrary to nature. And yet we say this in a special way about some sins.

Obj. 3. Everybody agrees about things that are in accord with nature. But not everybody agrees about virtuous acts, for things that are virtuous for some are vicious for others. Therefore, not all virtuous acts belong to the natural law.

On the contrary, Damascene says in his work *On Orthodox Faith* that "virtues are natural."[16] Therefore, virtuous acts are also subject to the natural law.

I answer that we can speak about virtuous acts in two ways: in one way as virtuous; in a second way as we consider such acts in their own species.

---

[14]In the body of the article.   [15]ST I–II, Q. 90, A. 2.

[16]*On Orthodox Faith* III, 14 (PG 94:1045).

Therefore, if we are speaking about virtuous acts as virtuous, then all virtuous acts belong to the natural law.[17] For I have said that everything to which human beings are inclined by their nature belongs to the natural law. But everything is by its nature inclined to the activity that its form renders fitting. For example, fire is inclined to heat things. And so, since the rational soul is the specific form of human beings, everyone has an inclination from one's nature to act in accord with reason. And this is to act virtuously. And so in this regard, all virtuous acts belong to the natural law, since one's own reason by nature dictates that one act virtuously.

But if we should be speaking about virtuous acts as such and such, namely, as we consider them in their own species, then not all virtuous acts belong to the natural law. For we do many things virtuously to which nature does not at first incline us, but which human beings by the inquiry of reason have discovered to be useful for living righteously.

Reply Obj. 1. Moderation concerns the natural desires for food and drink and sex, which desires are indeed ordered to the natural common good, just as other prescriptions of the natural law are ordered to the moral common good.

Reply Obj. 2. We can call the nature proper to human beings the nature of human beings. And so all sins, insofar as they are contrary to reason, are also contrary to nature, as Damascene makes clear in his work *On Orthodox Faith.*[18] Or else we can call the nature common to human beings and other animals the nature of human beings. And so we speak of certain particular sins being contrary to nature. For example, the sexual intercourse of males, which we specifically call the sin contrary to nature, is contrary to the sexual union of male and female, and such sexual union is natural for all animals.

Reply Obj. 3. The argument of this objection is valid regarding virtuous acts as such and such. For then, because of the different conditions of human beings, some acts may be virtuous for some persons, as proportionate and suitable for them, which are nonetheless vicious for other persons, as disproportionate for them.

FOURTH ARTICLE
Is the Natural Law the Same for All Human Beings?

We thus proceed to the fourth article. It seems that the natural law is not the same for all human beings, for the following reasons:

---

[17]ST I–II, Q. 94, A. 2.

[18]*On Orthodox Faith* II, 4 and 30 (PG 94:876, 976).

Obj. 1. The *Decretum* says that "the natural law is contained in the [Old] Law and the Gospel."[19] But what is contained in the Law and the Gospel is not in the common possession of all, since Rom. 10:16 says: "Some do not heed the Gospel." Therefore, the natural law is not the same for all human beings.

Obj. 2. "We call things in accord with law just," as the *Ethics* says.[20] But the same work says that nothing is so universally just that it is not otherwise for some.[21] Therefore, even the natural law is not the same for all human beings.

Obj. 3. Things to which human beings' nature inclines them belong to the natural law, as I have said before.[22] But nature inclines different human beings to different things. For example, nature inclines some to desire pleasures, others to desire honors, others to desire other things. Therefore, the natural law is not the same for all human beings.

On the contrary, Isidore says in his *Etymologies*: "The natural law is common to all peoples."[23]

I answer that things to which nature inclines human beings belong to the natural law, as I have said before,[24] and one of the things proper to human beings is that their nature inclines them to act in accord with reason. And it belongs to reason to advance from the general to the particular, as the *Physics* makes clear.[25] And regarding that process, theoretical reason proceeds in one way, and practical reason in another way. For inasmuch as theoretical reason is especially concerned about necessary things, which cannot be otherwise disposed, its particular conclusions, just like its general principles, are true without exception. But practical reason is concerned about contingent things, which include human actions. And so the more reason goes from the general to the particular, the more exceptions we find, although there is some necessity in the general principles. Therefore, truth in theoretical matters, both first principles and conclusions, is the same for all human beings, although some know only the truth of the principles, which we call universal propositions, and not the truth of the conclusions. But truth in practical matters, or practical rectitude, is the same for all human beings only regarding the general principles, not regarding the particular conclusions. And not all of those with practical rectitude regarding particulars know the truth in equal measure.

---

[19]Gratian, *Decretum* I, dist. 1, preface.   [20]Aristotle, *Ethics* V, 1 (1129b12).
[21]Ibid., 7 (1134b32).   [22]ST I–II, Q. 94, AA. 2, 3.
[23]*Etymologies* V, 4 (PL 82:199).   [24]ST I–II, Q. 94, AA. 2, 3.
[25]Aristotle, *Physics* I, 1 (184a16–27).

Therefore, the truth or rectitude regarding the general principles of both theoretical and practical reason is the same for all persons and known in equal measure by all of them. And the truth regarding the particular conclusions of theoretical reason is the same for all persons, but some know such truth less than others. For example, it is true for all persons that triangles have three angles equal to two right angles, although not everybody knows this.

But the truth or rectitude regarding particular conclusions of practical reason is neither the same for all persons nor known in equal measure even by those for whom it is the same. For example, it is correct and true for all persons that they should act in accord with reason. And it follows as a particular conclusion from this principle that those holding goods in trust should return the goods to the goods' owners. And this is indeed true for the most part, but it might in particular cases be injurious, and so contrary to reason, to return the goods (e.g., if the owner should be seeking to attack one's country). And the more the particular conclusion goes into particulars, the more exceptions there are (e.g., if one should declare that entrusted goods should be returned to their owners with such and such safeguards or in such and such ways). For the more particular conditions are added to the particular conclusion, the more ways there may be exceptions, so that the conclusion about returning or not returning entrusted goods is erroneous.

Therefore, we should say that the natural law regarding general first principles is the same for all persons both as to the principles' rectitude and as to knowledge of them. And the natural law regarding particulars, which are, as it were, conclusions from the general principles, is for the most part the same for all persons both as to its rectitude and as to knowledge of it. Nonetheless, it can be wanting in rather few cases both as to its rectitude and as to knowledge of it. As to rectitude, the natural law can be wanting because of particular obstacles, just as natures that come to be and pass away are wanting in rather few cases because of obstacles. And also as to knowledge of the natural law, the law can be wanting because emotions or evil habituation or evil natural disposition has perverted the reason of some. For example, the Germans of old did not consider robbery wicked, as Caesar's *Gallic Wars* relates,[26] although robbery is expressly contrary to the natural law.

Reply Obj. 1. We should not understand the cited statement to mean that all the matters included in the Law and the Gospel belong to the natural law, since the Law and the Gospel transmit to us many things above

---

[26]Julius Caesar, *Gallic Wars* VI, 23.

nature. Rather, we should understand the statement to mean that the Law and the Gospel completely transmit to us the things that belong to the natural law. And so Gratian, after saying that "the natural law is contained in the Law and the Gospel," immediately adds by way of example: "And everyone is thereby commanded to do to others what one wishes to be done to oneself."

Reply Obj. 2. We should understand the cited statement of the Philosopher regarding things just by nature as conclusions derived from general principles, not as the general principles. And such conclusions are correct for the most part and are wanting in rather few cases.

Reply Obj. 3. As the power of reason in human beings rules and commands other powers, so reason needs to direct all the natural inclinations belonging to other powers. And so it is universally correct for all persons to direct all their inclinations by reason.

FIFTH ARTICLE
Can the Natural Law Vary?

We thus proceed to the fifth article. It seems that the natural law can vary, for the following reasons:

Obj. 1. A gloss on Sir. 17:9, "He [God] supplied them with instruction and the law of life," says: "He wanted the [Old] Law to be written in order to correct the natural law."[27] But what is corrected is changed. Therefore, the natural law can vary.

Obj. 2. The killing of innocent human beings as well as adultery and theft are contrary to the natural law. But God altered these precepts. For example, God on one occasion commanded Abraham to slay his innocent son, as Gen. 22:2 relates. And God on another occasion commanded the Jews to steal vessels the Egyptians had lent them, as Ex. 12:35–6 relates. And God on another occasion commanded Hosea to take a fornicating wife, as Hos. 1:2 relates. Therefore, the natural law can vary.

Obj. 3. Isidore says in his Etymologies that "the common possession of all property and the same freedom for all persons belong to the natural law."[28] But we perceive that human laws have altered these precepts. Therefore, it seems that the natural law can vary.

On the contrary, the *Decretum* says: "The natural law originates with rational creatures. It does not vary over time and abides without change."[29]

I answer that we can understand the mutability of the natural law in two ways. We can understand it in one way by things being added to it.

---

[27] *Glossa ordinaria*, on Sir. 17:9 (PL 109:876; 113:1201).

[28] *Etymologies* V, 4 (PL 82:199).   [29] Gratian, *Decretum* I, dist. 5, preface.

And then nothing prevents the natural law changing, since both divine law and human laws add to natural law many things beneficial to human life.

We can understand the mutability of the natural law in a second way by way of subtraction, namely, that things previously subject to the law cease to be so. And then the natural law is altogether immutable as to its first principles. And as to its secondary precepts, which we said are proper proximate conclusions, as it were, from the first principles,[30] the natural law is not so changed that what it prescribes is not for the most part completely correct. But it can be changed regarding particulars and in rather few cases, due to special causes that prevent observance of such precepts, as I have said before.[31]

Reply Obj. 1. We say that written law has been given to correct the natural law either because the written law supplements what the natural law lacked, or because the natural law in the hearts of some regarding particulars had been corrupted insofar as they thought that things by nature evil were good. And such corruption needed correction.

Reply Obj. 2. All human beings, without exception, both the innocent and the guilty, die when natural death comes. And God's power indeed inflicts such natural death on human beings because of original sin, as 1 Sam. 2:6 says: "The Lord causes death and life." And so, at the command of God, death can without any injustice be inflicted on any human being, whether guilty or innocent.

Likewise, adultery is sexual intercourse with another man's wife, whom the law handed down by God has allotted to him. And so there is no adultery or fornication in having intercourse with any woman at the command of God.

And the argument is the same regarding theft, which consists of taking another's property. One does not take without the consent of the owner (i.e., steal) anything that one takes at the command of God, who is the owner of all property.

Nor is it only regarding human affairs that everything God commands is owed to him. Rather, regarding things of nature, everything God does is also in one respect natural, as I said in the First Part.[32]

Reply Obj. 3. We speak of things belonging to the natural law in two ways. We speak of them belonging in one way because nature inclines us to them. For example, one should not cause injury to another. We speak of them belonging in a second way because nature did not introduce the contrary. For example, we could say that it belongs to the natural law that human beings are naked, since nature did not endow them with clothes,

---

[30]ST I–II, Q. 94, A. 4. [31]Ibid. [32]ST I, Q. 105, A. 6, *ad* 1.

which human skill created. And it is in the latter way that we say that "the common possession of all property and the same freedom for all persons" belong to the natural law, namely, that the reason of human beings, not nature, introduced private property and compulsory servitude. And so the natural law in this respect varies only by way of addition.

SIXTH ARTICLE
Can the Natural Law Be Excised
from the Hearts of Human Beings?

We thus proceed to the sixth article. It seems that the natural law can be excised from the hearts of human beings, for the following reasons:

Obj. 1. A gloss on Rom. 2:14, "When the Gentiles, who do not have the law," etc., says: "The law of righteousness, which sin had wiped out, is inscribed on the inner human being renewed by grace."[33] But the law of righteousness is the natural law. Therefore, the natural law can be wiped out.

Obj. 2. The law of grace is more efficacious than the law of nature. But sin destroys the law of grace. Therefore, much more can the natural law be wiped out.

Obj. 3. What law establishes is rendered just, as it were. But human beings have established many things contrary to the natural law. Therefore, the natural law can be excised from the hearts of human beings.

On the contrary, Augustine says in his *Confessions*: "Your law is inscribed on the hearts of human beings, and indeed no wickedness wipes it out."[34] But the law inscribed on the hearts of human beings is the natural law. Therefore, the natural law cannot be wiped out.

I answer that, as I have said before,[35] there belong to the natural law, indeed primarily, very general precepts, precepts that everyone knows, and more particular, secondary precepts, which are like proximate conclusions from first principles. Therefore, regarding the general principles, the natural law in general can in no way be excised from the hearts of human beings. But the natural law is wiped out regarding particular actions insofar as desires or other emotions prevent reason from applying the general principles to particular actions, as I have said before.[36]

And the natural law can be excised from the hearts of human beings regarding the other, secondary precepts, either because of wicked opinions, just as errors in theoretical matters happen regarding necessary

---

[33]*Glossa ordinaria*, on Rom. 2:14 (PL 114:476); Peter Lombard, *Glossa*, on Rom. 2:14 (PL 191:1345).   [34]*Confessions* II, 4 (PL 32:678).
[35]ST I–II, Q. 94, AA. 4, 5.   [36]ST I–II, Q. 77, A. 2.

conclusions or because of evil customs or corrupt habits. For example, some did not think robbery a sin,[37] or even sins against nature to be sinful, as the Apostle also says in Rom. 1:24–8.

Reply Obj. 1. Sin wipes out the natural law regarding particulars but not in general, except perhaps regarding secondary precepts of the natural law, in the way I mentioned.[38]

Reply Obj. 2. Although grace is more efficacious than nature, nature is nonetheless more essential to human beings and so more abiding.

Reply Obj. 3. The argument of this objection is valid regarding the secondary precepts of the natural law, contrary to which some lawmakers have passed wicked statutes.

Question 95
On Human Law

FIRST ARTICLE
Was It Beneficial That Human Beings Establish Laws?

We thus proceed to the first inquiry. It seems that it was not beneficial that human beings establish laws, for the following reasons:

Obj. 1. The purpose of every law is to make human beings good, as I have said before.[1] But admonitions induce human beings willingly to live rightly more than laws do coercively. Therefore, there was no need to establish laws.

Obj. 2. The Philosopher says in the *Ethics*: "Human beings have recourse to judges as justice-in-the-flesh."[2] But justice-in-the-flesh is better than the inanimate justice contained in laws. Therefore, it would have been better to commit the execution of justice to the decisions of judges than to establish laws to supplement their decisions.

Obj. 3. Every law directs human actions, as is evident from what I have said before.[3] But since human acts regard particular things, which are potentially infinite, only the wise, who regard particulars, can sufficiently contemplate the things that belong to the direction of human acts. Therefore, it would have been better that the decisions of wise persons direct human actions than that any established law should. Therefore, there was no need to establish human laws.

On the contrary, Isidore says in his *Etymologies*: "Laws were established so that fear of them curb human audacity, and that innocence be safe in

---

[37]ST I–II, Q. 94, A. 4.   [38]In the body of the article.

[1]ST I–II, Q. 92, A. 1.   [2]*Ethics* V, 4 (1132a22).   [3]ST I–II, Q. 90, AA. 1, 2.

the midst of the wicked, and that the fear of punishment restrain the ability of the wicked to inflict harm."[4] But the human race most needs such things. Therefore, it was necessary to establish human laws.

I answer that, as is evident from what I have said before,[5] human beings by nature have a capacity for virtue, but they need to arrive at the very perfection of virtue by some training.[6] Just so, we perceive that industriousness helps them regarding their necessities (e.g., food and clothing). And nature gives them the sources to provide these necessities, namely, reason and hands, not the full complement of the necessities that nature gives other animals, for whom nature has sufficiently provided covering and food.

But human beings are not readily self-sufficient in regard to this training, since the perfection of virtue consists chiefly of human beings' restraint from excessive pleasures, toward which they are most prone. And this is especially true of youths, for whom training is more efficacious. And so human beings receive such training, whereby they arrive at virtue, from others. And indeed regarding youths prone to virtuous acts by good natural disposition or habituation (or, rather, a gift from God), paternal training, which consists of admonitions, suffices. But some persons are wicked and prone to vices, and cannot be easily persuaded by words. Therefore, force and fear were needed to restrain them from evil. Consequently, at least desisting from evil deeds, they would both leave others in peace and be themselves at length brought by such habituation to do voluntarily what they hitherto did out of fear, and so become virtuous. But such training, which compels by fear of punishment, is the training administered by laws. And so it was necessary to establish laws in order that human beings live in peace and have virtue. For, as the Philosopher says in the *Politics*: "As human beings, if perfect in virtue, are the best of animals, so are they, if cut off from law and justice, the worst of all animals."[7] This is because human beings, unlike other animals, have the defensive armor of reason to complement their disordered desires and beastly rages.

Reply Obj. 1. Voluntary admonitions induce well-disposed human beings to virtue better than compulsion does, but there are some who are not induced to virtue unless they be compelled.

---

[4]*Etymologies* V, 20 (PL 82:202).   [5]ST I–II. Q. 63, A. 1; Q. 94, A. 3.
[6]Thomas generally uses the word *disciplina* to mean instruction. But the instruction at issue here is practical in the fullest sense, with coercion the punishment for noncompliance. Therefore, we translate *disciplina* in this and like contexts as "training."   [7]*Politics* I, 1 (1253a31–3).

Reply Obj. 2. The Philosopher says in the *Rhetoric*: "It is better that law direct all things than that they be left to the decisions of judges."[8] And this is so for three reasons. First, indeed, it is easier to find the few wise persons sufficient to establish right laws than the many wise persons necessary to judge rightly about particular matters. Second, lawmakers consider over a long time what to impose by law, but judges reach decisions about particular deeds as cases spontaneously arise. And human beings can more easily perceive what is right by considering many instances than they can by considering only one deed. Third, lawmakers decide in general and about future events, but presiding judges decide current cases, and love or hatred or covetousness affects such decisions. And so their decisions are perverted.

Therefore, since few embody the justice required of a judge, and since that justice can be perverted, it was necessary that law determine, whenever possible, what judges should decide, and commit very few matters to the decisions of human beings.

Reply Obj. 3. "We need to commit to judges" certain particular details, which laws cannot encompass, as the Philosopher also says in the *Rhetoric*,[9] such as, "whether alleged deeds have or have not been done," and the like.

Second Article
Is Every Human Law Derived from the Natural Law?

We thus proceed to the second inquiry. It seems that not every human law is derived from the natural law, for the following reasons:

Obj. 1. The Philosopher says in the *Ethics* that "it does not at all matter originally whether one effects legal justice in this or that way."[10] But regarding obligations to which the natural law gives rise, it does matter whether one effects justice in this or that way. Therefore, not all the things established by human laws are derived from the natural law.

Obj. 2. Positive law differs from natural law, as Isidore makes clear in his *Etymologies*,[11] and the Philosopher makes clear in the *Ethics*.[12] But things derived as conclusions from the general principles of the natural law belong to the natural law, as I have said before.[13] Therefore, things proper to human law are not derived from the natural law.

Obj. 3. The natural law is the same for all persons. For the Philosopher says in the Ethics that "natural justice has the same force everywhere."[14]

---

[8]*Rhetoric* I, 1 (1354a31–4). [9]Ibid., (1354b13). [10]*Ethics* V, 7 (1134b20).
[11]*Etymologies* V, 4 (PL 82:199). [12]*Ethics* V, 7 (1134b18–9).
[13]ST I–II, Q. 94, A. 4. [14]*Ethics* V, 7 (1134b19–20).

Therefore, if human laws were to be derived from the natural law, human laws would likewise be the same for all persons. But such a conclusion is evidently false.

Obj. 4. We can assign reasons for things derived from the natural law. But "one cannot assign reasons for all the statutes rulers have decreed," as the Jurist says.[15] Therefore, some human laws are not derived from the natural law.

On the contrary, Cicero says in his *Rhetoric*: "Fear and reverence for the laws have prescribed things derived from nature and approved by custom."[16]

I answer that Augustine says in his work *On Free Choice*: "Unjust laws do not seem to be laws."[17] And so laws have binding force insofar as they have justice. And we say regarding human affairs that things are just because they are right according to the rule of reason. But the primary rule of reason is the natural law, as is evident from what I have said before.[18] And so every human law has as much of the nature of law as it is derived from the natural law. And a human law diverging in any way from the natural law will be a perversion of law and no longer a law.

But we should note that we can derive things from the natural law in two ways: in one way as conclusions from its first principles; in a second way as specifications of certain general principles. Indeed, the first way is like the way in which we draw conclusions from first principles in theoretical sciences. And the second way is like the way that craftsmen in the course of exercising their skill adapt general forms to specific things. For example, a builder needs to adapt the general form of a house to this or that shape of a house. Therefore, some things are derived from general principles of the natural law as conclusions. For example, one can derive the prohibition against homicide from the general principle that one should do no evil to anyone. And some things are derived from general principles of the natural law as specifications. For example, the natural law ordains that criminals should be punished, but that criminals be punished in this or that way is a specification of the natural law.

Therefore, human laws are derived from the natural law in both ways. Things derived from the natural law in the first way are not only contained in human laws as established by those laws, but they also have part of their binding force from the natural law. But things derived from the natural law in the second way have all of their binding force from human law.

---

[15]*Digest* I, title 3, law 20.   [16]*Rhetoric* II, 53.

[17]*On Free Choice* I, 5, n. 11 (PL 32:1227).   [18]ST I–II, Q. 91, A. 2, *ad* 2.

Reply Obj. 1. The Philosopher is speaking about the things laws decreed by determining or specifying one of the precepts of the natural law.

Reply Obj. 2. The argument of this objection is valid regarding things derived from the natural law as conclusions.

Reply Obj. 3. The general principles of the natural law cannot be applied to all peoples in the same way because of the great variety of human affairs. And so there are different positive laws for different peoples.

Reply Obj. 4. We should understand the Jurist's statement to regard things decreed by rulers about particular specifications of the natural law. And the judgments of experienced and prudent persons are indeed related to such specifications as certain principles underlying their judgments, namely, inasmuch as they immediately perceive what is the most fitting particular specification. And so the Philosopher says in the *Ethics* that "we should" in such matters "attend to the intuitive statements and opinions of the experienced and the mature or prudent no less than to their arguments."[19]

THIRD ARTICLE

**Does Isidore Appropriately Describe
the Characteristics of Positive Law?**

We thus proceed to the third inquiry. Isidore says: "Laws should be virtuous, just, possible by nature, in accord with a country's customs, suitable to time and place, necessary, useful, so clear that they contain nothing obscure to cause deception, and decreed for the common benefit of all citizens, not the private benefit of some."[20] It seems that he in this way inappropriately describes the characteristics of positive law, for the following reasons:

Obj. 1. Isidore previously had explained the characteristics of law in terms of three conditions: "Laws should be everything constituted by reason if befitting religion, suitable for training, and useful for the commonweal."[21] Therefore, he later unnecessarily added further conditions of law.

Obj. 2. Justice is a virtue, as Cicero says in his work *On Duties.*[22] Therefore, Isidore needlessly adds "just" after he mentioned "virtuous."

Obj. 3. Isidore contradistinguished written laws from customs.[23] Therefore, he ought not to have posited in the definition of law that laws be "in accord with a country's customs."

Obj. 4. We call things necessary in two ways. Things that cannot be otherwise, are absolutely necessary, and such necessary things are not

---

[19]*Ethics* VI, 11 (1143b11–13).   [20]*Etymologies* V, 21 (PL 82:203).   [21]Ibid., 3 (PL 82:199).   [22]*On Duties* I, 7   [23]*Etymologies* II, 10 (PL 82:131); V, 3 (PL 82:199).

subject to human judgment. And so such necessity does not belong to human law. Other things are necessary for ends, and such necessity is the same as usefulness. Therefore, Isidore needlessly posits both "necessary" and "useful" as characteristics of law.

On the contrary, there stands the authority of Isidore himself.

I answer that we need to determine the form of any means in relation to the end desired. For example, the form of a saw is such as to be suitable for cutting wood, as the *Physics* makes clear.[24] Likewise, everything ruled and measured needs to have a form apportioned to its rule or measure. And human law has both, since it is both something ordered to an end and a rule or measure ruled or measured by a higher measure. And the higher measure is indeed of two kinds, namely, the divine law and the natural law, as is evident from what I have said before.[25] But the end of human law is the benefit of human beings, as the Jurist also says.[26] And so indeed Isidore first posited three things as conditions of human law, namely, that human law benefit religion (i.e., as human law is properly related to the divine law), that human law be suitable for training (i.e., as human law is properly related to the natural law), and that human law be useful for the commonweal (i.e., as human law is properly related to human usefulness).

And all the other conditions that he later mentions are traceable to these three things. For what he calls virtuous is a reference to what befits religion. And by adding that human laws be "just, possible by nature, in accord with a country's customs, suitable to the place and time," he indicates that the laws should be suitable for training. For we indeed first consider human training in relation to the order of reason, which order is implied in what he calls just. Second, we consider human training in relation to the capacity of human agents. For training ought to be suitable to each according to the capacity of each, including natural capacity. (For example, one should not impose the same training on children that one imposes on adults.) And training ought to be suitable according to human customs, since human beings do not live in society by themselves, not manifesting their behavior to others. Third, in relation to requisite circumstances, he says: "suitable to the place and time."

And the additional words, "necessary," "useful," and so forth, refer to what facilitates the commonweal. For example, necessity refers to removing evils, usefulness to acquiring benefits, and clarification to preventing harm that could arise from the laws themselves.

---

[24]Aristotle, *Physics* II, 9 (200a10–3, b5–9).

[25]ST I–II, Q. 95, A. 1; ST I–II, Q. 93, A. 3.   [26]*Digest* I, title 3, law 25.

And he indicates that human laws are ordered to the common good, as I have previously affirmed,[27] in the last part of the definition.

Reply Objs. 1–4. The answer makes clear the replies to the objections.

FOURTH ARTICLE
Does Isidore Appropriately Designate Kinds of Human Law?[28]

We thus proceed to the fourth inquiry. It seems that Isidore does not appropriately designate kinds of human law, for the following reasons:

Obj. 1. Isidore includes in human law "the common law of peoples," which he so names, as he says, because "almost every people possesses it."[29] But "natural law is common to all peoples," as he himself says.[30] Therefore, "the common law of peoples is contained in the natural law rather than positive human law.

Obj. 2. Things that have the same binding force seem to differ only materially, not formally. But "statutes, plebiscites, decrees of the senate," and the other like things Isidore describes[31] all have the same binding force. Therefore, they seem to differ only materially. But artisans should pay no attention to such differences, since there can be an endless number of them. Therefore, Isidore inappropriately introduces such divisions.

Obj. 3. As there are rulers and priests and soldiers in political communities, so human beings also have other public duties. Therefore, as Isidore posits "military law" and "public law" (which govern priests and magistrates),[32] so he should also posit other laws pertaining to other public duties.

Obj. 4. We should ignore accidental things. But it is accidental to laws whether they are framed by this or that human being. Therefore, Isidore inappropriately posits a division of laws by the names of their framers,[33] namely, that one is called the Cornelian law, another the Falcidian law, and so forth.

On the contrary, the authority of Isidore suffices.

I answer that we can intrinsically distinguish each thing by what belongs to its nature. For example, the nature of animal includes a soul that is rational or nonrational. And so we properly and intrinsically distinguish animals by whether they are rational or irrational, and not by whether they are black or white, which are characteristics altogether outside the nature of animals.

And many characteristics belong to the nature of human laws, and we can properly and intrinsically distinguish human laws by any of those

---

[27]ST I–II, Q. 90, A. 2.   [28]*Etymologies* V, 4 (PL 82:199ff.).
[29]Ibid., 6 (PL. 82:200).   [30]Ibid., 4 (PL 82:199).   [31]Ibid., 9 (PL 82:200).
[32]Ibid., 7 and 8 (PL 82:200).   [33]Ibid., 15 (PL 82:201).

things. For example, it first of all belongs to the nature of human laws that they be derived from the natural law, as is evident from what I have said before.[34] And we in this respect divide positive laws into the common law of peoples and the laws of particular commonwealths by the two ways in which things may be derived from the natural law, as I have said before.[35] For precepts derived from the natural law as conclusions from its general principles belong to the common law of peoples (e.g., just buying and selling, and the like, without which human beings cannot live sociably with one another). And living sociably with others belongs to the natural law, since human beings are by nature social animals, as the *Politics* proves.[36] But precepts derived from the natural law by way of particular specifications belong to the laws of particular commonwealths, whereby each commonwealth specifies things suitable for itself.

Second, it belongs to the nature of human laws that they be ordered to the common good of a political community. And we can in this respect distinguish human laws by the different kinds of persons who perform particular tasks for the common good (e.g., priests, who pray to God for the people; rulers, who govern the people; soldiers, who fight for the safety of the people). And so special laws are adapted for such persons.

Third, it belongs to the nature of human laws that they be established by those who govern the political community, as I have said before.[37] And we in this respect distinguish human laws by the different forms of governing political communities. And as the Philosopher says in the *Politics*,[38] one of these forms is monarchy (i.e., rule by one person). And we understand the laws of monarchical regimes as royal decrees. And aristocracy (i.e., rule by the best persons or aristocrats) is another form of government. And we understand the laws of aristocratic regimes as the authoritative legal opinions of the wise, and also as the decrees of the senate. And oligarchy (i.e., rule by a few rich and powerful persons) is another form of government. And we understand the laws of oligarchical regimes as magisterial law, also called law by dignitaries. And another form of government is by the people, which form we call democracy. And we understand the laws of democratic regimes as laws by the people. (Tyranny is another form of government, an altogether corrupt form, and so we do not understand the laws of tyrannical regimes as any law.) There is also a form of government that is a mixture of the good forms, and this mixed form of government is the best. And we

---

[34]ST I–II, Q. 95, A. 2.   [35]Ibid.   [36]Aristotle, *Politics* I, 1 (1253a2–3).
[37]ST I–II, Q. 90, A. 3.   [38]*Politics* III, 7 (1279a23–b10).

understand the laws of such regimes as law "prescribed by elders and the people," as Isidore says.[39]

Fourth, it belongs to the nature of human laws that they direct human actions. And we in this respect distinguish laws, which we sometimes designate by their authors, by the laws' different subject matter. For example, we distinguish the Julian Law on adultery,[40] the Cornelian Law on assassination,[41] and the like, because of their subject matter, not because of their authors.

Reply Obj. 1. The common law of peoples is indeed natural for human beings in one respect, insofar as it is rational, since it is derived from the natural law as conclusions not very remote from general principles of the natural law. And so human beings easily agree about such matters. But we distinguish the common law of peoples from the natural law, especially from what is common to all animals.

Reply Objs. 2–4. The replies to these objections are evident from what I have said.[42]

Question 96
On the Power of Human Laws

First Article
Should Human Laws Be Framed in
Particular Rather than General Terms?

We thus proceed to the first inquiry. It seems that human laws should be framed in particular rather than general terms, for the following reasons:

Obj. 1. The Philosopher says in the *Ethics* that "things of the legal order consist of everything laws decree about individual matters, and likewise of judicial decisions,"[1] which also concern particular matters, since judges hand down decisions on particular cases. Therefore, laws are framed both in general and in particular terms.

Obj. 2. Laws direct human actions, as I have said before.[2] But human actions consist of particular things. Therefore, laws should be framed in particular rather than general terms.

Obj. 3. Laws are the rules and measures of human actions, as I have said before.[3] But measures should be most certain, as the *Metaphysics*

---

[39]*Etymologies* II, 10 (Pl 82:130); V, 10 (PL 82:200).
[40]Justinian, *Digest* XLVIII, title 5.   [41]Ibid., title 8.   [42]In the body of the article.
[1]*Ethics* V, 7 (1134b23–4).   [2]ST I–II, Q. 90, AA. 1, 2.   [3]Ibid.

says.[4] Therefore, since nothing about human actions can be so universally certain as not to be wanting in particular cases, it seems that laws need to be framed in particular rather than general terms.

On the contrary, the Jurist says: "Laws need to be framed to suit things that more frequently happen, and laws are not framed to suit things that can happen once in a while."[5]

I answer that everything for an end needs to be proportioned to the end. But the end of law is the common good, since "laws should be framed for the common benefit of citizens, not for any private benefit," as Isidore says in his *Etymologies.*[6] And so human laws need to be proportioned to the common good. But the common good consists of many things. And so laws need to regard many things, both persons, matters, and times. For the political community consists of many persons, and its good is procured by many actions. Nor is it instituted to endure only for a short time but to last for all time through successive generations of citizens, as Augustine says in *The City of God.*[7]

Reply Obj. 1. The Philosopher in the *Ethics* posits three parts of legal justice (i.e., positive law).[8] For there are certain prescriptions framed only in general terms, and these are general laws. And regarding such laws, he says that "legal justice indeed does not originally differentiate in particulars but does once established."[9] For example, captives are ransomed at a fixed price.

And there are some laws that are general in one respect and particular in another. And we call such laws privileges, that is, private laws, since they regard particular persons, and yet the power of these laws extends to many matters. And it is regarding these that the Philosopher adds: "And, further, everything laws decree in particular cases."[10]

And we call some things legal because general laws are applied to particular cases, not because the applications are laws. For example, judges hand down decisions that we consider legally binding. And it is regarding such that the Philosopher adds: "And judicial decisions."[11]

Reply Obj. 2. Something directive needs to direct several things, and so the Philosopher says in the Metaphysics that all the things belonging to a genus are measured by the one of them that primarily belongs to the genus.[12] For if there were to be as many rules or measures as things

[4]*Metaphysics* X, 1 (1053a1–8).　[5]*Digest* I, title 3, laws 3, 4.

[6]*Etymologies* II, 10 (PL 82:131); V, 21 (PL 82:203).

[7]*The City of God* XXII, 6 (PL 41:759).　[8]*Ethics* V, 7 (1134b20–4).

[9]Ibid., 7 (1134b20–1).　[10]Ibid., 7 (1134b23).　[11]Ibid., 7 (1134b24).

[12]*Metaphysics* X, 1 (1052b18–22).

measured or ruled, a rule or measure, which is that one thing enable many things to be known, would cease to be of any use. And so a law would have no usefulness if it were to cover only a single action. For wise persons give individual commands to direct individual actions, but law is a general command, as I have said.[13]

Reply Obj. 3. "One should not look for the same certainty in all things," as the *Ethics* says.[14] And so in the case of contingent things like natural events and human affairs, there is sufficient certainty if things are true for the most part, even though they sometimes fail to happen in relatively few cases.

SECOND ARTICLE

Does It Belong to Human Laws to Prohibit All Vices?

We thus proceed to the second inquiry. It seems that it belongs to human laws to prohibit all vices, for the following reasons:

Obj. 1. Isidore says in his *Etymologies* that "laws have been established in order to curb human audacity out of fear of them."[15] But human audacity would not be sufficiently curbed unless laws were to prohibit everything evil. Therefore, human laws ought to prohibit everything evil.

Obj. 2. The aim of lawmakers is to make citizens virtuous. But citizens can be virtuous only if they are curbed of all vices. Therefore, it belongs to human law to curb all vices.

Obj. 3. Human law is derived from natural law, as I have said before.[16] But all vices are contrary to the natural law. Therefore, human law ought to prohibit all vices.

On the contrary, Augustine says in his work *On Free Choice*: "It seems to me that laws written for the people's governance rightly permit such things, and that God's providence punishes them."[17] But God's providence punishes only vices. Therefore, human laws, by not prohibiting some vices, rightly permit them.

I answer that laws are established as certain rules or measures of human actions, as I have already said.[18] But measures should be homogeneous with what they measure, as the *Metaphysics* says,[19] since different kinds of things are measured by different kinds of measures. And so laws need also to be imposed on human beings according to their condition, since laws ought to be "possible regarding both nature and a country's customs," as

---

[13]ST I–II, Q. 92, A. 2, obj. 1 (citing Justinian).

[14]Aristotle, *Ethics* I, 3 (1094b13–22).　　[15]*Etymologies* V, 20 (PL 82:202).

[16]ST I–II, Q. 95, A. 2.　　[17]*On Free Choice* I, 5, n. 13 (PL 32:1228).

[18]ST I–II, Q. 90, AA. 1, 2.　　[19]*Metaphysics* X, 1 (1053a24–30).

Isidore says.[20] And the power or ability to act results from internal habituation or disposition, since the virtuous and those without virtuous habits do not have the same power to act. Just so, children and adults do not have the same power to act, and so the law is not the same for children and adults. For example, many things are permitted children that the law punishes in adults, or even that public opinion censures. And likewise, many things are tolerated in persons of imperfect virtue that would not be tolerated in virtuous persons.

[margin note: cannot have too high expectations]

And human law is established for the collectivity of human beings, most of whom have imperfect virtue. And so human law does not prohibit every kind of vice, from which the virtuous abstain. Rather, human law prohibits only the more serious kinds of vice, from which most persons can abstain, and especially those vices that inflict harm on others, without the prohibition of which human society could not be preserved. For example, human laws prohibit murders, thefts, and the like.

Reply Obj. 1. Audacity seems to belong to attacks on others. And so audacity belongs chiefly to the sins that inflict injury on neighbors, and human law prohibits such sins, as I have said.[21]

Reply Obj. 2. Human laws aim to induce human beings to virtue little by little, not all at once. And so the laws do not immediately impose on the many imperfect citizens what already belongs to virtuous citizens, namely, that citizens abstain from everything evil. Otherwise, the imperfect citizens, unable to endure those commands, would erupt into worse evil things. Just so, Prov. 30:33 says: "Those who blow their nose too strongly, emit blood." And Mt. 9:17 says: "If one should put new wine," that is, the precepts of a perfect life, "into old wineskins," that is, imperfect human beings, "the wineskins burst, and the wine is spilled," that is, the precepts are despised, and human beings burst into worse evil things out of contempt.

Reply Obj. 3. The natural law is our participation in the eternal law, but human law falls short of the eternal law. For Augustine says in his work *On Free Choice*: "The laws framed for the governance of political communities permit and leave unpunished many things that God's providence punishes. Nor, indeed, should we criticize what the laws do do because of the fact that they do not do everything."[22] And so also human laws cannot prohibit everything that the natural law prohibits.

---

[20]*Etymologies* II, 10 (PL 82:131); V, 21 (PL 82:203).

[21]In the body of the article.

[22]*On Free Choice* I, 5, n. 13 (PL 32:1228).

THIRD ARTICLE
Do Human Laws Command Every Virtuous Action?

We thus proceed to the third article. It seems that human laws do not command every virtuous action, for the following reasons:

Obj. 1. Vicious actions are the contrary of virtuous actions. But human laws do not prohibit all vices, as I have said.[23] Therefore, human laws also do not command every virtuous action.

Obj. 2. Virtuous actions come from virtue. But virtue is the aim of laws, and so what comes from virtue cannot fall within legal precepts. Therefore, human laws do not command every virtuous action.

Obj. 3. Laws are ordered to the common good, as I have said.[24] But some virtuous actions are ordered to private, not the common, good. Therefore, laws do not command every virtuous action.

On the contrary, the Philosopher says in the *Ethics*: "Laws command courageous and moderate and kind behavior, and likewise regarding other virtues and vices, commanding the former and forbidding the latter."[25]

I answer that we distinguish specific virtues by their objects, as is evident from what I have said before.[26] But we can relate all the objects of virtues either to the private good of a person or to the common good of the people. For example, one can perform courageous acts either to preserve the political community or to uphold the rights of one's friends, and similarly with other virtuous acts. And laws are ordered to the common good, as I have said.[27] And so there are no virtues regarding whose actions laws could not command. But laws do not command regarding every action of every virtue. Rather, they only command things that can be ordered to the common good, whether immediately, as when things are done directly for that good, or mediately, as when lawmakers ordain things belonging to good training, which trains citizens to preserve the common good of justice and peace.

Reply Obj. 1. Human laws do not by strict command prohibit every vicious action, just as they do not command every virtuous action. But human laws prohibit some acts of particular vices, just as they command some acts of particular virtues.

Reply Obj. 2. We call actions virtuous in two ways. We call them virtuous in one way because persons perform virtuous deeds. For example, just actions consist of doing just things, brave actions consist of doing brave things. And human laws command virtuous acts in this way. We call

---

[23]ST I–II, Q. 96, A. 2.   [24]ST I–II, Q. 90, A. 2.   [25]*Ethics* V, 1 (1129b19–25).
[26]ST I–II: Q. 54, A. 2; Q. 60, A. 1; Q. 62, A. 2.
[27]ST I–II, Q. 90, A. 2.

actions virtuous in a second way because persons perform virtuous deeds as virtuous persons do. And the actions of virtuous persons always come from virtue and do not fall within legal precepts, although lawmakers aim to induce such behavior.

Reply Obj. 3. There are no virtues whose actions cannot be ordered to the common good, either directly or indirectly, as I have said.[28]

FOURTH ARTICLE

Does Human Law Impose Obligation on Human Beings in the Court of Conscience?

We thus proceed to the fourth article. It seems that human law does not impose obligation on human beings in the court of conscience, for the following reasons:

Obj. 1. Lower powers cannot impose laws on the courts of higher powers. But the power of human beings, which establishes human laws, is inferior to God's power. Therefore, human law cannot impose laws on the court of God, that is, the court of conscience.

Obj. 2. The judgment of conscience depends most of all on God's commandments. But human laws sometimes nullify God's commandments, as Mt. 15:6 says: "You have nullified God's commandment for the sake of your traditions." Therefore, human laws do not impose obligation regarding conscience.

Obj. 3. Human laws often bring defamation and injury to human beings. Just so, Is. 10:1–2 says: "Woe to those who establish wicked laws and inscribe injustices when they write laws, in order to oppress the poor in the courts and do violence in cases involving the lowly of my people." But all are permitted to avoid oppression and violence. Therefore, human laws do not impose obligation on human beings regarding conscience.

On the contrary, 1 Pet. 2:19 says: "It is a blessing if one, suffering unjustly, endures sorrows for the sake of conscience."

I answer that laws established by human beings are either just or unjust. If just, they indeed have obligatory force in the court of conscience from the eternal law, from which they are derived. Just so, Prov. 8:15 says: "Kings rule through me, and lawmakers decree justice." And we call laws just from three perspectives: (1) from their end, namely, when they are ordained for the common good; (2) from their authority, namely, when the laws enacted do not surpass the power of the lawmakers; (3) from their form, namely, when they impose proportionately equal burdens on citizens for the common good.

---

[28]In the body of the article.

And laws are unjust in two ways. They are unjust in one way by being contrary to the human good in the foregoing respects. Laws may be unjust regarding their end, as when authorities impose burdensome laws on citizens to satisfy the authorities' covetousness or vainglory rather than to benefit the community. Or laws may be unjust regarding the authority to make them, as when persons enact laws that exceed the power committed to them. Or laws may be unjust regarding their form, as when burdens, even if ordered to the common good, are disproportionately imposed on the people. And such laws are acts of violence rather than laws, since "unjust laws do not seem to be laws," as Augustine says in his work *On Free Choice.*[29] And so such laws do not oblige in the court of conscience, except perhaps to avoid scandal or civil unrest, to avoid which human beings ought to yield even their rights. Just so, Mt. 5:40–1 says: "If someone has taken your coat from you, give the person your cloak as well, and if someone has forced you to go one mile, go with the person another two."

Laws can be unjust in a second way by being contrary to the divine good (e.g., the laws of tyrants inducing their subjects to worship idols or to do anything else contrary to the divine law). And it is never permissible to obey such laws, since "we ought to obey God rather than human beings," as Acts 5:29 says.

Reply Obj. 1. The Apostle says in Rom. 13:1–2: "All human power is from God, and so those who resist the power" in matters belonging to its scope "resist God's ordinance." And so such persons become guilty in respect to their conscience.

Reply Obj. 2. The argument of this objection is valid about human laws ordained contrary to God's commandments. And the scope of human power does not extend to such laws. And so one should not obey human laws in such matters.

Reply Obj. 3. The argument of this objection is valid about laws that inflict unjust burdens on citizens, and also the scope of power granted by God does not extend to such laws. And so human beings are not obliged in such cases to obey the laws if it be possible to resist them without giving scandal or causing greater harm.

FIFTH ARTICLE
Is Everyone Subject to the Law?

We thus proceed to the fifth article. It seems that not everyone is subject to the law, for the following reasons:

---

[29]*On Free Choice* I, 5, n. 11 (PL 32:1227).

Obj. 1. Only those for whom laws are established are subject to the law. But the Apostle says in 1 Tim. 1:9 that "laws are not established for the righteous." Therefore, the righteous are not subject to human law.

Obj. 2. Pope Urban says, and the *Decretum* maintains: "No reason demands that those guided by private law be constrained by public law."[30] But all spiritual persons, who are sons and daughters of God, are guided by the private law of the Holy Spirit. Just so, Rom. 8:14 says: "Those moved by the Spirit of God are God's children." Therefore, not everyone is subject to human law.

Obj. 3. The Jurist says that "rulers are exempt from the laws."[31] But those exempt from the law are not subject to it. Therefore, not everyone is subject to the law.

On the contrary, the Apostle says in Rom. 13:1: "Let every soul be subject to higher powers." But any persons not subject to the law that higher powers establish seem not to be subject to the powers. Therefore, all persons should be subject to human law.

I answer that, as is evident from what I have said before,[32] two things belong to the nature of law: first, indeed, that law be the rule of human actions; second, that law have coercive power. Therefore, human beings can be subject to the law in two ways. They can be subject to law in one way as the ones regulated by the rule. And in this regard, all those subject to a power are subject to the laws the power establishes. But one may not be subject to a power in two ways. One may not be subject to a power in one way because one is absolutely free from subjection to the power. And so those belonging to one political community or kingdom are not subject to the laws of the ruler of another political community or kingdom, since such persons are not subject to that ruler's dominion. One may not be subject to a power in a second way insofar as one is ruled by a higher law. For example, a person subject to a proconsul ought to be ruled by the proconsul's commands but not regarding matters from which the emperor exempted the person. For regarding the latter, a person directed by a higher command is not bound by the command of an inferior power. And so those absolutely subject to the law may not be bound by the law regarding matters about which they are ruled by a higher law.

We say in a second way that some are subject to the law as the coerced to the power coercing. And in this respect, only the wicked, not the virtuous and righteous, are subject to the law. For what is coerced and forced is contrary to the will. But the will of the virtuous is in accord, and the

---

[30]Gratian, *Decretum* II, cause 19, q. 2, c. 2. [31]*Digest* I, title 3, law 31.
[32]ST I–II, Q. 90: AA. 1, 2; A. 3, *ad* 2.

will of the wicked in discord, with the law. And so only the wicked, not the virtuous, are subject to the law in this respect.

Reply Obj. 1. The argument of this objection is valid about being subject to the law by way of coercion. For then "the law is not established for the righteous," since "they are a law unto themselves" because "they manifest what the law requires written in their hearts," as the Apostle says in Rom. 2:14–5. And so the law does not have the coercive force in their regard that the law has regarding the wicked.

Reply Obj. 2. The law of the Holy Spirit is superior to every human law. And so spiritual persons, insofar as they are guided by the law of the Holy Spirit, are not subject to human law regarding things contrary to the Holy Spirit's guidance. But it belongs to the Holy Spirit's guidance that spiritual persons be subject to human laws, as 1 Pet. 2:13 says: "Be subject to every human creature for God's sake."

Reply Obj. 3. We say that rulers are exempt from the law regarding its coercive force, since, properly speaking, one is not coerced by oneself, and law has coercive force only by the power of a ruler. Therefore, we say that rulers are exempt from the law because no one can pass sentence on them if they act contrary to the law. And so a gloss on Ps. 51:4, "I have sinned against you alone," etc., says that "there is no one who is competent to judge the deeds of a king."[33]

But regarding the directive power of law, rulers are subject to the law by their own will. Just so, the *Decretals* say: "Rulers should follow the law that they decree for others. And the authority of a wise man says: 'Obey the law you yourself decreed.'[34]"[35] Also, the Lord reproves "those who preach and do not practice" and "those who impose heavy burdens on others but do not themselves want to lift a finger to move them," as Mt. 23:3–4 relates. And so, regarding God's judgment, rulers are not exempt from the law regarding its directive power, and they should willingly, not by coercion, fulfill the law.

Also, rulers are above the law insofar as they can, if it be expedient, alter the law and dispense from it at certain times and places.

SIXTH ARTICLE
Are Those Subject to the Law Permitted to Act Contrary to the Letter of the Law?

We thus proceed to the sixth article. It seems that those subject to the law are not permitted to act contrary to the letter of the law, for the following reasons:

---

[33]*Glossa ordinaria*, on Ps. 51:4 (PL 113:919); Peter Lombard, *Glossa*, on Ps. 51:4 (PL 191:486).   [34]Denis Cato, *Concise Opinions and Distichs on Morals*, preliminary opinion 53.   [35]Gregory IX, *Decretals* I, title 2, c. 6.

Obj. 1. Augustine says in his work *On True Religion*: "Although human beings judge about temporal laws when they decree them, the subjects will not be permitted to judge about them after they have been decreed and established. Rather, subjects should judge according to the laws."[36] But if one disregards the letter of the law, claiming that one preserves the lawmaker's aim, such a one seems to judge about the law. Therefore, those subject to the law are not permitted to disregard the letter of the law in order to preserve the lawmaker's aim.

Obj. 2. Only those who frame laws are competent to interpret them. But human beings subject to the law are not competent to frame them. Therefore, such human beings are not competent to interpret them. Rather, such human beings ought always to act according to the letter of the law.

Obj. 3. Every wise person knows how to explain the person's aim in words. But we ought to esteem wise those who frame laws, since wisdom says in Prov. 8:15: "Kings rule through me, and the framers of laws decree justice." Therefore, we should judge about the lawmaker's aim only by the words of the law.

On the contrary, Hilary says in his work *On the Trinity*: "We should understand the meaning of statements from the reasons for making them, since speech ought to be governed by things, not things by speech."[37] Therefore, we ought to pay more attention to the lawmaker's aim than to the very words of the law.

I answer that, as I have said before,[38] every law is ordered to the commonweal and has the force and nature of law insofar as it is so ordered. But a law has no power to bind morally insofar as it falls short being so ordered. And so the Jurist says: "No aspect of law or favor of equity allows us to render severe by a harsher interpretation contrary to the benefit of human beings things wholesomely introduced for their benefit."[39] And it often happens that observing the law is generally beneficial to the commonweal but most harmful to it in particular cases. Therefore, since lawmakers cannot envision all particular cases, they direct their aim at the common benefit and establish laws regarding things that generally happen. And so one should not observe a law if a case happens to arise in which observance of the law would be harmful to the commonweal. For example, if a law should decree that the gates of a besieged city remain shut, this is for the most part for the benefit of the commonweal. But if a situation should arise in which enemy soldiers are pursuing some citizens defending the city, it would be most harmful to the community if the gates

---

[36]*On True Religion* 31 (PL 34:148).   [37]*On the Trinity* IV, n. 14 (PL 10:107).
[38]ST I–II, Q. 96, A. 4.   [39]*Digest* I, title 3, law 25.

were not to be opened to admit the defenders. And so, contrary to the letter of the law, the city gates should be opened in such a situation in order to preserve the commonweal, which is the lawmaker's intention.

And yet we should note that not everyone is competent to interpret what may be useful or not useful for the community if observance of the letter of the law does not risk a sudden danger that needs to be immediately resolved. Rather, only rulers are competent to make such interpretations, and they have authority in such cases to dispense citizens from laws. On the other hand, if there be a sudden danger that does not allow enough time to be able to have recourse to a superior, the very necessity includes an implicit dispensation, since necessity is not subject to the law.

Reply Obj. 1. Those who in cases of necessity act contrary to the letter of the law do not judge about the law itself. Rather, they judge about particular cases, in which they perceive that they should not observe the letter of the law.

Reply Obj. 2. Those who follow the lawmaker's aim do not, absolutely speaking, interpret the law. Rather, they interpret the law regarding particular cases in which evidence of harm makes it clear that the lawmaker intended otherwise than the letter of the law. For if they have any doubt, they ought to act according to the letter of the law or consult superiors.

Reply Obj. 3. No human being's wisdom is so great as to be able to contemplate every single case. And so one cannot adequately express in words the things suitable for an intended end. And if a lawmaker could contemplate all cases, the lawmaker, to avoid confusing citizens, need not express all of them. Rather, the lawmaker should establish laws regarding what generally happens.

Question 97
On Revision of Laws

First Article
Should Human Law Be Revised in Any Way?

We thus proceed to the first inquiry. It seems that human law should be revised in no way, for the following reasons:

Obj. 1. Human law is derived from the natural law, as I have said before.[1] But the natural law remains immutable. Therefore, human law ought to remain immutable.

Obj. 2. Measures ought to be most permanent, as the Philosopher says

---

[1] ST I–II, Q. 95, A. 2.

in the *Ethics*.[2] But human law is the measure of human actions, as I have said before.[3] Therefore, human law ought to remain without change.

Obj. 3. It belongs to the nature of law to be just and upright, as I have said before.[4] But things once upright are always upright. Therefore, things once law ought always to be law.

On the contrary, Augustine says in his work *On Free Choice:* "Temporal law, although just, can be justly revised over time."[5]

I answer that, as I have said before,[6] human law is a dictate of reason directing human actions. And so there can be two reasons why laws may be rightly revised: one, indeed, regarding reason; the second regarding human beings, whose actions laws regulate. One reason indeed regards reason, since it seems to be natural for reason to advance step-by-step from the imperfect to the perfect. And so we perceive, regarding theoretical sciences, that the first philosophers transmitted imperfect doctrines that later philosophers corrected. So also is this the case in practical matters. For the first lawmakers, who strove to discover things useful for the human community but were unable of themselves to consider everything, instituted imperfect laws that were deficient in many respects. And later lawmakers revised those laws, establishing laws that could fail to serve the commonweal in fewer cases.

And regarding human beings, whose actions laws regulate, laws can be rightly revised to suit the changed conditions of human beings, and different things are expedient for human beings according to their different circumstances. Just so, Augustine in his work *On Free Choice* poses this example:

> If a people should be well-tempered and serious and most diligently mindful of the commonweal, a law is rightly framed that permits such a people to choose magistrates to administer the commonwealth. Then, if the same people, corrupted over time, sell their votes and entrust their governance to scoundrels and criminals, the power to bestow offices is rightly taken away from such a people, and the power to bestow the offices falls to the choice of a few good persons.[7]

Reply Obj. 1. The natural law is a participation in the eternal law, as I have said before,[8] and so the natural law remains immutable. And the natural law has this immutability from the immutability and perfection of

---

[2]*Ethics* V, 5 (1133a25).   [3]ST I–II, Q. 90, AA. 1, 2.   [4]ST I–II, Q. 90, A. 2.

[5]*On Free Choice* I, 6, n. 14 (PL 32:1229).   [6]ST I–II, Q. 91, A. 3.

[7]*On Free Choice* I, 6, n. 14 (PL 32:1229).

[8]ST I–II: Q. 91, A. 2; Q. 96, A. 2, *ad* 3.

the divine reason that establishes human nature. But human reason is mutable and imperfect.

And besides, the natural law consists of universal precepts that always abide, while laws established by human beings consist of particular precepts that regard different situations that arise.

Reply Obj. 2. Measures ought to be as permanent as possible. But there cannot be anything altogether immutably permanent in mutable things. And so human laws cannot be altogether immutable.

Reply Obj. 3. We predicate upright of material things in an absolute sense, and so they stay upright as far as it is in their power. But we speak of the rectitude of laws in relation to the commonweal, to which the same things are not always duly proportionate, as I have said before.[9] And so such rectitude changes.

SECOND ARTICLE
Should Human Laws Always Be Revised for Something Better?

We thus proceed to the second article. It seems that human laws should always be revised for something better, for the following reasons:

Obj. 1. Human reason devises human laws, just as it devises human skills. But prior rules regarding other skills are modified for better rules. Therefore, we should also do the same regarding human laws.

Obj. 2. We can provide for the future from things of the past. But many unsuitable things would result if human laws were not revised by adding better provisions, since the laws of antiquity were unsophisticated in many respects. Therefore, it seems that laws should be revised as often as something better presents itself to be made law.

Obj. 3. Human laws are framed for the particular actions of human beings. But regarding such actions, we can gain complete knowledge only by experience, which "takes time," as the *Ethics* says.[10] Therefore, it seems that better things can occur over time and should be enacted as laws.

On the contrary, the *Decretum* says: "It is foolish and rather detestably shameful to allow the traditions of our forefathers to be modified."[11]

I answer that, as I have said,[12] human laws are revised insofar as their revision serves the commonweal. But the very revision of laws, considered as such, involves some detriment to the commonweal. For custom avails very much for the observance of laws, since we regard things done contrary to common custom, even if those things be in themselves slight, as rather serious. And so the binding force of law is diminished when laws

---

[9]In the body of the article.   [10]*Ethics* II, 1 (1103a16).

[11]Gratian, *Decretum* I, dist. 12, c. 5.   [12]ST I–II, Q. 97, A. 1.

are revised, since custom is removed. And so human laws should never be revised unless the commonweal gains in one respect as much as it loses in the other. And such indeed is the case either because a very great and very clear benefit results from the new law, or because there is a very great necessity due either to the fact that the existing law is clearly unjust, or to the fact that observance of the existing law is most harmful. And so the Jurist says that "in establishing new laws, the benefit of departing from laws long perceived as just ought to be evident."[13]

Reply Obj. 1. The rules relating to skills derive their efficacy only from reason, and so prior rules should be revised whenever a better reason presents itself. But "laws have their greatest power from custom," as the Philosopher says in the *Politics*.[14] And so we should not rush to revise laws.

Reply Obj. 2. The argument of this objection rightly concludes that laws should be revised. But they should be revised for the sake of a great benefit or necessity, not for the sake of any betterment, as I have said.[15]

Reply Obj. 3. The same reply applies to this objection.

THIRD ARTICLE
Can Customs Obtain the Force of Law?

We thus proceed to the third article. It seems that customs cannot obtain the force of law or abolish laws, for the following reasons:

Obj. 1. Human law is derived from the natural law and the divine law, as is evident from what I have said before.[16] But human customs cannot alter the natural law or the divine law. Therefore, they also cannot alter human law.

Obj. 2. Moral good cannot come out of many wicked acts. But those who first begin to act contrary to a law act wickedly. Therefore, many such acts do not produce something morally good. But law is something morally good, since law regulates human actions. Therefore, customs cannot abolish laws so that the customs obtain the force of law.

Obj. 3. Framing laws belongs to public persons, whose business it is to govern a community, and so private persons cannot make law. But customs flourish through the acts of private persons. Therefore, customs cannot obtain the force of law so as to abolish laws.

On the contrary, Augustine says in a letter: "We should consider the customs of God's people and the prescriptions of our ancestors as laws. And as those who disobey God's laws should be punished, so also should

---

[13]*Digest* I, title 4, law 2.   [14]*Politics* II, 5 (1269a20–4).
[15]In the body of the article.   [16]ST I–II: Q. 93, A. 3; Q. 95, A. 2.

those who contemn ecclesiastical customs."[17]

I answer that all laws come from the reason and will of lawmakers: the divine and natural laws, indeed, from the reasonable will of God, and human laws from human wills regulated by reason. But the deeds of human beings as much as their words indicate their reason and will regarding things to be done. For example, everyone seems to desire as good what one carries out in deed. And human words evidently alter and also explain laws insofar as the words explain the internal movements and thoughts of human reason. And so also even acts, especially when repeated so as to constitute custom, can alter and explain laws, and cause things to obtain the force of law, namely, insofar as repeated external acts most effectively manifest internal movements of the will and the thoughts of reason. For things done repeatedly seem to proceed from deliberate judgments of reason. And so custom has the force of law and abolishes law and interprets law.

Reply Obj. 1. The natural law and the divine law come from the divine will, as I have said.[18] And so only divine authority, not customs that come from the wills of human beings, can alter those laws. And so no custom can obtain the force of law in opposition to the divine and natural laws, as Isidore says in his *Synonyms*: "Let custom yield to authority; let law and reason prevail over wicked customs."[19]

Reply Obj. 2. Human laws are wanting in particular cases, as I have said before.[20] And so one can sometimes act outside the law, namely, in cases in which the laws are wanting, and yet the actions will not be morally evil. And when such instances are repeated because of alterations in human beings, then customs indicate that laws are no longer useful, just as it would be evident that laws are no longer useful if expressly contrary laws were to be promulgated. But if the same reason for which the original law was useful still persists, the law prevails over the custom, not the custom over the law. There may be an exception if the law seems useless simply because it is not "possible according to a country's customs," which was one of the conditions of law.[21] For it is difficult to destroy a people's customs.

Reply Obj. 3. The people among whom a custom is introduced can be in two situations. For if a people is free, that is, self-governing, the consent of the whole people, which custom indicates, counts more in favor of a particular legal observance than the authority of its ruler, who only has the power to frame laws insofar as the ruler acts in the name of the

---

[17]*Letter 36,* to Casulanus (PL 33:136).   [18]In the body of the article.

[19]*Synonyms* II, n. 80 (PL 83:863).   [20]ST I–II, Q. 96, A. 6.

[21]ST I–II, Q. 95, A. 3.

people. And so the whole people can establish laws, but individual persons cannot.

But if a people should not have the free disposition to frame laws for itself or to abolish laws imposed by a higher power, the very customs prevailing in such a people still obtain the force of law insofar as those who have the power to impose laws on the people tolerate the customs. For rulers thereby seem to approve what the customs introduce.

FOURTH ARTICLE

Can the People's Rulers Dispense Subjects from Human Laws?

We thus proceed to the fourth article. It seems that the people's rulers cannot dispense subjects from human laws, for the following reasons:

Obj. 1. Laws are established "for the commonweal," as Isidore says.[22] But the common good should not be cast aside for the private convenience of a particular person, since "the good of the people is more godlike than the good of one human being," as the Philosopher says in the *Ethics.*[23] Therefore, it seems that no one should be dispensed to act contrary to the people's common law.

Obj. 2. Dt. 1:17 commands those with authority over others: "You shall listen to the lowly as well as the mighty, nor shall you regard who anyone is, since your judgment is God's." But to grant to one what is denied to all seems to be regard for who the person is. Therefore, the people's rulers cannot give such dispensations, since this is contrary to a precept of the divine law.

Obj. 3. Human law, if just, needs to be in accord with the natural and divine laws; otherwise, it would not "be fitting for religion" or "be suitable for training," which are prerequisites of law, as Isidore says.[24] But no human being can dispense anyone from the divine and natural laws. Therefore, neither can any human being dispense someone from a human law.

On the contrary, the Apostle says in 1 Cor. 9:17: "Dispensation has been entrusted to me."

I answer that dispensing, properly speaking, signifies allotting common goods to individuals. And so we also call the heads of households dispensers, since they with due weight and in due measure distribute to each member of their households both duties and things necessary for living. Therefore, we also say regarding any political community that one dispenses, since that one in a way ordains how individuals should fulfill a general precept. And a precept generally for the convenience of the

---

[22]*Etymologies* II, 10 (PL 82:131); V, 3 (PL 82:199).   [23]*Ethics* I, 2 (1094b9–10).
[24]*Etymologies* II, 10 (PL 82:131); V, 3 (PL 82:199).

community may sometimes be unsuitable for a particular person or in a particular case, either because it would prevent something better, or because it would even bring about some evil, as is evident from what I have said before.[25] But it would be most dangerous to commit this to the discretion of each individual, except, perhaps, when there is a clear and present danger, as I have said before.[26] And so those empowered to rule a people have the power to dispense from human laws that rest on the rulers' authority, namely, as regards persons or situations in which the law is wanting, to grant permission not to observe precepts of the law.

But if rulers should grant this permission at their mere whim, without the persons or situations warranting it, they will be unfaithful or unwise dispensers. Rulers will be unfaithful dispensers if they do not aim at the common good, and they will be unwise dispensers if they ignore the reason for granting dispensations. And so the Lord says in Lk. 12:42: "Who, do you think, is the faithful and wise dispenser that a master sets over his household?"

Reply Obj. 1. One ought not to be dispensed from observing general laws at the prejudice of the common good. Rather, dispensations should be granted for the purpose of benefiting the common good.

Reply Obj. 2. There is no regard for who persons are if unequal things are dispensed to persons who are unequal. And so when the condition of persons requires that special things be reasonably accorded them, there is no regard for who the persons are if special favors are granted them.

Reply Obj. 3. The natural law as consisting of general precepts, which are never wanting, cannot be dispensed. But human beings sometimes dispense from other precepts of the natural law, which are conclusions, as it were, from the general precepts (e.g., dispensing from the obligation to repay loans owed to traitors, or the like).

But every human being is subject to the divine law as private persons are subject to public law. And so, as only rulers or their representatives can dispense from human laws, so only God or his special representatives can dispense from precepts of the divine law.

Questions 98–108

[Questions 98–105 deal with the Old Law. Questions 106–8 deal with the New Law and its relation to the Old Law. Only AA. 1–3, 8–12 of Q. 100, and A. 1 of Q. 105 are translated here.]

---

[25]ST I–II, Q. 96, A. 6.   [26]Ibid.

Question 100
On the Moral Precepts of the Old Law

FIRST ARTICLE
Do All the Moral Precepts of the
Old Law Belong to the Natural Law?

We thus proceed to the first inquiry. It seems that not every moral precept of the Old Law belongs to the natural law, for the following reasons:

Obj. 1. Sir. 17:9 says: "In addition, he [God] bequeathed them instruction and the law that brings life." But we contradistinguish instruction from the natural law, since we do not learn that law. Rather, we know that law by an impulse from nature. Therefore, not every moral precept of the Old Law belongs to the natural law.

Obj. 2. The divine law is more complete than human law. But human law adds things pertaining to good morals to things belonging to the natural law. And this is evidenced by the fact that the natural law is the same for all human beings, but the things pertaining to good morals established by human law are different for different peoples. Therefore, there was a much stronger reason why the divine law should have added to the natural law things pertaining to good morals.

Obj. 3. As natural reason leads human beings to particular good morals, so also does faith. And so also Gal. 5:6 says that "faith acts through charity." But faith is not contained in the natural law, since things belonging to faith surpass natural reason. Therefore, not every moral precept of the divine law belongs to the natural law.

On the contrary, the Apostle says in Rom. 2:14: "The Gentiles, who do not have the [Old] Law, by nature do the things belonging to the Law." But we need to understand this about things pertaining to good morals. Therefore, all the moral precepts of the Old Law belong to the natural law.

I answer that moral precepts of the Old Law, as distinguished from its ceremonial precepts and its precepts governing the administration of justice, concern things that as such belong to good morals. And since we speak of human morals in relation to reason, which is the specific source of human acts, we call those morals good that are in accord with reason, and those morals bad that are not. And as every judgment of theoretical reason derives from the natural knowledge of first principles, so also every judgment of practical reason derives from certain naturally known first principles, as I have said before.[1] And one can in various ways proceed from these principles to judge about different things.

---

[1] ST I–II, Q. 94, AA. 2, 4.

For example, there are some things regarding human acts so explicit that, by applying the general and first principles, we can with rather little reflection at once approve or disapprove them. And there are some things that, in order to be judged morally, require much reflection on various circumstances, which only the wise, not everyone, is qualified to study carefully. Just so, considering particular scientific conclusions belongs only to philosophers, not to everybody. And there are some things that human beings need the help of divine instruction in order to judge, as is the case regarding articles of faith.

But the moral precepts of the Old Law concern things that pertain to good morals, and such precepts are in accord with reason. And every judgment of human reason is derived from natural reason. Therefore, all the moral precepts of the Old Law evidently need to belong to the natural law, albeit in different ways.

For example, the natural reason of each person at once judges that some things as such are to be done or not to be done (e.g., "Honor thy father and thy mother,"[2] "Thou shalt not kill,"[3] "Thou shalt not steal"[4]). And such precepts belong to the natural law absolutely.

And there are some things that the wise after more careful reflection judge should be done. And these things belong to the natural law but in such a way that they need instruction, whereby the wiser teach those less wise (e.g., "Rise up at the presence of a grey head, and honor the person of the elderly,"[5] and such like).

And there are some things that human reason needs divine instruction to judge, and we thereby learn about divine things (e.g., "Thou shalt not make for thyself a graven image or any likeness,"[6] "Thou shalt not take the name of the Lord thy God in vain"[7]).

Reply to Objs. 1–3. And this answer makes clear the replies to the objections.

SECOND ARTICLE
Do the Moral Precepts of the Old Law Concern All Virtuous Acts?

We thus proceed to the second article. It seems that the moral precepts of the Old Law do not concern all virtuous acts, for the following reasons:

Obj. 1. We call observance of the precepts of the Old Law justification, as Ps. 119:8 says: "I shall observe your ways of justification." But justification is the execution of justice. Therefore, the moral precepts of the Old Law concern only acts of justice.

---

[2]Ex. 20:12; Dt. 5:16.   [3]Ex. 20:13; Dt. 5:17.   [4]Ex. 20:15; Dt. 5:19.
[5]Lev. 19:32   [6]Ex. 20:4; Dt. 5:8.   [7]Ex. 20:7; Dt. 5:11.

Obj. 2. What falls under a precept has the nature of something owed. But the nature of something owed belongs only to justice, whose particular act is to render to everyone what is owed to that person, and not to other virtues. Therefore, the moral precepts of the Old Law concern only acts of justice, not the acts of other virtues.

Obj. 3. Every law is established for the common good, as Isidore says.[8] But of virtues, only justice regards the common good, as the Philosopher says in the *Ethics*.[9] Therefore, the moral precepts of the Old Law concern only justice.

On the contrary, Ambrose says that "sin is transgression of the divine law and disobedience of the heavenly commandments."[10] But sins run contrary to all virtuous acts. Therefore, the divine law has ordinances regarding all virtuous acts.

I answer that since legal precepts are ordered to the common good, as I have maintained before,[11] they need to be distinguished by different kinds of political communities. And so also the Philosopher teaches in the *Politics* that one kind of laws needs to be framed for a political community ruled by a king, and a different kind of laws needs to be framed for a political community where the people or some powerful persons in the community rule.[12] And there is one kind of community to which human law is ordered, and another kind to which divine law is ordered.

For human law is ordered to a political community, which consists of human beings in relation to one another. And human beings are related to one another by external actions, whereby they are in communion with one another. And such communion belongs to the nature of justice, which, properly speaking, gives direction to a human community. And so human law lays down precepts only regarding acts of justice, and it prescribes other virtuous acts, if at all, only insofar as those acts take on an aspect of justice, as the Philosopher makes clear in the *Ethics*.[13]

But the community for which divine law provides consists of human beings in relation to God, whether in the present or the future life. And so divine law lays down precepts regarding everything that rightly orders human beings for communion with God. But human beings are united to God by their reason or mind, in which is the image of God. And so the divine law lays down precepts about everything that rightly orders human beings' reason. And all virtuous acts bring this about. For example, intellectual virtues rightly order acts of reason, as such, and moral virtues

---

[8]*Etymologies* II, 10 (PL 82:131); V, 21 (PL 82:203).   [9]*Ethics* V, 1 (1130a3–5).
[10]*On Paradise* 8 (PL 14:292).   [11]ST I–II, Q. 90, A. 2.
[12]*Politics* IV, 1 (1289a11–25).   [13]*Ethics* V, 1 (1129b12–25).

rightly order acts of reason regarding internal emotions and external actions. And so the divine law fittingly lays down precepts about the acts of every virtue. But the divine law does so in such a way that some things, without which the order of virtue, that is, the order of reason, cannot be observed, fall under the obligation of precepts, while things belonging to the well-being of complete virtue fall under the admonition of counsels.

Reply Obj. 1. Keeping the commandments of the Old Law even regarding the acts of virtues other than justice have the nature of justification, since it is just that human beings obey God, or even that everything belonging to human beings be subject to reason.

Reply Obj. 2. Justice, properly speaking, concerns what one human being owes to another, but every other virtue concerns the duty lower powers owe to reason. And by reason of such duty, the Philosopher in the *Ethics* speaks of justice in a metaphorical sense.[14]

Reply Obj. 3. What I have said about different kinds of community makes clear the reply to this objection.[15]

THIRD ARTICLE
Do We Trace All the Moral Precepts of
the Old Law to the Ten Commandments?

We thus proceed to the third article. It seems that we do not trace all the moral precepts of the Old Law to the Ten Commandments, for the following reasons:

Obj. 1. As Mt. 22:37, 39 says, the first and chief precepts of the Old Law are: "Thou shalt love the Lord thy God" and "Thou shalt love thy neighbor." But these two precepts are not included in the Decalogue. Therefore, not all the moral precepts of the Old Law are included in the Decalogue.

Obj. 2. We do not trace the moral precepts of the Old Law to its ceremonial precepts. Rather, we do the converse. But one of the commandments, namely, "Remember that thou keep holy the Sabbath,"[16] is ceremonial. Therefore, we do not trace all the moral precepts of the Old law to all the commandments of the Decalogue.

Obj. 3. The moral precepts of the Old Law concern all virtuous acts. But the Decalogue includes only precepts pertaining to acts of justice, as is evident to anyone who examines them one by one. Therefore, the Decalogue does not include all the moral precepts of the Old Law.

On the contrary, a gloss on Mt. 5:11, "Blessed are you when they have reviled you," etc., says that Moses, after laying down the Ten

---

[14]Ibid., V, 11 (1138b5–14).   [15]In the body of the article.
[16]Ex. 20:8, Dt. 5:12.

Commandments, explains them in particulars.[17] Therefore, all the precepts of the Old Law are particulars of the Decalogue.

I answer that the Decalogue differs from the other precepts of the Old Law in that God himself is said to have laid down the Decalogue for the people but laid down the other precepts for them through Moses. And the precepts whose knowledge human beings possess from God himself belong to the Decalogue. But the precepts they can know from the first general principles with rather little reflection, as well as those divinely infused faith reveals, are such.

Therefore, two kinds of precepts are not reckoned among precepts of the Decalogue. The first kind consists of the first and general precepts, and these precepts need no further promulgation than their inscription on natural reason as self-evident, as it were (e.g., human beings should do evil to no one, and such like). And the second kind consists of the precepts that the wise by careful study discover belong to reason, since God communicates these precepts to the people through the instruction of the wise. Still, both of these kinds of precepts are included in the Decalogue, albeit in different ways. For the first and general precepts are included as first principles in proximate conclusions, and, conversely, the precepts known through the wise are included as conclusions in first principles.

Reply Obj. 1. These two precepts are first and general precepts of the natural law self-evident to human reason, whether by nature or by faith. And so all precepts of the Decalogue are traceable to these two precepts as conclusions to general first principles.

Reply Obj. 2. The commandment to observe the Sabbath is moral in one respect, namely, that human beings devote some time to divine things, as Ps. 46:10 says: "Be still and perceive that I am God." And we reckon the commandment to observe the Sabbath among the moral precepts of the Decalogue in this respect, but not as to the appointed day, since the commandment in the latter respect is ceremonial.

Reply Obj. 3. The nature of obligation regarding virtues other than justice is more hidden than the nature of obligation regarding justice. And so we do not know the precepts regarding the other virtues as well as we know the precepts regarding acts of justice. And so acts of justice fall specifically within the commandments of the Decalogue, which are the chief elements of the Old Law.

---

[17]*Glossa ordinaria*, on Mt. 5:11 (PL 114:90).

EIGHTH ARTICLE
Can Human Beings Be Dispensed from the Commandments of the Decalogue?

We thus proceed to the eighth article. It seems that human beings can be dispensed from the commandments of the Decalogue, for the following reasons:

Obj. 1. The commandments of the Decalogue belong to the natural law. But what is just by nature is wanting in some cases and can be changed, just like human nature, as the Philosopher says in the *Ethics*.[18] But deficiencies of law in particular cases are reasons for dispensing from the law, as I have said before.[19] Therefore, human beings can be dispensed from commandments of the Decalogue.

Obj. 2. As human beings are to the human laws they establish, so is God to the law he establishes. But human beings can dispense from the laws they establish. Therefore, since God established the commandments of the Decalogue, it seems that he can dispense from them. But ecclesiastical superiors take the place of God on earth, for the Apostle says in 2 Cor. 2:10: "For I have also in the person of Christ pardoned what I have pardoned, if anything, for your sakes." Therefore, ecclesiastical superiors also can dispense from the commandments of the Decalogue.

Obj. 3. A prohibition against homicide is included in the commandments of the Decalogue. But human beings seem to dispense from this commandment. For example, the precepts of human law permit human beings such as criminals and enemies to be killed. Therefore, the commandments of the Decalogue can be dispensed.

Obj. 4. Sabbath observance is included in the commandments of the Decalogue. But there was a dispensation regarding this commandment, since 1 Mc. 2:41 says: "And they laid plans on that day, saying: 'We shall fight against all those who will come to war against us on the Sabbath ' " Therefore, the commandments of the Decalogue can be dispensed.

On the contrary, Is. 24:5 reproves some because "they have changed the Law and broken the everlasting covenant." But it seems that we should most understand this about the commandments of the Decalogue. Therefore, the commandments of the Decalogue cannot be dispensed.

I answer that, as I have said before,[20] there ought to be dispensations from precepts whenever there arise particular cases in which observance of the letter of the law would be contrary to the intention of the lawmaker. And first and foremost, the intention of any lawmaker is indeed directed to the common good. And second, the intention of a lawmaker is directed

---

[18]*Ethics* V, 7 (1134b28–9).   [19]ST I–II. Q. 96, A. 6, Q. 97, A. 4.   [20]Ibid.

to the order of justice and virtue, which preserves and attains the common good. Therefore, if precepts be laid down that include the very preservation of the common good or the very order of justice and virtue, the precepts include the intention of the lawmaker and so cannot be dispensed from. For example, if a community were to have a precept that no one should subvert the commonwealth or betray the political community to its enemies, or that no one should do unjust or evil things, such precepts could not be dispensed from.

But if other precepts subordinate to the latter were to be laid down that specify particular ways to preserve the common good or the order of justice and virtue, such precepts could be dispensed from. The precepts could be dispensed from insofar as their nonobservance in particular cases would not cause prejudice to the first precepts, which include the intention of the lawmaker. For example, if a political community, to preserve the commonwealth, were to decree that citizens stand guard on each street of a besieged city, some citizens could be dispensed for the sake of a greater benefit.

And the commandments of the Decalogue include the very aim of the lawmaker, namely. God. For the commandments of the first tablet, which direct human beings in relation to God, include the very order to human beings' common and ultimate good, that is, God. And the commandments of the second tablet include the very order of justice to be observed in human society, namely, that nothing improper be done to anyone, and that one should render to others what is their due. For we should so understand the commandments of the Decalogue. And so the commandments of the Decalogue cannot be dispensed from at all.

Reply Obj. 1. The Philosopher is not speaking about the just by nature that includes the very order of justice, since the principle that justice should be observed is never wanting. But he is speaking about specific ways of observing justice, which are wanting in particular cases.

Reply Obj. 2. The Apostle says in 2 Tim. 2:13: "God remains faithful, nor can he deny his very self." But he would deny his very self if he were to remove the very order of his justice, since he is justice itself. And so God cannot so dispense human beings that they would be permitted not to be properly related to God, or that they would be permitted not to be subject to the order of his justice regarding precepts that direct human beings in their relation to one another.

Reply Obj. 3. The Decalogue prohibits the killing of human beings insofar as such killing has the nature of being undeserved, for then the commandment includes the very nature of justice. And human law cannot make it lawful that human beings be killed undeservedly. But it is not undeserved that criminals and enemies of the commonwealth be killed.

And so this is not contrary to the commandment of the Decalogue, nor is such killing murder, which the commandment prohibits, as Augustine says in his work *On Free Choice*.[21] And likewise, it is not theft or robbery, which a commandment of the Decalogue prohibits, if property is taken from one who ought to relinquish it.

And so when the children of Israel at the command of God took away the spoils of the Egyptians,[22] there was no theft, since the spoils were due the Israelites by reason of God's judgment. Likewise, Abraham, when he agreed to kill his son,[23] did not consent to murder, since it was proper that Isaac be killed at the command of God, who is the Lord of life and death. God himself is the one who inflicts death on all human beings, just and unjust, for the sin of our first parent, and human beings will not be murderers if they should by divine authority execute God's judgment, just as God is not a murderer. And likewise, Hosea, having sexual intercourse with a fornicating wife or an adulterous woman,[24] is not an adulterer or fornicator, since he had intercourse with a woman who was his by the command of God, who is the author of the institution of marriage.

Therefore, the commandments of the Decalogue, regarding the nature of justice that they include, cannot be changed. But specifications applying the commandments to particular acts, namely, specifications whether this or that be murder, theft, or adultery, are indeed variable. The specifications sometimes change only because of divine authority, namely, regarding matters that God alone instituted, such as marriage and the like. The specifications also sometimes change because of human authority, as in matters committed to the jurisdiction of human beings. For in this but not every respect, human beings take the place of God.

Reply Obj. 4. The cited way of thinking was an interpretation of the commandment rather than a dispensation. For we should not understand that those who do deeds necessary for the human weal violate the Sabbath, as the Lord proves in Mt. 12:3–5.

NINTH ARTICLE
Does the Way of Virtue Fall under Command of the Law?

We thus proceed to the ninth article. It seems that the way of virtue does fall under command of the law, for the following reasons:

Obj. 1. The way of virtue consists of persons doing just deeds justly, and brave deeds bravely, and the like regarding other virtues. But Dt. 16:20 commands: "You shall carry out just deeds justly." Therefore,

---

[21]*On Free Choice* I, 4, n. 9 (PL 32:1226).   [22]Ex. 12:35–6.
[23]Gen. 22:1–12.   [24]Hos. 1:2–11.

the way of virtue falls under command of the law.

Obj. 2. What belongs to the lawmaker's intention falls most under the law's command. But the lawmaker chiefly aims to make human beings virtuous, as the *Ethics* says.[25] And it belongs to the virtuous to act virtuously. Therefore, the way of virtue falls under command of the law.

Obj. 3. Properly speaking, the way of virtue seems to consist of acting willingly and with pleasure. But this falls under command of the divine law, for Ps. 100:2 says: "Serve the Lord in gladness," and 2 Cor. 9:7 says: "Do not act out of sadness or necessity, for the Lord loves a cheerful giver." And a gloss on the latter says: "Do cheerfully the good you do, and then you act well. But if you act with sadness, the good is done from you, not by you."[26] Therefore, the way of virtue falls under command of the law.

On the contrary, one can act in a virtuous way only if one should possess a virtuous habit, as the Philosopher makes clear in the *Ethics.*[27] But anyone transgressing the command of a law deserves punishment. Therefore, if the way of virtue falls under command of the law, one without a virtuous habit would deserve punishment no matter what he or she does. But this is contrary to the aim of the law, which strives to induce human beings to virtue by habituating them to good deeds. Therefore, the way of virtue does not fall under command of the law.

I answer that commands of the law have the power to compel compliance, as I have said before.[28] Therefore, what the law compels falls directly under command of the law. And the law compels compliance by fear of punishment, as the *Ethics* says,[29] since that for which legal punishment is inflicted falls strictly under command of the law. And the divine law and human law are differently disposed in regard to ordaining punishment. For legal punishment is inflicted only for things regarding which lawmakers have the power to judge, since the law punishes by passing sentence. And human beings, who lay down human laws, have the power to judge only regarding external acts, since "human beings perceive sensibly perceptible things," as 1 Sam. 16:7 says. But only God, who lays down the divine law, has the power to judge regarding interior movements of the will, as Ps. 7:9 says: "God scrutinizes our desires and emotions."

Therefore, we should accordingly say that both divine law and human law concern the way of virtue in one respect, that the divine law but not human law concerns the way of virtue in another respect, and that neither

---

[25]Aristotle, *Ethics* II, 1 (1103b3–6).

[26]*Glossa ordinaria*, on 2 Cor. 9:17 (PL 114:564); Peter Lombard, *Glossa*, on 2 Cor. 9:17 (PL 192:63).   [27]*Ethics* II, 4 (1105a17–21); V, 8 (1135b24).

[28]ST I–II, Q. 90, A. 3, *ad* 2.   [29]Aristotle, *Ethics* X, 9 (1179b11–8).

the divine law nor human law concerns the way of virtue in a third respect.

And the way of virtue consists of three things, as the Philosopher says in the *Ethics*.[30] And the first of these is whether one acts knowingly. And both the divine law and human law judge this, since one does accidentally what one does unknowingly. And so both the divine law and human law deem deeds worthy of punishment or pardon depending on the person's knowledge or ignorance.

The second consideration is whether one acts willingly, that is, by choice and by choosing to do something for its own sake. And we thereby signify two interior movements, namely, of willing and intending, about which I have spoken before.[31] And only the divine law, not human law, judges these two interior movements. For human law does not punish one who wants to kill and does not, but the divine law does, as Mt. 5:22 says: "Those who are angry with their brother will be liable to judgment."

And the third consideration is whether one has the power to act firmly and consistently and does so. And such firmness, properly speaking, belongs to habits, namely, that one act by reason of ingrained habit. And in this respect, the way of virtue does not fall under command of the law, whether the divine law or human law. For example, neither human beings nor God punish as transgressors of the law those who give requisite honor to their parents but do not have the habit of filial piety.

Reply Obj. 1. The way one performs just acts falling under command of the law is that the deeds be done according to the ordinance of the law, not that they be done by reason of the habit of justice.

Reply Obj. 2. The intention of a lawmaker concerns two things. One is indeed what lawmakers strive to induce by legal commands, and this is virtue. And the second is what lawmakers intend legal commands to impose, and this is what leads or disposes citizens to virtue, that is, virtuous acts. For the end of precepts and what precepts lay down are not the same thing, just as ends and means are not the same in regard to other things.

Reply Obj. 3. It falls under a command of the divine law that we perform virtuous acts ungrudgingly, since those who act begrudgingly act unwillingly. And to act with pleasure, that is, joyfully or cheerfully, falls under the command of the law in one respect, namely, insofar as pleasure results from love of God and neighbor, which falls under the command of the law. But to act with pleasure does not fall under the command of the law in another respect, namely, insofar as habits result in pleasure, since "pleasure in deeds is evidence that persons have become habituated," as

---

[30]Ibid., II, 4 (1105a31–b5).   [31]ST I–II, QQ. 8, 12.

the Ethics says.[32] For acts can be pleasurable either because of their end or because of suitable habits.

Does the Way of Charity Fall under Command of the Divine Law?

We thus proceed to the tenth article. It seems that the way of charity does fall under command of the divine law, for the following reasons:

Obj. 1. Mt. 19:17 says: "If you wish to enter into life, keep the commandments." And it seems from this that keeping the commandments suffices to lead human beings into life. But good deeds do not suffice to lead human beings into life unless the deeds are done out of charity. For 1 Cor. 13:3 says: "If I have distributed all my goods to feed the poor, and if I have delivered my body to be burned, it profits me nothing if I should not have charity." Therefore, the way of charity is included in what the law commands.

Obj. 2. It belongs strictly to the way of charity that everything be done for God. But this falls under command of the law, for the Apostle says in 1 Cor. 10:31: "Do everything for the glory of God." Therefore, the way of charity falls under command of the law.

Obj. 3. If the way of charity does not fall under command of the law, then one can fulfill commands of the law without possessing charity. But what can be done without charity can be done without grace, which always accompanies charity. Therefore, one can fulfill commands of the law without grace. But this is the error of Pelagius, as Augustine makes clear in his work *On Heresies*.[33] Therefore, the way of charity is included in what the law commands.

On the contrary, those who do not keep the commands of the law commit mortal sin. Therefore, if the way of charity falls under command of the law, then those who do anything otherwise than out of charity commit mortal sin. But those who do not possess charity do not act out of charity. Therefore, those who do not possess charity commit mortal sins in their every deed, however good the deed is by its nature. But this conclusion is improper.

I answer that there have been conflicting views on this matter. For example, some have said that the way of charity is absolutely under command of the law.[34] Nor is it impossible to keep this command if one does not possess charity, since such people can dispose themselves so that God infuses charity in them. Nor does a person commit mortal sin whenever

---

[32]Aristotle, *Ethics* II, 3 (1104b3–9).   [33]*On Heresies* 88 (PL 42:47–8).

[34]E.g., Albert the Great, *Commentary on the Sentences* III, dist. 36, a. 6.

the person does something by its nature good, since the command that one act out of charity is an affirmative precept and morally obliges only when one possesses charity, not at all times. And others have said that the way of charity does not at all fall under command of the law.

And both of these opinions are true in some respect. For we can consider acts of charity in two ways. We can consider them in one way insofar as they are acts of charity as such. And they in this respect fall under commands of the law that lay down specific commands (e.g., "Thou shalt love the Lord thy God,"[35] and "Thou shalt love thy neighbor"[36]). And the first opinion is true in this respect. For it is not impossible to observe these precepts, which concern acts of charity, since human beings can dispose themselves to possess charity and can exercise charity after they have possessed it.

We can consider acts of charity in a second way insofar as they are the way of acts of other virtues, that is, as acts of other virtues are ordered to charity, which is "the purpose of commands," as 1 Tim. 1:5 says. For I have said before that the intended end is a formal modality of acts ordered to the end.[37] And the second opinion, that the way of charity does not fall under the command of the law, is true in this respect, that is to say, that the commandment "Honor thy father"[38] only commands that one honor one's father, not that one honor one's father out of charity. And so those who honor their fathers, even if they do not possess charity, do not become transgressors of the precept to honor one's father, although they are transgressors of the precept regarding acts of charity. And they deserve punishment because of the latter transgression.

Reply Obj. 1. The Lord said: "If you wish to enter into life, keep all the commandments," not: "If you wish to enter into life, keep one commandment." And the commandment to love God and neighbor is included in the commandments.

Reply Obj. 2. That one love God with one's whole heart is included in the commandment of charity, to which commandment it belongs to relate everything to God. And so human beings can fulfill the precept of charity only by relating everything to God. Therefore, those honoring their parents are morally obliged to do so out of charity by force of the commandment "Thou shalt love the Lord thy God with all thy heart,"[39] not by force of the commandment "Honor thy parents."[40] And although these are two commandments that do not oblige at all times, they can oblige at different times. And so one may fulfill the precept about honoring one's

---

[35]Dt. 6:5.   [36]Lev. 19:18.   [37]ST I–II, Q. 12: A. 1, *ad* 3; A. 4, *ad* 3.
[38]Ex. 20:12; Dt. 5:16.   [39]Dt. 6:5.   [40]Ex. 20:12; Dt. 5:6.

parents without transgressing the precept about omitting the way of charity.

Reply Obj. 3. Human beings cannot keep all the commandments of the law unless they fulfill the precept of charity, which is not done without grace. And so what Pelagius said, that human beings fulfill the law without grace, is impossible.

ELEVENTH ARTICLE
Do We Appropriately Mark Out Other Moral Precepts of the Law besides the Decalogue?

We thus proceed to the eleventh article. It seems that we do not appropriately mark out other moral precepts of the Law besides the Decalogue, for the following reasons:

Obj. 1. The Lord says in Mt. 22:40: "The whole law and the prophets depend on the two precepts of love." But the Ten Commandments explain these two precepts. Therefore, there need not be other moral precepts.

Obj. 2. We distinguish moral precepts from ceremonial precepts and precepts governing the administration of justice, as I have said.[41] But specifying general moral precepts belongs to ceremonial precepts and precepts governing the administration of justice, and general moral precepts are included in, or even presupposed by, the Decalogue, as I have said.[42] Therefore, it is inappropriate that there be other moral precepts besides the Decalogue.

Obj. 3. Moral precepts concern every kind of virtuous act, as I have said before.[43] Therefore, as the Old Law lays down moral precepts pertaining to worship, generosity, mercy, and chastity, in addition to the Decalogue, so also should the Old Law have laid down precepts pertaining to other virtues (e.g., courage, sobriety, and the like). But we do not find such in the Old Law. Therefore, we do not appropriately mark out in the Old Law other moral precepts besides the Decalogue.

On the contrary, Ps. 19:8 says: "The law of the Lord is spotless, converting souls." But other moral precepts added to the Decalogue also preserve human beings from the stain of sin and convert their souls to God. Therefore, it also belonged to the Old Law to lay down other moral precepts.

I answer that, as is clear from what I have said before,[44] ceremonial precepts and precepts governing the administration of justice derive their force only from their institution, since it did not seem to matter whether things should be done in this way or that before the precepts were instituted. But

---

[41]ST I–II, Q. 99, A. 3.   [42]ST I–II, Q. 100, A. 3.   [43]ST I–II, Q. 100, A. 2.
[44]ST I–II, Q. 99, A. 3.

moral precepts have efficacy from the very dictates of natural reason even if the precepts were never laid down in the Old Law. And there are three classes of moral precepts. For some moral precepts are most certain and so evident to reason that they need no promulgation. For example, such are the commandments to love God and neighbor, and the like, as I have said before,[45] and these commandments are the ends of the commandments, as it were. And so no one's reason can judge erroneously about them. And some moral precepts are more specific, and everyone, even ordinary people, can at once easily perceive their reasonableness. And yet they need to be promulgated, since human reason in a few instances may be led astray regarding them. And such are the commandments of the Decalogue. And there are some moral precepts whose reasonableness is evident only to the wise but not so evident to everyone. And these are the moral precepts added to the Decalogue, precepts laid down by God for the people through Moses and Aaron.

But because evident things are the sources for knowing things that are not evident, we trace the moral precepts added to the Decalogue to the commandments of the Decalogue[46] as corollaries. For example, the First Commandment of the Decalogue prohibits worship of strange gods, and precepts are added thereto prohibiting things ordered to the worship of idols. Thus Dt. 18:10 relates: "Let there be among you none who would purify their sons and daughters by fire, nor let there be any wizard or witch, nor let anyone consult fortune-tellers or diviners, nor let anyone seek truth from the dead."

And the Second Commandment prohibits perjury. And Lev. 24:15–6 adds a prohibition of blasphemy thereto, and Dt. 13:1–11 adds a prohibition of false teaching.

And all the ceremonial precepts are added to the Third Commandment.

And the precept about honoring the elderly, as Lev. 19:32 says, "Rise in the presence of a hoary head, and honor the person of the elderly," is added to the Fourth Commandment about honoring one's parents. And more generally, all the precepts prescribing that we show respect to our betters and kindness to our equals or inferiors are added to that commandment.

---

[45]ST I–II , Q. 100, A. 3; A. 4, *ad* 1.

[46]Thomas follows the Vulgate numbering and division of the commandments. What the Vulgate enumerates as the First Commandment, the King James Version enumerates as the First and Second Commandments, and what the Vulgate enumerates as the Ninth and Tenth Commandments, the King James Version enumerates as the Tenth Commandment.

And there is a prohibition of hate or any violence against our neighbor, as Lev. 19:16 says, "You shall not stand against the blood of your neighbor," and there is also a prohibition of hatred of one's brother, as Lev. 19:17 says, "You shall not hate your brother in your heart." These prohibitions are added to the Fifth Commandment, which concerns the prohibition of homicide.

And there is a precept prohibiting prostitution, as Dt. 23:17 says, "There will be no prostitute among the daughters of Israel nor whoremonger among the sons of Israel," and there is also a precept prohibiting the sin against nature, as Lev. 18:22–23 says, "You shall not have sexual intercourse with a fellow male or any beast." These precepts are added to the Sixth Commandment, which concerns the prohibition of adultery.

And there is a precept prohibiting interest-taking, as Dt. 23:19 says, "You shall not lend to your brother at interest," and there is a prohibition against fraud, as Dt. 25:13 says, "You shall not put different weights in your sack." And more generally, there are all the precepts that pertain to prohibiting trickery and robbery. These precepts are added to the Seventh Commandment, which prohibits theft.

And there is a prohibition against passing false judgment, as Ex. 23:2 says, "Nor shall you depart from the truth by yielding to the judgment of the majority," and there is a prohibition of lying, as Ex. 23:7 says, "You shall avoid lying." And there is a prohibition of detraction, as Lev. 19:16 says, "You shall not be a detractor or scandalmonger among the people." These prohibitions are added to the Eighth Commandment, which concerns the prohibition of false testimony.

And no other precepts are added to the last two commandments, since these commandments prohibit all evil coveting without exception.

Reply Obj. 1. The commandments of the Decalogue are directed to the love of God and neighbor by reason of the clear nature of the obligations, but other precepts are so directed by reason of their less evident nature.

Reply Obj. 2. Ceremonial precepts and precepts governing the administration of justice specify commandments of the Decalogue by force of the precepts' institution and not by force of an inclination from nature, as the additional moral precepts do.

Reply Obj. 3. Legal precepts are ordered to the common good, as I have said before.[47] And virtues directing us in relation to others pertain directly to the common good, and likewise the virtue of chastity, inasmuch as the reproductive act promotes the common good of the species. Therefore,

---

[47]ST I–II, Q. 90, A. 2.

the commandments of the Decalogue and the precepts added thereto are laid down regarding those virtues. And regarding acts of courage, commanders exhorting troops in a war undertaken for the common good give the troops commands, as Dt. 20:3 makes clear when priests are commanded to say: "Do not be afraid, do not retreat." Likewise, the prohibition of acts of gluttony is committed to paternal admonition, since such acts are contrary to the good of the household. And so Dt. 21:20 says in the person of parents: "He contemns listening to our admonitions, he wastes himself in extravagances and lusts and feasting."

TWELFTH ARTICLE
Did the Moral Precepts of the
Old Law Make Human Beings Just?

We thus proceed to the twelfth article. It seems that the moral precepts of the Old Law made human beings just, for the following reasons:

Obj. 1. The Apostle says in Rom. 2:13: "For those who observe the Law will be made just, and those who merely listen to the Law have not been." But we call those who fulfill the precepts of the Law observers of the Law. Therefore, fulfilling the precepts of the Law made human beings just.

Obj. 2. Lev. 18:5 says: "Keep my laws and judgments, and human beings, if they do so, will thereby have life." But human beings have spiritual life by being just. Therefore, fulfilling the precepts of the Law made human beings just.

Obj. 3. The divine law is more efficacious than human law. But human law makes human beings just, since there is a justice in fulfilling precepts of that law. Therefore, precepts of the Law made human beings just.

On the contrary, the Apostle says in 2 Cor. 3:6: "The letter of the Law kills." But as Augustine says in his work *On the Spirit and Letter of the Law,*[48] we also understand the statement of the Apostle to refer to the moral precepts of the Law. Therefore, the moral precepts of the Old Law did not make human beings just.

I answer that we properly and primarily predicate health of what possesses health, and secondarily of what signifies or preserves health. Just so, we primarily and properly predicate justification of the very process that makes human beings just, and we can secondarily and improperly, as it were, predicate justification of what signifies justice or disposes to justice. And the precepts of the Old Law evidently made human beings just in the latter two respects, namely, inasmuch as the precepts disposed human beings to the justifying grace of Christ, and the precepts also signified

---

[48]*On the Spirit and Letter of the Law* 14 (PL 44:215).

that grace. This is so because, as Augustine says in his work *Against Faustus*,[49] "the life of that people foretold and prefigured Christ."

But if we should speak of justification in the strict sense, then we need to note that we can understand justice as habitual or actual, and we accordingly speak of justification in two ways. We indeed speak of justification in one way as human beings who acquire the habit of justice become just. And we speak of justification in a second way as human beings perform just deeds, so that justification in this respect is simply the execution of justice. And we can understand justice, like other virtues, as either acquired or infused, as is evident from what I have said before.[50] And deeds indeed produce the acquired virtue of justice, but God himself by infusing his grace produces the infused virtue of justice. And the latter justice is the true justice about which we are now speaking, regarding which one is called just with God, as Rom. 4:2 says: "If works of the Law made Abraham just, he has reason to boast, but not with God." Therefore, the moral precepts of the Old Law, which concern human acts, could not produce such justice. And so the moral precepts could not make human beings just by producing such justice.

And if we should understand justification to mean the execution of justice, then all the precepts of the Old Law made human beings just in one way or another. For example, the ceremonial precepts in general indeed included justice as such, namely, insofar as they were observed for the worship of God, although those precepts in particular included justice as such only because the divine law so specified. And so we say that such precepts made human beings just only by the devotion or the obedience of those carrying out the precepts.

And the moral precepts and the precepts governing the administration of justice, either in general or in particular, included matter pertaining to justice as such. And the moral precepts included matter pertaining to justice as such regarding general justice, that is, "all virtue," as the *Ethics* says.[51] And the precepts governing the administration of justice pertain to particular justice, which concerns the interactions of human life that transpire among human beings in their relations to one another.

Reply Obj. 1. The Apostle in the cited text understands justification to mean the execution of justice.

Reply Obj. 2. The cited text says that the human beings who fulfilled the precepts of the Law had life thereby in that they did not incur the penalty of death that the Law inflicted on transgressors. And the Apostle in Gal. 3:12 quotes the passage in this sense.

---

[49]*Against Faustus* XXII, 24 (PL 42:417).   [50]ST I–II, Q. 63, A. 4.

[51]Aristotle, *Ethics* V, 1 (1129b30–1).

Reply Obj. 3. The precepts of human law make human beings just by acquired justice, and we are presently speaking only about justice with God, not about acquired justice.

Question 105
On the Reason for Precepts Governing the Administration of Justice

FIRST ARTICLE
Did the Old Law Ordain Fitting Precepts Regarding Rulers?

We thus proceed to the first inquiry. It seems that the Old Law did not ordain fitting precepts regarding rulers, for the following reasons:

Obj. 1. "The right order of the people depends chiefly on the chief ruler," as the Philosopher says in the *Politics*.[1] But we do not find in the Law how the supreme ruler ought to be established, although we find prescriptions regarding inferior officials. First, indeed, we find the prescription in Ex. 18:21–2: "Provide wise men from all the people," etc. And we find the prescription in Num. 11:16–7: "Gather for me seventy men from the elders of Israel," etc. And we find the prescription in Dt. 1:13–8: "Give me wise and knowledgeable men from among you," etc. Therefore, the Old Law inadequately ordained rulers of the people.

Obj. 2. "It belongs to the best to lead to the best things," as Plato says.[2] But the best regime of a political community or any people is to be governed by a king, since such a regime most represents the divine regime, in which God governs the world from its beginning. Therefore, the Law should have established a king for the people and not have left this to their choice, as Dt. 17:14–6 permits: "When you shall say, 'I shall establish a king over me,' you shall establish him," etc.

Obj. 3. Mt. 12:25 says: "Every kingdom divided against itself shall be laid low." And this was also evidenced by trial and error in the history of the Jewish people, regarding whom the division of the kingdom brought about its destruction. But law should aim chiefly at things pertaining to the commonweal of the people. Therefore, the Law should have prohibited division of the kingdom under two kings. Nor should even divine authority have introduced such a division, since we read in 1 Kgs. 11:29–31 that it was introduced by the authority of the prophet Ahijah of Shiloh.

Obj. 4. As priests are instituted for the benefit of the people regarding things that pertain to God, as Heb. 5:1 makes clear, so also rulers are

---

[1]*Politics* III, 4 (1278b8–10).   [2]Cf. *Timaeus* 29A; 29E.

instituted for the benefit of the people regarding human affairs. But certain things (e.g., tithes and first fruits and many other like things) were allotted to the priests and Levites of the Old Law as a means of their livelihood. Therefore, certain things should likewise have been ordained for the rulers of the people to provide them with a livelihood. And this is especially so because the rulers were prohibited from accepting bribes, as Ex. 23:8 makes clear: "You shall not take bribes, which blind even the wise and pervert the responses of the just."

Obj. 5. As a kingdom is the best regime, so tyranny is the most corrupt regime. But the Lord by establishing a king established tyrannical law, for 1 Sam. 8:11–7 says: "This will be the law of the king who will reign over you: he will take away your sons," etc. Therefore, the Old Law made inappropriate provision regarding the institution of rulers.

On the contrary, Num. 24:5 commends the people of Israel for the beauty of its institutions: "How beautiful are your tabernacles, O Jacob, and your tents, O Israel." But the beauty of the institutions of a people depends on the right institution of its rulers. Therefore, the Old Law made the right institution for the people regarding its rulers.

I answer that we should note two things regarding the right institution of rulers in any political community or people. The first is that all citizens should participate in the regime, since this maintains civic peace, and since all citizens love and protect such an institution, as the *Politics* says.[3] The second is what we note regarding the types of regimes, that is, forms of government. And although regimes have different forms, as the Philosopher notes in the *Politics*,[4] the chief forms are a kingdom, in which one person rules by reason of the person's virtue, and aristocracy (i.e., government by the best), in which a few persons rule by reason of their virtue. And so the best institution of rulers belongs to a city or kingdom in which one person is chosen by reason of his virtue to rule over all, and other persons govern under him by reason of their virtue. And yet such a regime belongs to all citizens, both because its rulers are chosen from the citizens, and because all citizens choose its rulers. For this is the best constitution, a happy mixture of kingdom, since one person rules; and of aristocracy, since many govern by reason of their virtue; and of democracy (i.e., government by the people), since rulers can be chosen from the people, and since the choice of rulers belongs to the people.

And the divine law established such a regime. For Moses and his successors governed the people, individually ruling over all, as it were, and this regime is a form of kingdom. And seventy-two elders were chosen by

---

[3]Aristotle, *Politics* II, 6 (1270b17–9).   [4]Ibid., III, 5 (1279a32–b10).

reason of their virtue, for Dt. 1:15 says: "I took wise and honorable men from your tribes and constituted them rulers." And this was aristocratic. And the regime was democratic in that the rulers were chosen from all the people, for Ex. 18:21 says: "Provide wise men from all the people," etc., and in that the people chose the rulers, and so Dt. 1:13 says: "Take wise men from among you," etc. And so the best institution of rulers was the one that the Old Law established.

Reply Obj. 1. The people were ruled under the special care of God, and so Dt. 7:6 says: "The Lord your God chose you to be a special people." And so God reserved to himself the institution of the chief ruler. And Num. 27:16 relates that Moses sought this: "Let the Lord God of the spirits of all flesh provide a man to rule this people." And so the ordinance of God established Joshua to rule after Moses. And we read about the Judges who succeeded Joshua, as Jgs. 3:9–10, 15 makes clear, that God "raised up a savior for the people," and that "the spirit of God was in them." And so the Lord did not commit the choice of a king to the people. Rather, he reserved the choice to himself, as Dt. 17:15 says: "You shall constitute as king the one the Lord your God has chosen."

Reply Obj. 2. A kingdom, if it be not corrupted, is the best regime for the people. But a kingdom easily degenerates into tyranny because of the great power granted a king, unless the one granted such power should have complete virtue. For it belongs only to the virtuous to bear themselves well when favored by good fortune, as the Philosopher says in the *Ethics*.[5] And few persons have complete virtue, and the Jews were particularly cruel and prone to avarice, through which vices human beings most fall into tyranny. And so the Lord at the beginning did not establish a king with complete power over the people but established judges and governors to protect them. But he, almost indignantly, granted the people a king when they petitioned for one, as 1 Sam. 8:7 makes clear by what he said to Samuel: "They have not rejected you but me, that I not rule over them."

Nonetheless, he from the beginning established regarding the institution of kingship, indeed first of all, the means of choosing a king. And he established two things in this regard, namely, that they await the judgment of the Lord in choosing a king, and that they not make a foreigner king, since such kings are usually little attached to the people over whom they are appointed, and so do not care about them.

Second, he ordained regarding kings when established how they should conduct themselves regarding themselves, namely, that they not have many horses or wives or immense riches, since rulers descend to

---

[5]*Ethics* IV, 3 (1124a30–b4).

tyranny and abandon justice by coveting such things.

Third, he established how they should dispose themselves toward God, namely, that they should always read and meditate on God's Law and always fear and obey God.

Fourth, he established how they should dispose themselves toward their subjects, namely, that they not in their pride contemn or oppress their subjects, and that they not deviate from justice.

Reply Obj. 3. The division of the kingdom and plurality of kings was inflicted on the people as punishment for their many rebellions, which they especially undertook against the just David, rather than for their benefit. And so Hos. 13:11 says: "In my wrath, I shall give you a king." And Hos. 8:4 says: "They reigned, but not by my will; rulers appeared, and I did not know them."

Reply Obj. 4. Priests were appointed to perform the sacred ministry by successive generations from father to son. And this was done so that they be held in greater respect if not anyone of the people could become a priest, since the honor they received added to respect for the divine worship. And so special things, in tithes and first fruits and even oblations and sacrifices, needed to be allotted to them as the means of their livelihood. But rulers were taken from the whole people, as I have said,[6] and so they had fixed possessions of their own as the means of their livelihood, and especially since the Lord also prohibited kings from having excessive wealth or displaying magnificence. The Lord prohibited these things both because it was difficult not to be incited by them to pride and tyranny, and because common people did not usually strive much for them if the rulers were not very rich, and if the rulers' office was laborious and full of anxiety. And so the occasion for sedition was removed.

Reply Obj. 5. The divine institution of kingship did not give to the kings of Israel any right to make tyrannical law. Rather, the Lord foretold that the kings of Israel, who, degenerating into tyranny and preying on their subjects, made evil laws to suit themselves, would claim a right to make such laws. And 1 Sam. 8:17 makes this clear: "And you will be the king's slaves," which belongs strictly to tyranny in that tyrants rule over their subjects as if their subjects were their slaves. And so Samuel said this to deter the people from seeking a king, for a subsequent verse, v. 19, says: "The people would not listen to the voice of Samuel."

But a good king may without tyranny have occasion to take sons away and establish them as tribunes or centurions, and to take many things from his subjects, in order to secure the common good.

---

[6]In the body of the article

3

Justice

In ST II–II, Q. 57, Thomas says that right is the object of justice, which directs human beings in their relations with others (A. 1). He distinguishes natural right, which consists of rendering to others things equivalent by their nature, and positive right, which consists of rendering to others things equivalent by private or public agreement (A. 2); the common right of peoples (the jus gentium*), which consists of rendering to others things commensurate by reason of their consequences (A. 3); parental right and master-slave right, which consist of rendering to others things commensurate by reason of children or slaves belonging to their parents or masters in certain respects (A. 4).*

In ST II–II, Q. 58, Thomas defines justice as the perpetual and constant will to render to others their rights (A. 1), and justice is always in relation to others (A. 2). Justice is a virtue (A. 3) and belongs to the will (A. 4). Justice in general is virtue in general insofar as justice directs the acts of other virtues to the common good (A. 5), but justice is essentially different from other virtues (A. 6). There is also particular justice (A. 7), which concerns external actions and things (A. 8). Justice is not about governing emotions (A. 9), and the mean of justice is a real mean, not a mean of reason (A. 10). Just acts render to others what is owed to them (A. 11). Justice is the greatest moral virtue (A. 12).

In ST II–II, Q. 61, Thomas distinguishes two kinds of particular justice: commutative justice, which consists of just exchanges between individuals; and distributive justice, which consists of just distributions of common goods to individuals (A. 1). The mean of commutative justice is arithmetic, and the mean of distributive justice is geometric (A. 2). Commutative justice and distributive justice have different subject matters: the former concerns activities involving exchanges, and the latter activities involving distributions (A. 3).

---

[1]The Latin word *jus* means law or right. In at least the first article of this question, Thomas seems to be using *jus* in the latter sense. But since it is law that establishes right, right and law are correlative. In subsequent articles of the question, we have continued to translate *jus* as "right," although "law" would there also seem to fit the contexts (e.g., "common law of peoples" for "common right of peoples").

ST II–II Justice
Question 57
On Right[1]

FIRST ARTICLE
Is Right the Object of Justice?

We thus proceed to the first inquiry. It seems that right is not the object of justice, for the following reasons:

Obj. 1. The jurist Celsus says that "establishing right is skill in establishing goodness and fairness."[2] But skills as such are intellectual virtues, and so the skill of establishing right is not the object of justice. Therefore, right is not the object of justice.

Obj. 2. Isidore says in his *Etymologies*: "Law is a species of establishing right."[3] But law is the object of practical wisdom rather than the object of justice. And so also the Philosopher designates lawmaking part of practical wisdom.[4] Therefore, right is not the object of justice.

Obj. 3. Justice chiefly renders human beings subject to God, for Augustine says in his work *On the Morals of the Church*: "Justice is love that serves God alone and for that reason rightly governs other things, which are subject to human beings."[5] But right belongs only to human affairs, not divine matters, for Isidore says in his *Etymologies*: "Divine law makes allowances, but human law establishes right."[6] Therefore, right is not the object of justice.

On the contrary, Isidore says in the same work that "right is called such because it is just."[7] But just deeds are the object of justice, for the Philosopher says in the *Ethics* that "all human beings agree about calling justice the habit whereby they perform just deeds."[8] Therefore, right is the object of justice.

I answer that in contrast to other virtues, it is the object of justice to direct human beings in their relations with one another. For justice signifies a certain equality, as the very name indicates, since we commonly speak of equal things being exactly right. And things have equality in relation to other things. But other virtues perfect human beings only

---

[2]Justinian, *Digest* I, title 1, c. 1.   [3]*Etymologies* V, 3, n. 1 (PL 82:199).

[4]*Ethics* VI, 8 (1141b25–9).   [5]*On the Morals of the Church* 15 (PL 32:1322).

[6]*Etymologies* V, 2, n. 2 (PL 82:198). Isidore literally says that divine law is *fas,* that is, divine law or divine right. The point is that divine law makes allowances for the human condition and does not (impossibly) insist on strict quid pro quo, and we have freely translated the quotation accordingly.

[7]Ibid., V, 3, n. 1 (PL 82:199).   [8]*Ethics* V, 1 (1129a7–11).

regarding things that befit human beings in their own individual regard.

Therefore, we understand the rectitude of the acts of other virtues, for which, as their proper objects, the other virtues strive, only in relation to the human beings performing the acts. But the relation of acts of justice to other persons, in addition to the acts' relation to the human beings performing the acts, constitutes the rectitude of the acts. For we call our deeds just if they return quid pro quo to others (e.g., the payment of wages due for services rendered).

Therefore, we call just, as possessing the rectitude of justice, things that are the termini of acts of justice, even apart from how the human agent performs them. But in the case of other virtues, we specify things as right only if the human agent performs the things in a certain way. And so we specify the object of justice as such beyond that of other virtues, and we call just things the object. And so right is clearly the object of justice.

Reply Obj. 1. We are wont to adapt words from their original use to signify other things. For example, we first use the word *medicine* to signify a remedy administered to the sick to cure them and then extend the term to signify the skill that accomplishes this. Just so, the word *right* was first used to signify the very things that are just. And the word was later extended to signify the skill whereby lawmakers know what is just. And the word was further extended to signify the courts where *right* is adjudicated, as, for example, we speak of persons appearing in courts of law. And we also further speak of decisions by officials administering justice as establishing right, even if their decisions are evil.

Reply Obj. 2. A plan for the things a craft produces externally, the plan we call the rule of the craft, preexists in the mind of artisans. Just so, a plan for the just deeds reason specifies, a rule of practical wisdom, so to speak, preexists in the mind of lawmakers. And we call the lawmakers' plan, if expressed in written form, a statute, for a statute is a "written decree," as Isidore says.[9] And so a statute is not, strictly speaking, the very right established but a plan establishing the right.

Reply Obj. 3. Justice signifies equality. But we cannot give equal recompense to God. And so we cannot return to God what is just in the fullest sense. And so, properly speaking, we speak of divine law as making allowances, not as in the case of [strict] right, since God is clearly satisfied if we fulfill his law as far as we can. Nonetheless, justice aims for human beings, as far as they can, to repay God by completely subjecting their souls to him.

---

[9]*Etymologies* V, 3, n. 2 (PL 82:199).

SECOND ARTICLE
Do We Appropriately Divide Right
into Natural and Positive Right?

We thus proceed to the second inquiry. It seems that we inappropriately so divide right, for the following reasons:

Obj. 1. What is natural cannot be changed, and all peoples so judge. But there is no such thing in human affairs, since all rules of human law are wanting in particular cases, nor are they in force everywhere. Therefore, there is no natural right.

Obj. 2. We call anything produced by the human will something positive. But nothing is just simply because it is produced by a human will; otherwise, the human will could not be unjust. Therefore, since the just and right mean the same thing, it seems that there is no positive right.

Obj. 3. Divine right, since it surpasses human nature, is not natural right. Likewise, divine right, since it relies on divine rather than human authority, is not positive right. Therefore, we inappropriately divide right into only two kinds of right, natural and positive.

On the contrary, the Philosopher says in the *Ethics* that "part of political justice is indeed natural, and part legal,"[10] that is, established by positive law.

I answer that, as I have said before,[11] right or justice consists of rendering to others things equivalent by some measure of equality. And equivalent things can be rendered to others in two ways. Things can indeed be so rendered to them in one way by the very nature of the things, as, for example, when one gives so much in order to receive so much. And we call this natural right.

Things are equivalent to, or commensurate with, other things in a second way by agreement or mutual consent, namely, when one deems oneself content to receive so much. And this can indeed happen in two ways. It happens in one way by private agreement, as something confirmed by a contract between private persons. It can happen in a second way by public agreement, as, for example, when the whole people agree that things be considered equivalent to, or commensurate with, other things, or when a ruler in charge of the people and acting on its part so ordains. And we call this positive right.

Reply Obj. 1. What is natural for things having an immutable nature needs to be always and everywhere such. But the nature of human beings is mutable. And so what is natural for human beings can sometimes be wanting. For example, it is natural equity to return entrusted things to

---

[10]*Ethics* V, 7 (1134b18–9).   [11]ST II–II, Q. 57, A. 1.

their owners, and so this principle should always be observed if human nature were always righteous. But since the will of human beings may sometimes be evil, there are cases in which entrusted things should not be returned to their owners lest human beings having a wicked will use the things wickedly (e.g., if a madman or enemy of the commonwealth should demand return of his weapons).

Reply Obj. 2. The human will can, by common agreement, make something just in the case of things as such compatible with natural justice. And positive right plays a role in such things. And so the Philosopher says in the *Ethics* that legal justice "concerns things about which it initially makes no difference whether they are done in this or that way, but it does matter when they are prescribed as law."[12] But if something of itself should be incompatible with natural justice, the human will cannot make it just. For example, such would be the case if laws should decree that it is permissible to steal or commit adultery. And so Is. 10:1 says: "Woe to those who establish wicked laws."

Reply Obj. 3. We call decrees promulgated by God divine right. And divine right indeed partially concerns things just by nature, although their justice is unknown to human beings, and partially concerns things just by divine institution. And so also we can distinguish divine right by these two kinds of just things, just as we can distinguish human right by them. For divine law commands certain things because they are good and prohibits certain things because they are evil. And other things are good or evil because divine law commands or forbids them.

THIRD ARTICLE
Is the Common Right of Peoples
[*Jus gentium*] the Same as Natural Right?

We thus proceed to the third inquiry. It seems that the common right of peoples is the same as natural right, for the following reasons:

Obj. 1. Human beings agree only about things natural to them. But all human beings agree about the common right of peoples, for the Jurist says that "the common right of peoples is the right that all peoples recognize."[13] Therefore, the common right of peoples is natural right.

Obj. 2. Human slavery is natural, since some human beings are by nature slaves, as the Philosopher says in the *Politics.*[14] But slavery belongs to the common right of peoples, as Isidore says.[15] Therefore, the common right of peoples is natural right.

---

[12]*Ethics* V, 7 (1134b20–4).   [13]*Digest* I, title 1, c. 1.   [14]*Politics* I, 2 (1254a15).
[15]*Etymologies* V, 6, n. 1 (PL 82:199).

Obj. 3. We divide right into natural right and positive right, as I have said.[16] But the common right of peoples is not positive right, since all peoples have never agreed to establish any right by mutual agreement. Therefore, the common right of peoples is natural law.

On the contrary, Isidore says that "right is either natural or proper to a political community or common to all peoples."[17] And so he distinguishes the common right of peoples from natural right.

I answer that, as I have said before,[18] right or natural justice consists of things equated or commensurate with other things. And this can be so in two ways. It can happen in one way as we consider things absolutely. For example, men are by their nature commensurate with women in begetting offspring, and parents are commensurate with children in rearing the latter.

Things are by nature commensurate with others in a second way by reason of their consequences, not as we consider them absolutely. For example, dominion over property is such. For if we should consider a particular plot of farmland absolutely, there is no reason why it should belong to one person rather than to another. But if we should consider the plot of farmland with respect to its opportune cultivation and settled use, the land in this respect commensurately belongs to one person rather than another, as the Philosopher makes clear in the *Politics.*[19]

And to take possession of something absolutely is proper both to human beings and to other animals. And so the right we call natural in the first way is common to us and to other animals. And the common right of peoples is distinct from the right called natural in the above sense, because, as the Jurist says,[20] "The latter right is common to all animals, the former only to human beings." But considering things in relation to their consequences belongs to reason. And so the jurist Gaius says: "All peoples cherish what natural reason establishes with all human beings, and we call such the common right of peoples."[21]

Reply Obj. 1. The answer makes clear the reply to obj. 1.

Reply Obj. 2. There is no natural reason, absolutely speaking, why this person rather than that person should be a slave. But there is only a beneficial result, since it is useful that particular persons be ruled by those wiser, and that the former assist the latter, as the *Politics* says.[22] And so the slavery associated with the common right of peoples is natural in the second way, not the first.

---

[16]ST II–II, Q. 57, A. 2.   [17]*Etymologies* V, 4, n. 1 (PL 82:199).
[18]ST II–II, Q. 57, A. 2.
[19]*Politics* II, 2 (1263a21–4).   [20]*Digest* I, title 1, c. 1.   [21]Ibid., c. 9.
[22]Aristotle, *Politics* I, 2 (1255b5–9).

Reply Obj. 3. Since natural reason dictates things belonging to the common right of peoples (e.g., things having approximate equality), such things do not need any particular institution. Rather, natural reason instituted them, as the cited authority of Gaius said.[23]

FOURTH ARTICLE
Should We Distinguish Paternal Right and Master-Slave Right as Special Kinds of Right?

We thus proceed to the fourth inquiry. It seems that we should not distinguish paternal right and master-slave right as special kinds of right, for the following reasons:

Obj. 1. It belongs to justice "to render to each what belongs to each," as Ambrose says in his work *On Duties.*[24] But right is the object of justice, as I have said.[25] Therefore, right belongs to everyone. And so we should not distinguish paternal right and master-slave right as special kinds of right.

Obj. 2. Law is the plan for what is just, as I have said.[26] But law concerns the common good of a political community or kingdom, as I have maintained before,[27] not the private good of one person or one household. Therefore, there should not be any special right or justice, whether paternal or master-slave, since masters and fathers belong to households, as the *Politics* says.[28]

Obj. 3. Human beings belong to many other different ranks. For example, some are soldiers, some priests, some rulers. Therefore, we should specify what is just for them.

On the contrary, the Philosopher in the *Ethics* specifically distinguishes master-slave and paternal justice and the like from political justice.[29]

I answer that we speak of right or justice as the commensuration of some things to other things. And we can speak of things being other in two ways. We can speak of them in one way as absolutely other, as altogether different. Such is evidently the case of two persons neither of whom is subject to the other, although both are subject to the ruler of their political community. And among such, there is justice without qualification, as the Philosopher says in the *Ethics.*[30]

We speak of things being other in a second way, not absolutely other but as one thing belongs to the other. And regarding human life, children

---

[23]At the conclusion of the body of this article.

[24]*On Duties* I, 24, n. 115 (PL 16:57).   [25]ST II–II, Q. 57, A. 1.   [26]Ibid., *ad* 2.

[27]ST I–II, Q. 90, A. 2.   [28]Aristotle, *Politics* I, 2 (1253b5–8).

[29]*Ethics* V, 6 (1134b8–9).   [30]Ibid., (1134a26).

belong to their fathers in this way, since they are in a way parts of their fathers, as the *Ethics* says.[31] And slaves belong to their masters, since slaves are their masters' instruments, as the *Politics* says.[32] And so fathers are not related to their children as absolutely other. And so the paternal relationship has a certain justice, namely, paternal justice, but not justice absolutely. And by the same argument, the master-slave relationship has a certain justice, namely, master-slave justice, not justice absolutely.

And wives belong to their husbands, since husbands are related to their wives as to their own bodies, as the Apostle makes clear in Eph. 5:28. Nonetheless, wives are more distinct from their husbands than children are from fathers, or slaves from masters, since wives are partners in the social life of marriage. And so there is more of the character of justice between husbands and wives than between fathers and children, or masters and slaves, as the Philosopher says.[33] But husbands and wives have a direct relation to a household community, as the *Politics* says.[34] Therefore, there is between them household justice rather than political justice in the absolute sense.

Reply Obj. 1. It belongs to justice for human beings to render to others what is due them, but this assumes that the one rendering is distinct from the one receiving. For we do not call giving to oneself what is owed to oneself justice in the strict sense. And since what belongs to children belongs to their fathers, and what belongs to slaves belongs to their masters, there is no justice in the strict sense between fathers and children or between masters and slaves.

Reply Obj. 2. Children as such belong to their parents, and likewise slaves as such belong to their masters. But both children and slaves considered as human beings are as such subsistent and distinct from other human beings. And so insofar as they are human beings, there is justice in their regard in that respect. And there are also for this reason laws regarding the relations of fathers to their children and of masters to their slaves. But insofar as both belong to others, the complete nature of justice or right is lacking.

Reply Obj. 3. All other distinctions between persons in political communities bear a direct relationship to the communities and their rulers. And so there is justice in the fullest sense in regard to those persons. But we distinguish such justice by different duties. And so also we speak of

---

[31]Ibid., VIII, 12 (1161b18–9).

[32]Aristotle, *Politics* I, 2 (1253b32; 1254a14–5).

[33]*Ethics* V, 6 (1134b15–8).

[34]Aristotle, *Politics* I, 2 (1253b6–11).

military right or magisterial right or priestly right because things proper to every condition of persons are due persons in accord with their particular stations, not because such rights fall short of justice absolutely, as when we speak of paternal right and master-slave right.

Question 58
On Justice

FIRST ARTICLE
Do We Appropriately Define Justice as the Constant and Perpetual Will to Render to Others What Is Due Them?

We thus proceed to the first inquiry. It seems that jurists inappropriately define justice as "the constant and perpetual will to render to others what is due them,"[1] for the following reasons:

Obj. 1. The Philosopher says in the *Ethics* that justice is "the habit whereby human beings act justly and do so willingly."[2] But the will designates the power or its acts. Therefore, we inappropriately call justice the will.

Obj. 2. The rectitude of the will is not the will. Otherwise, if the will were to be its rectitude, then no will would be wicked. But "justice is rectitude," as Anselm says in his work *On Truth*.[3] Therefore, justice is not the will.

Obj. 3. Only God's will is everlasting. Therefore, if justice is perpetual will, there will be justice only in God.

Obj. 4. Everything perpetual, since it is immutable, is constant. Therefore, it is superfluous to posit both perpetual and constant in the definition of justice.

Obj. 5. Rendering to others what is due them belongs to rulers. Therefore, if justice be rendering to others what is due them, then justice will belong only to rulers. And this conclusion is inappropriate.

Obj. 6. Augustine says in his work *On the Morals of the Church* that "justice is love serving God alone."[4] Therefore, justice does not render to other human beings what is theirs.

I answer that the aforementioned definition of justice is appropriate if we understand it correctly. For inasmuch as virtues are habits that are the sources of action, we need to define virtue as good action regarding the particular matter of a virtue. And justice concerns things in relation to others as its particular matter, as I shall make clear later.[5] And so the definition,

---

[1]Justinian, *Digest* I, title 1, c. 10.   [2]*Ethics* V, 1 (1129a7–11).
[3]*On Truth* 12 (PL 158:480).   [4]*On the Morals of the Church* 15 (PL 32:1322).
[5]ST II–II, Q. 58, AA. 2, 8.   [6]*Etymologies* X, n. 125 (PL 82:380).

when it speaks of "rendering to others what is their due," touches on acts of justice in relation to the particular matter and object of justice, since Isidore says in his *Etymologies*: "We call human beings just because they respect what is just."[6] But for any act regarding any matter to be virtuous, the act needs to be voluntary and steadfast and enduring. For the Philosopher says in the *Ethics* that virtuous acts require, above all else, that "one act knowingly"; second, that one act "by choice and for a proper end"; third, that "one act steadfastly."[7] And the first point is included in the second, since "what one does in ignorance, one does involuntarily," as the *Ethics* says.[8] And so the will is first designated in the definition of justice in order to show that acts of justice need to be voluntary. And constancy and perpetuity are added to the definition in order to designate the steadfastness of the acts.

And so the aforementioned definition is the complete definition of justice, save that acts are substituted for the habit, which the acts specify, since we speak of habits in relation to acts. And if one were to want to put this into the proper form of a definition, one could then say that justice is the habit whereby one with a constant and perpetual will renders to others what is due them. And this is almost the same definition as the one the Philosopher gives in the *Ethics* when he says that "justice is the habit whereby we say that one acts justly by choice."[9]

Reply Obj. 1. Will in the cited text designates acts, not the power. And writers usually define habits by acts, as, for example, Augustine says in his *Commentary on the Gospel of John* that the habit of faith consists of "believing what one does not see."[10]

Reply Obj. 2. Justice is only the same as rectitude insofar as it causes rectitude, but it is not essentially the same. For justice is the habit whereby one acts justly and willingly.

Reply Obj. 3. We can speak of the will being perpetual in two ways. A will is perpetual in one way regarding its very act if that act perdures forever, and then only God's will is perpetual. A will is perpetual in a second way regarding its object, namely, in that one perpetually wills to do things. And the nature of justice requires this kind of perpetual will. For example, it does not satisfy the nature of justice that one be willing in the course of conducting business to observe justice for an hour, since there scarcely exists a person who would wish to act unjustly in every matter. Rather, justice requires that human beings have a will to observe justice perpetually and in every matter.

---

[7]*Ethics* II, 4 (1105a31–b5).   [8]Ibid., III, 1 (1109b35–1110a1).
[9]Ibid., V, 5 (1134a1–3).
[10]*Commentary on the Gospel of John*, tr. 40, n. 9 (PL 35:1690).

Reply Obj. 4. Since we do not understand perpetuity to mean the perpetual duration of the will's act, it is not superfluous to add the notion of constancy to the definition of justice. As we in speaking of perpetual will denote that one has a perpetual intention to observe justice, so also we in speaking of constant will denote that one persists steadfastly in such a purpose.

Reply Obj. 5. Judges render what belongs to individuals by commanding and directing individuals, since "judges are justice-in-the-flesh, and rulers guardians of justice," as the *Ethics* says.[11] But subjects render to others what is due them by observing the commands and directions.

Reply Obj. 6. Love of neighbor is included in love of God, as I have said before.[12] Just so, human beings' service of God includes rendering to others what is due them.

SECOND ARTICLE
Does Justice Always Consist of Relations to Others?

We thus proceed to the second inquiry. It seems that justice does not always consist of relations to others, for the following reasons:

Obj. 1. The Apostle says in Rom. 3:22 that "the justice of God is through faith in Jesus Christ." But we do not speak of faith in terms of the relation of human beings to one another. Therefore, we do not speak of justice in such terms.

Obj. 2. Augustine says in his work *On the Morals of the Church* that it belongs to justice that human beings in serving God "rightly govern the other things subject to them."[13] But sense appetite is subject to human beings, as Gen. 4:7 says: "Your appetite [for sin] will be subject to you, and you shall master it." Therefore, it belongs to justice to master one's own appetites, and so there will be justice in relation to oneself.

Obj. 3. God's justice is eternal. But nothing else has been coeternal with God. Therefore, justice does not essentially consist of the relations of human beings to one another.

Obj. 4. As actions in relation to others need to be rightly directed, so also do actions in relation to oneself. But justice rightly directs actions, as Prov. 11:5 says: "The justice of the pure directs their way." Therefore, justice concerns both one's actions in relation to others and one's actions in relation to oneself.

On the contrary, Cicero says in his work *On Duties* that it is the nature of justice "to maintain the social relations of human beings and their common life."[14] But this signifies regard for others. Therefore, justice regards

---

[11]Aristotle, *Ethics* V, 4 (1132a21–5); V, 6 (1134b1–2).   [12]ST II–II, Q. 25, A. 1.
[13]*On the Morals of the Church* 15 (PL 32:1322).   [14]*On Duties* I, 7.

only our relations to others.

I answer that, as I have said before,[15] justice by its nature concerns our relations to others, since its name denotes equality. For things are equal to other things, not to themselves. And since it belongs to justice to direct human acts rightly, as I have said,[16] the otherness that justice requires needs to belong to different things capable of action. And actions belong to subsistent and whole entities, not, strictly speaking, to parts and forms, or faculties. For example, we do not properly say that hands strike things, but that human beings strike things with their hands. Nor, strictly speaking, do we say that heat warms things, but that fire warms things by heating them. Nonetheless, we say metaphorically that hands strike things, and that heat warms things.

Therefore, strictly speaking, justice requires distinct individual subsistent substances and so consists only of the relations of human persons to one another. But we metaphorically understand the different sources of action in one and the same human being (e.g., reason and the concupiscible and irascible powers) as if they were different efficient causes. And so we say metaphorically that justice belongs to one and the same human being insofar as reason commands the irascible and concupiscible powers, and insofar as those powers obey reason, and generally insofar as we attribute to each part of a human being what belongs to it. And so the Philosopher in the *Ethics* calls this justice "metaphorical."[17]

Reply Obj. 1. The justice accomplished in us by faith is the justice that makes the ungodly just. And this justice indeed consists of the proper order of the parts of the soul, as I have said before when I was treating of the justification of the ungodly.[18] And this belongs to metaphorical justice, which can belong even to one living a solitary life.

Reply Obj. 2. And the foregoing makes clear the reply to the second objection.

Reply Obj. 3. God's justice is from eternity as to his eternal will and purpose, and justice chiefly consists of this. But God's justice is not from eternity in its effects, since nothing is coeternal with God.

Reply Obj. 4. The actions of human beings regarding themselves are sufficiently well directed if the other moral virtues rightly direct the emotions. But actions in relation to others need special direction both in relation to those causing the actions and in relation to those others. And so regarding such actions, there is a particular virtue, namely, justice.

---

[15]ST II–II, Q. 57, A. 1.

[16]ST I–II: Q. 60, A. 2; Q. 61, A. 3; Q. 113, A. 1.

[17]*Ethics* V, 11 (1138b5–14).   [18]ST I–II, Q. 113, A. 1.

THIRD ARTICLE
Is Justice a Virtue?

We thus proceed to the third inquiry. It seems that justice is not a virtue, for the following reasons:

Obj. 1. Lk. 17:10 says: "When you have done all the things commanded of you, say: 'We are useless servants; we have done what we should have done.'" But doing virtuous deeds is not useless, since Ambrose says in his work *On Duties*: "We speak of usefulness as the acquisition of godliness, not as the value of monetary gain."[19] Therefore, doing what one ought to do is not a virtuous deed. But doing what one ought to do is a deed of justice. Therefore, justice is not a virtue.

Obj. 2. What one does out of necessity is not meritorious. But rendering to others what is theirs, which belongs to justice, is necessary. Therefore, rendering to others what is theirs is not meritorious. But we merit by virtuous acts. Therefore, justice is not a moral virtue.

Obj. 3. Every moral virtue concerns actions. But things externally caused are things that are produced, not actions, as the Philosopher makes clear in the *Metaphysics*.[20] Therefore, since it belongs to justice to produce an external deed that is in itself just, it seems that justice is not a moral virtue.

On the contrary, Gregory says in his work *Morals* that "the entire structure of good deeds arises in four virtues,"[21] namely, moderation, practical wisdom, courage, and justice.

I answer that human virtues make human acts and human beings themselves good, and this indeed belongs to justice. For the actions of human beings are rendered good because they achieve the rule of reason, which correctly directs human acts. And so since justice correctly directs human actions, it evidently renders the deeds of human beings good. And Cicero says in his work *On Duties*: "We chiefly call human beings good by reason of their justice."[22] And so "the luster of virtue is greatest in it," as he says in the same place.

Reply Obj. 1. When one does what one ought, one brings no useful gain to the other in relation to whom one does what one ought. Rather, one only abstains from harming the other. But one does profit oneself insofar as one does spontaneously and readily what one ought to do, which is to act virtuously. And Wis. 8:7 says that the wisdom of God "teaches sobriety and justice, practical wisdom and virtue, than which nothing is more useful for human beings," namely, virtuous human beings, "in living well."

---

[19]*On Duties* II, 6, n. 23 (PL 16:109).   [20]*Metaphysics* IX, 8 (1050a30–b2).
[21]*Morals* II, 49, n. 76 (PL 75:592).   [22]*On Duties* I, 7.

Reply Obj. 2. There are two kinds of necessity. One kind is the necessity of coercion, and this necessity, because it is contrary to acting willingly, takes away the character of merit. And the other kind is the necessity deriving from the obligation of precepts or the necessity of means for ends, namely, when one cannot attain a virtuous end without doing a particular deed. And the latter kind of necessity does not exclude the character of merit, since one does willingly what is necessary in the latter way. But the latter necessity excludes the glory of doing more than one's duty, as 1 Cor. 9:16 says: "If I have preached the Gospel, this is no credit to me, since the obligation to do so was imposed on me."

Reply Obj. 3. Justice concerns external things as to their use in relation to others, not as to their production, which belongs to skill.

FOURTH ARTICLE
Does Justice Inhere in the Will as Its Subject?

We thus proceed to the fourth inquiry. It seems that justice does not inhere in the will as its subject, for the following reasons:

Obj. 1. We sometimes call justice truth. But truth belongs to the intellect, not the will. Therefore, justice does not inhere in the will as its subject.

Obj. 2. Justice concerns things in relation to others. But directing things in relation to other things belongs to reason. Therefore, justice inheres in the power of reason as its subject rather than in the will.

Obj. 3. Justice is not an intellectual virtue, since it is not related to knowledge. And so we conclude that it is a moral virtue. But the subjects of moral virtues are powers that are rational by participation, that is, the irascible and concupiscible powers, as the Philosopher makes clear in the *Ethics*.[23] Therefore, justice inheres in the irascible and concupiscible powers rather than in the will as its subject.

On the contrary, Anselm says that "justice is rectitude of the will observed for its own sake."[24]

I answer that the power whose acts a virtue aims to direct rightly is the subject of the virtue. But justice is not ordered to direct any cognitive act, since we are not called just because we correctly know things. And so the subject of justice is not the intellect or reason, which is a cognitive power.

But since we are called just because we do things rightly, and the proximate sources of action are appetitive powers, justice needs to inhere in an appetitive power as its subject. And there are two kinds of appetite, namely, the will, which belongs to reason, and the sense appetites resulting from sense perceptions. And sense appetites are divided into the

---

[23]*Ethics* 1, 13 (1102b30).   [24]*On Truth* 12 (PL 158:482).

irascible and concupiscible powers, as I maintained in the First Part.[25] And rendering to others what is theirs cannot issue from a sense appetite, since sense perception does not reach far enough to be able to consider the relation of one thing to another. Rather, such consideration belongs to reason. And so justice cannot inhere in the irascible and concupiscible powers but can only inhere in the will as its subject. And so the Philosopher defines justice by acts of the will, as what I have said before makes clear.[26]

Reply Obj. 1. Because the will is a rational appetite, the rectitude of reason, which we call truth, when impressed on the will, retains the name of truth because of the close connection of the will to reason. And so we sometimes call justice truth.

Reply Obj. 2. The will is carried to its object after reason understands the object. And so since reason directs things in relation to other things, the will can will things in relation to others, which belongs to justice.

Reply Obj. 3. "All appetitive powers," as the *Ethics* says,[27] and not only the irascible and concupiscible powers, are rational by participation. For every appetitive power obeys reason, and the will is one of the appetitive powers. And so the will can be the subject of moral virtues.

FIFTH ARTICLE
Is Justice Virtue in General?

We thus proceed to the fifth inquiry. It seems that justice is not virtue in general, for the following reasons:

Obj. 1. Justice is classified with other kinds of virtue, as Wis. 8:7 makes clear: "She [wisdom] teaches sobriety and justice, practical wisdom and virtue." But the general is neither the specific nor listed with the specific contained in the general. Therefore, justice is not virtue in general.

Obj. 2. We designate moderation and courage, like justice, cardinal virtues. But we do not designate moderation and courage virtue in general. Therefore, we should in no respect designate justice virtue in general.

Obj. 3. Justice is always in relation to others, as I have said before.[28] But sin against one's neighbor is not sin in general but contradistinguished from sin against oneself. Therefore, justice is likewise not virtue in general.

On the contrary, the Philosopher says in the *Ethics* that "justice is every virtue."[29]

I answer that, as I have said before,[30] justice directs human beings in relation to others. And this happens in two ways. It happens in one way

---

[25]ST I, Q. 81, A. 2.   [26]ST II–I, Q. 58, A 1, obj. 1.   [27]See n. 23, supra.
[28]ST II–II, Q. 58, A. 2.   [29]*Ethics* V, 1 (1130a9–10).   [30]ST II–II, Q. 58, A. 2.

in relation to others individually. It happens in a second way in relation to others in general, namely, as those serving a community serve everyone in the community. Therefore, there can be justice in the strict sense in both ways. But everyone in a community is clearly related to the community as a part to the entire community. And parts belong to the whole. And so also every good of the part can be directed to the good of the whole. Therefore, we can in this respect relate the good of any virtue, whether a virtue directing human beings in relation to themselves or a virtue directing human beings in relation to other individual persons, to the common good, regarding which justice directs. And so the acts of every virtue can belong to justice insofar as justice directs human beings regarding the common good. And in this respect, we call justice virtue in general. And because it belongs to law to direct human beings regarding the common good, as I have maintained before,[31] we call justice in general, in the aforementioned way, legal justice. We do so because human beings by observing justice are in accord with the law, which directs the acts of every virtue toward the common good.

Reply Obj. 1. Justice is specific and listed alongside other virtues insofar as it is a special virtue, as I shall explain later,[32] and not insofar as it is virtue in general.

Reply Obj. 2. Moderation and courage belong to sense appetites, namely, the concupiscible and irascible powers. And the objects of such powers are particular goods, just as the objects of the senses are particular things. But justice inheres in the intellectual appetite as its subject, and the object of the intellectual appetite can be good in general, which the intellect can understand. And so justice, unlike moderation and courage, can be virtue in general.

Reply Obj. 3. Things regarding oneself can be related to others, especially to the common good. And so also we can call legal justice, insofar as it is directed toward the common good, virtue in general. And we can for the same reason call injustice sin in general. And so 1 Jn. 3:4 says that "every sin is lawlessness."

Sixth Article
Is Justice in General Essentially Identical with All Virtue?

We thus proceed to the sixth inquiry. It seems that justice in general is essentially identical with all virtue, for the following reasons:

Obj. 1. The Philosopher says in the *Ethics* that legal justice "is identical with every virtue, but their modality is not the same."[33] But things that

---

[31]ST I–II, Q. 90, A. 2.   [32]ST II–II, Q. 58, A. 7.
[33]*Ethics* V, 1 (1130a12–3).

differ only in modality or conceptually do not differ essentially. Therefore, justice is essentially the same as all virtue.

Obj. 2. Any virtue that is not essentially the same as all virtue is part of virtue.[34] But the aforementioned justice, as the Philosopher says in the same place, "is the whole of virtue, not part of virtue." Therefore, the aforementioned justice is essentially the same as all virtue.

Obj. 3. Habits do not differ essentially because virtues direct their acts to higher ends. For example, the habit of moderation is essentially the same even if its acts are ordered to the divine good. But it belongs to legal justice that the acts of all virtues be ordered to a higher end, namely, the common good of the people, which surpasses the good of an individual person. Therefore, it seems that legal justice is essentially all virtue.

Obj. 4. Every good of parts can be directed to the good of the whole. And so it seems to be empty and pointless if the good of parts is not directed to the good of the whole. But what concerns virtue cannot be such. Therefore, it seems that no act could belong to any virtue that does not belong to justice in general, which directs acts toward the common good. And so it seems that justice in general is essentially the same as all virtue.

On the contrary, the Philosopher says in the *Ethics*: "Many are indeed capable of exercising virtue in their own regard but incapable of doing so in matters that relate to others."[35] And he says in the *Politics* that "the virtue of a good person and a good citizen are not absolutely the same."[36] But the virtue of a good citizen is justice in general, which directs one toward the common good. Therefore, justice in general is not the same as virtue in general, and one can possess the one without possessing the other.

I answer that we speak of things being general in two ways. We speak of things being general in one way by predication. For example, animal is something general in human beings and horses and the like. And general in this sense needs to be essentially the same as the things in which it is something general, since genera belong to the essence of their species and are part of their species' definitions.

We speak of things being general in a second way regarding their causal power. For example, universal causes are general regarding all their effects, like the sun regarding all material substances, which its power illumines and affects. And general in this sense does not need to be essentially the same as the things in relation to which it is something general, since the essences of such causes and their effects differ.

---

[34]Ibid. (1130a9–10).   [35]Ibid. (1129b33–1130a1).
[36]*Politics* III, 2 (1277a22).

And it is the latter sense, as I have said before,[37] that we say that legal jus-tice is virtue in general, namely, insofar as legal justice directs the acts of other virtues to its end, which is to induce all other virtues by commanding them. For as we can call charity virtue in general insofar as charity directs the acts of all virtues to the divine good, so also we can call legal justice virtue in general insofar as legal justice directs the acts of all virtues to the common good. Therefore, as charity, which regards the divine good as its object, is essentially a special virtue, so also legal justice is essen-tially a special virtue insofar as legal justice concerns the common good as its object. And so legal justice resides chiefly and architectonically, as it were, in rulers, and secondarily and ministerially, as it were, in subjects.

But we can call any virtue legal justice insofar as that justice, indeed essentially particular but general regarding its causal power, relates virtu-ous acts to the common good. And in this sense, legal justice is essentially the same as all virtue, although conceptually different. And the Philosopher is speaking in this sense.[38]

Reply Objs. 1–2. And so the replies to objs. 1 and 2 are clear.

Reply Obj. 3. The argument of this objection is valid about legal justice in the cited sense, as we call the virtues legal justice commands legal justice.

Reply Obj. 4. Every virtue by its nature directs its acts to its peculiar end. But that a virtue be directed to a higher end, whether always or sometimes, does not belong to that virtue by its nature. Rather, another, higher virtue needs to give such direction to a higher end. And so a virtue higher and essentially distinct from every other virtue needs to direct all virtues toward the common good, and that higher virtue is legal justice.

SEVENTH ARTICLE
Besides Justice in General, Is There Particular Justice?

We thus proceed to the seventh inquiry. It seems that there is no particu-lar justice besides justice in general, for the following reasons:

Obj. 1. Nothing regarding virtues is superfluous, just as there is nothing superfluous regarding nature. But justice in general suffices to direct every-thing in relation to others. Therefore, no particular justice is necessary.

Obj. 2. We do not distinguish special virtues by whether one or many things are involved. But legal justice directs human beings in relation to others regarding things that belong to the people, as what I have said before makes clear.[39] Therefore, there is no other species of justice that

---

[37]ST II–II, Q. 58, A. 5.   [38]See obj. 1.

[39]ST II–II, Q. 58, AA. 5, 6.

directs human beings in relation to others regarding matters that belong to individual persons.

Obj. 3. Household communities are in between individual persons and the people of a political community. Therefore, if there is a particular justice in relation to individual persons besides justice in general, there should by like reasoning be a household justice to direct human beings in relation to the common good of households. And we indeed do not say this. Therefore, there is no particular justice besides legal justice.

On the contrary, on Mt. 5:6, "Blessed are those who hunger and thirst for justice," Chrysostom says: "We call justice either virtue in general or the particular virtue contrary to avarice."[40]

I answer that, as I have said before,[41] legal justice is not essentially all virtue, and there need to be other virtues directly orienting human beings in regard to particular goods, in addition to legal justice, which directly orients human beings to the common good. And these other virtues can indeed be in relation to oneself or in relation to other individual persons. Besides legal justice, therefore, there should be particular virtues that direct human beings regarding themselves (e.g., the virtues of moderation and courage). Just so, besides legal justice, there should be a particular justice that directs human beings regarding things in relation to other individual persons.

Reply Obj. 1. Legal justice indeed suffices to direct human beings in their relations with others, directly regarding the common good and indirectly regarding the good of individual persons. And so there needs to be a particular justice directly orienting human beings to the good of other individual persons.

Reply Obj. 2. The common good of a political community and the individual good of individual persons do not differ only by reason of the number of persons involved. Rather, the two goods differ by a formal difference, for the nature of the common good and the nature of an individual good are different, just as the nature of a whole and the nature of parts of the whole are different. And so the Philosopher says in the *Politics*: "Those who say that a political community and households and the like differ only by larger or smaller, not specifically, are in error."[42]

Reply Obj. 3. As the Philosopher says in the *Politics*,[43] we distinguish household communities by three relationships, namely, "the relationship

---

[40]*Homilies on the Gospel of Matthew*, homily 15 (PG 57:227).
[41]ST II–II, Q. 58, A. 6.   [42]*Politics* I, 1 (1252a7–10).
[43]Ibid., 2 (1253b6–8).

of husband and wife, the relationship of fathers and children, and the relationship of master and slaves," and one person in each of these relationships belongs to the other. And so there is no justice absolutely in relation to such a person. Rather, there is a species of justice, namely, household justice, as the *Ethics* says.[44]

EIGHTH ARTICLE
Does Particular Justice Have Special Subject Matter?

We thus proceed to the eighth inquiry. It seems that particular justice has no special subject matter, for the following reasons:

Obj. 1. A gloss on Gen. 2:14, "The fourth river is the Euphrates," says: "Euphrates means fruitful. Nor does the text say through what place it flows, since justice belongs to all parts of the soul."[45] But this would not be so if justice were to have special subject matter, since any special subject matter belongs to a special power. Therefore, particular justice has no special subject matter.

Obj. 2. Augustine in his *Eighty-Three Questions* says that "there are four virtues of the soul whereby one lives spiritually in this life, namely, practical wisdom, moderation, courage, and justice," and he says that the fourth, justice, "is diffused through all the others."[46] Therefore, particular justice, which is one of the four cardinal virtues, has no special subject matter.

Obj. 3. Justice sufficiently directs human beings in their relations with others. But human beings can be directed in their relations with others in everything belonging to this life. Therefore, the subject matter of justice is general, not special.

On the contrary, the Philosopher in the *Ethics* designates particular justice as justice particularly regarding things that belong to life in society.[47]

I answer that everything that reason can rightly direct is the subject matter of moral virtue, which is defined by right reason, as the Philosopher makes clear in the *Ethics*.[48] And reason can rightly direct both internal emotions of the soul and external actions and the external things that human beings come to use. But we consider the relations of human beings to one another by their external actions and the external things that they share with one another, and we consider the rectitude of human beings in their own regard by their internal emotions. And so justice, since it is directed toward others, only concerns external actions and things

---

[44]Aristotle, *Ethics* V, 6 (1134b8–9).

[45]*Glossa ordinaria*, on Gen. 2:14 (PL 113:87).

[46]*Eighty-Three Questions*, q. 61, n. 4 (PL 40:51).

[47]*Ethics* V, 2 (1130b31–3).   [48]Ibid., II, 6 (1107a1–2).

regarding a special objective aspect, namely, as they relate human beings to one another, and does not regard the whole subject matter of moral virtue.

Reply Obj. 1. Justice indeed belongs essentially to one part of the soul, namely, the will, which indeed induces other parts of the soul to act at the will's command, and the will is the subject in which justice inheres. And so justice belongs to all parts of the soul as if by diffusion, not directly.

Reply Obj. 2. We understand cardinal virtues in two ways, as I have said before.[49] We understand them in one way insofar as they are special virtues having fixed subject matter. We understand them in a second way insofar as they signify general modalities of virtue. And Augustine in the cited text speaks of them in the latter way. For he says that practical wisdom is "knowledge of what we should seek or shun," moderation "restraint of the lust for fleeting pleasures," courage "strength of soul to resist transitory trials," justice "a love of God and neighbor overflowing to the other virtues."[50] And that is to say that justice is the common source of the whole ordering of our relations to others.

Reply Obj. 3. Internal emotions, which are part of the subject matter of moral virtue, are not as such directed toward others, which direction belongs to the nature of justice. Rather, we can direct the effects of our emotions, namely, our external actions, in relation to others. And so it does not follow that the subject matter of justice is general.

Ninth Article
Does Justice Concern Emotions?

We thus proceed to the ninth article. It seems that justice does, for the following reasons:

Obj. 1. The Philosopher says in the *Ethics* that "moral virtue concerns pleasure and anguish."[51] But pleasure (i.e., delight) and anguish are emotions, as I have maintained before when I treated of emotions.[52] Therefore, justice, as a moral virtue, concerns emotions.

Obj. 2. Justice directs actions rightly in relation to others. But we can direct such actions rightly only if we direct our emotions rightly, since disordered actions in relation to others result from disordered emotions. For example, adultery results from sexual lust, and theft from excessive love of money. Therefore, justice concerns emotions.

Obj. 3. Legal justice concerns relations to others in the same way that particular justice does. But legal justice concerns emotions. Otherwise, it

---

[49]ST I–II, Q. 61, AA. 3, 4.   [50]See n. 46, supra.   [51]*Ethics* II, 3 (1104b8–9).
[52]ST I–II: Q. 23, A. 4; Q. 31, A. 1; Q. 35, A. 1.

would not comprehend all virtues, some of which obviously concern emotions. Therefore, justice concerns emotions.

On the contrary, the Philosopher says in the *Ethics* that justice concerns actions.[53]

I answer that two things make clear the answer to this question. One, indeed, is the very subject of justice, that is, the will, whose movements or acts are not emotions, as I have maintained before.[54] Rather, we call only movements of sense appetites emotions. And so justice does not concern emotions, as do moderation and courage, which belong to the irascible and concupiscible sense appetites.

The second thing making clear the answer to this question regards the subject matter of justice. For justice concerns our relations with others. But our internal emotions are not directly related to others. And so justice does not concern emotions.

Reply Obj. 1. Not every moral virtue concerns pleasure and anguish as its subject matter. For example, courage concerns timidity and temerity. But every moral virtue is directed to pleasure and anguish as consequent ends. For the Philosopher says in the *Ethics*: "Pleasure and anguish are the chief end regarding which we say that everything such-and-such is evil, and everything such-and-such good."[55] And pleasure and anguish belong to justice in the latter way, since "a just person rejoices in just actions," as the *Ethics* says.[56]

Reply Obj. 2. External actions are in one respect in between external things, which are the subject matter of external actions, and internal emotions, which are the sources of external actions. And there may sometimes be deficiency in one extreme without deficiency in the other extreme. For example, one might steal the possession of another out of a desire to harm the other rather than a desire to possess the thing. Or, conversely, one might covet the possession of another without wanting to steal it. Therefore, it belongs to justice to direct actions rightly insofar as external things are the objects of the actions, but it belongs to other virtues, which concern emotions, to direct actions rightly insofar as the actions arise out of emotions. And so justice prohibits stealing the property of another as contrary to the equality that should be established regarding external things, while generosity prohibits stealing as a consequence of excessive desire of riches. But external actions are specified by the external things that are their objects, not by internal emotions. Therefore, strictly speaking, external actions are the subject matter of justice rather than of other moral virtues.

---

[53]*Ethics* V, 1 (1129a3–5).   [54]ST I–II: Q. 22, A. 3; Q. 59, A. 4.
[55]*Ethics* VII, 11 (1152b2–3).   [56]Ibid., I, 8 (1099a18–21).

Reply Obj. 3. The common good is the end of individual persons living in a political community, as the end of a whole is the end of each of its parts. But the end of an individual person is not the end of another. And so legal justice, which is directed to the common good, rather than particular justice, which is directed to the good of another individual person, can comprehend internal emotions, whereby human beings are in one respect disposed regarding themselves. But legal justice more importantly comprehends other virtues regarding their external actions, namely, insofar as "law commands us to perform courageous, moderate, and kind actions," as the *Ethics* says.[57]

TENTH ARTICLE
Is the Mean of Justice a Real Mean?

We thus proceed to the tenth inquiry. It seems that the mean of justice is not a real mean, for the following reasons:

Obj. 1. All the species of a genus retain the nature of the genus. But the *Ethics* defines moral virtue as "a habit of the will consisting of the mean that reason determines in relation to ourselves."[58] And so there is likewise in justice a mean of reason, not a real mean.

Obj. 2. There is no taking too much or too little regarding things that are absolutely good, and so there is no mean regarding them, as there evidently is in the case of virtues, as the *Ethics* says.[59] But justice concerns absolutely good things, as the *Ethics* says.[60] Therefore, there is no real mean in justice.

Obj. 3. We say that there are means of reason rather than real means in the case of other virtues because we understand those means in relation to different persons, since what is too much for one person is too little for another, as the *Ethics* says.[61] But we observe the same in the case of justice, for we inflict more punishment on one who strikes a ruler than on one who strikes a private citizen. Therefore, justice likewise has a mean of reason, not a real mean.

On the contrary, the Philosopher in the *Ethics* designates the mean of justice by an arithmetic proportion,[62] and such a mean is a real mean.

I answer that, as I have said before,[63] other moral virtues concern emotions, whose right direction we consider only in relation to the very human beings to whom the emotions belong, namely, as one recoils or

---

[57]Ibid., V, 1 (1129b19–25).   [58]Ibid., II, 6 (1106b36–1107a2).
[59]Ibid. (1107a22–7).   [60]Ibid., V, 1 (1129b5–6).
[61]Ibid., II, 6 (1106a36–b7).   [62]Ibid., V, 4 (1132a1–7, 25–30).
[63]ST II–II, Q. 58, A. 2, *ad* 4; A. 8; I–II, Q. 60, A. 2.

desires as one should in different circumstances. And so we understand the mean of such virtues only in relation to the virtuous person and not by the relation of one thing to another. And so there is only a mean determined by reason in relation to ourselves in those virtues. But the subject matter of justice consists of external actions insofar as they or the things used have the proper relation to other persons. And so the mean of justice consists of the equivalence of an external thing to an external person. But equality is a real mean between greater and lesser, as the *Metaphysics* says.[64] And so justice has a real mean.

Reply Obj. 1. The real mean of justice is also a mean of reason. And so justice retains the nature of moral virtue.

Reply Obj. 2. We can speak of absolutely good in two ways. We can speak of it in one way as good in every way, as, for example, virtues are good in every way. And then we do not understand means and extremes regarding things absolutely good.

We can speak of absolutely good in a second way because something is absolutely good, namely, by its nature, although it could become evil by misuse, as is evidently the case regarding riches and honors. And we can understand excess, defect, and mean in such things in relation to human beings, who can use them either well or ill. And it is in this sense that we say that justice concerns absolutely good things.

Reply Obj. 3. Injury inflicted on a ruler and injury inflicted on a private citizen are different things. And so each type of injury needs to be rectified by different kinds of punishment. And this pertains to a real distinction and not merely a distinction of reason.

ELEVENTH ARTICLE
Do Acts of Justice Consist of Rendering to Others What Is Theirs?

We thus proceed to the eleventh inquiry. It seems that acts of justice do not consist of rendering to others what is theirs, for the following reasons:

Obj. 1. Augustine in his work *On the Trinity* assigns "succoring the needy" to justice.[65] But in succoring the needy, we render to them what belongs to ourselves, not what belongs to them. Therefore, acts of justice do not consist of rendering to others what is theirs.

Obj. 2. Cicero says in his work *On Duties* that "beneficence, which we can call kindness and generosity," belongs to justice.[66] But it belongs to generosity to give to others what is one's own, not what belongs to others.

---

[64]Aristotle, *Metaphysics* X, 5 (1056a18–24).

[65]*On the Trinity* XIV, 9 (PL 42:1046).   [66]On *Duties* I, 7.

Therefore, acts of justice do not consist of rendering to others what is theirs.

Obj. 3. It belongs to justice both to give things in a proper way and to prohibit injurious actions like murder, adultery, and other such things. But rendering to others what is theirs seems to belong only to giving things. Therefore, the statement that acts of justice consist of rendering to others what is theirs does not sufficiently denote the acts.

On the contrary, Ambrose says in his work *On Duties*: "Justice consists of rendering to others what is theirs, of not laying claim to the property of another, of disregarding one's own benefit in order to respect common equity."[67]

I answer that, as I have said,[68] the subject matter of justice consists of external actions insofar as the order of justice equates them or the things they use to other persons. But we say that what is due others in equal proportion belongs to them. And so the proper act of justice consists only of rendering to others what is theirs.

Reply Obj. 1. Other, secondary virtues (e.g., mercy, generosity, and the like) are joined to justice, which is a cardinal virtue, as I shall explain later.[69] And so we attribute succoring the needy, which belongs to mercy or gratitude, and generous beneficence, which belongs to generosity, to justice as the chief virtue on which they are founded.

Reply Obj. 2. The foregoing makes clear the reply to obj. 2.

Reply Obj. 3. The Philosopher says in the *Ethics* that we by extension call everything excessive in matters of justice gain, just as we call everything deficient in such matters loss.[70] And we do so because justice is first and more commonly practiced in voluntary exchanges of things (e.g., buying and selling), regarding which we use the words gain and loss in the strict sense. And the words are then extended to everything regarding which there can be a matter of justice. And the same reasoning applies to rendering to others what is theirs.

TWELFTH ARTICLE
Is Justice the Most Important Moral Virtue?

We thus proceed to the twelfth inquiry. It seems that justice is not the most important moral virtue, for the following reasons:

Obj. 1. It belongs to justice to render to others what is theirs. But it belongs to generosity to give to others what is one's own, and this is more virtuous. Therefore, generosity is a greater virtue than justice.

Obj. 2. Only something more worthy adorns something else. But

---

[67]On *Duties* I, 24 (PL 16:57).   [68]ST II–II, Q. 58, AA. 8, 10.
[69]ST II–II, Q. 80.   [70]*Ethics* V, 4 (1132b11–20).

"magnanimity is the adornment" of justice and "of all virtues," as the *Ethics* says.[71] Therefore, magnanimity is more excellent than justice.

Obj. 3. Virtue concerns "the difficult" and "the desirable," as the *Ethics* says.[72] But courage concerns more difficult things than justice does, namely, "the risk of death," as the *Ethics* says.[73] Therefore, courage is more excellent than justice.

On the contrary, Cicero says in his work *On Duties*: "Justice has the greatest virtuous splendor, and we call human beings good by reason of it."[74]

I answer that if we should be speaking of legal justice, justice is clearly the most important moral virtue, since the common good surpasses the individual good of individual persons. And so the Philosopher says in the *Ethics*: "Justice seems to be the most distinguished virtue, and neither the evening nor the morning star is so wonderful."[75]

But even if we should be speaking of particular justice, justice is the most important moral virtue for two reasons. And we can understand the first reason in regard to the subject in which justice inheres, namely, in that justice inheres in the more excellent part of the soul, that is, the rational appetite, the will. But other moral virtues inhere in sense appetites, to which emotions, the subject matter of those virtues, belong.

We understand the second reason regarding the object. For we praise other moral virtues only by reason of virtuous persons themselves. But we praise justice insofar as virtuous persons are related rightly to others, and so justice is in one respect the good of others, as the *Ethics* says.[76] And so the Philosopher says in the *Rhetoric*: "The greatest virtues are necessarily those that are the most worthy in the eyes of others, since virtue is beneficent power. People most honor the brave and the just because courage benefits others in time of war, and justice benefits others both in war and in peace."[77]

Reply Obj. 1. Generous persons, although they give from what is theirs, do so as they consider their own virtuous good. But just persons give to others what belongs to others as just persons consider the common good. Moreover, one observes justice toward all, but generosity cannot be extended to everyone. And, again, generosity, where one gives from one's own possessions, is founded on justice, which upholds the right of owners to their possessions.

Reply Obj. 2. Magnanimity increases the goodness of justice insofar as the former adds to the latter virtue. But magnanimity without justice would not have any virtuous character.

---

[71]Ibid., IV, 3 (1124a1–4).   [72]Ibid., II, 3 (1105a9–13).
[73]Ibid., III, 6 (1115a24–27).   [74]*On Duties* I, 7.   [75]*Ethics* V, 1 (1129b27–9).
[76]Ibid. (1130a3–8).   [77]*Rhetoric* I, 8 (1366b3–7).

Reply Obj. 3. Courage concerns more difficult things but not better things, since it is useful only in time of war, while justice is useful both in peace and in war, as I have said.[78]

Question 61
On Particular Justice

[This question is divided into four articles, three of which are translated here.]

FIRST ARTICLE
Do We Appropriately Designate Distributive and Commutative Justice Species of Justice?

We thus proceed to the first inquiry. It seems that we inappropriately designate distributive and commutative justice species of justice, for the following reasons:

Obj. 1. What harms the people cannot be a species of justice, since justice is directed to the common good. But distributing the goods of the community to many persons harms the common good of the people both because the riches of the community are thereby depleted, and because the morals of citizens are thereby corrupted. For example, Cicero says in his work *On Duties*: "Those who receive benefits become worse and quicker to expect to receive benefits again and again."[1] Therefore, distributing common goods does not belong to any species of justice.

Obj. 2. Acts of justice consist of rendering to others what is theirs, as I have maintained before.[2] But in distributing goods, things that belonged to the community, not things that belonged to individuals, are newly distributed to individuals. Therefore, such does not belong to justice.

Obj. 3. Justice can belong to rulers or subjects, as I have maintained before.[3] But distributing common goods always belongs to rulers. Therefore, such distribution does not belong to justice.

Obj. 4. "Distributive justice regards common goods," as the *Ethics* says.[4] But common things belong to legal justice. Therefore, distributive justice is a species of legal justice, not of particular justice.

Obj. 5. The number of things affected does not distinguish specific virtues. But commutative justice consists of rendering things to individual

---

[78]At the conclusion of the body of the article.

[1]*On Duties* II, 15.   [2]ST II–II, Q. 58, A. 2.   [3]ST II–II, Q. 58, A. 6.
[4]Aristotle, *Ethics* V, 4 (1131b27–32).

persons, while distributive justice consists of giving things to many persons. Therefore, they are not different species of justice.

On the contrary, the Philosopher in the *Ethics* designates two parts of justice, and he says that "one part directs distributions, and the other part directs exchanges."[5]

I answer that, as I have said,[6] particular justice is directed to private persons, who are related to the political community as parts to a whole. And we can consider two relationships regarding parts. There is indeed one relationship of parts to other parts, and the relationship of one private person to another is such. And commutative justice, which consists of mutual exchanges between two persons, directs this relationship.

We consider a second relationship of a whole to its parts, and the relationship of community goods to individual persons is such. And distributive justice, which distributes common goods to individual persons proportionally, directs this relationship. And so there are two species of justice, namely, commutative and distributive justice.

Reply Obj. 1. As we praise moderation and condemn excess in the largess of private persons, so also rulers should observe moderation in the distribution of common goods, which distributive justice directs.

Reply Obj. 2. As parts and a whole are in one respect identical, so what belongs to a whole belongs in one respect to its parts. And so since common goods are distributed to individual persons, individual persons in a sense receive what is theirs.

Reply Obj. 3. The actual distribution of common goods belongs only to those in charge of the goods, but distributive justice also belongs to the subjects receiving the goods, namely, as the subjects are content with just distributions. But sometimes goods common to a household, not to the political community, are distributed, and the authority of a private person can accomplish such a distribution.

Reply Obj. 4. We specify movements by their final termini. And so it belongs to legal justice to direct the possessions of private persons to the common good, and, conversely, it belongs to particular justice to direct the common good to individual persons by distributing common goods to them.

Reply Obj. 5. We distinguish distributive and commutative justice both by the number of persons affected and by the different nature of the obligations involved. For common goods are due to individuals in one way, and private goods in another way.

---

[5]Ibid., 2 (1130b31–3).
[6]ST II–II, Q. 58, A. 7.

Second Article
Do We Understand the Mean in Distributive and Commutative Justice in the Same Way?

We thus proceed to the second inquiry. It seems that we do so understand their means, for the following reasons:

Obj. 1. Both distributive and commutative justice are included in particular justice, as I have said.[7] But we understand the mean in every part of moderation and courage in the same way. Therefore, we should understand the mean in distributive and commutative justice in the same way.

Obj. 2. The form of moral virtues consists of a mean determined by reason. Therefore, since each moral virtue has one form, it seems that we should understand the mean in both distributive and commutative justice in the same way.

Obj. 3. We understand the mean in distributive justice by considering the various excellences of persons. But we also consider the excellence of persons regarding commutative justice. For example, in the case of inflicting punishments, those who strike rulers are punished more than those who strike private persons. Therefore, we understand the mean in both distributive and commutative justice in the same way.

On the contrary, the Philosopher says in the *Ethics* that we understand the mean in distributive justice by "geometric proportionality,"[8] and the mean in commutative justice by "arithmetic proportionality."[9]

I answer that, as I have said,[10] distributive justice allots things to private persons insofar as what belongs to a whole belongs to its parts. And the greater the importance parts have in a whole, the greater, indeed, is the distribution allotted to the parts. And so regarding distributive justice, the more important the persons in a political community, the more common goods are allotted to them. And we indeed gauge the importance of persons in aristocratic regimes by the standard of virtue, of persons in oligarchic regimes by the standard of wealth, of persons in democratic regimes by the standard of freedom, and of persons in other regimes in other ways.

And so we do not understand the mean in distributive justice by the proportion of things to things. Rather, we understand that mean by the proportion of things to persons, namely, in such a way that as one person surpasses another, so also the goods allotted to one person surpass the goods allotted to another. And so the Philosopher says that such a mean is by "geometric proportionality," wherein we consider equality proportionally, not quantitatively. This is as if we should say that three is to two

---

[7]ST II–II, Q. 61, A. 1.   [8]*Ethics* V, 3 (1131b32–1132a7).
[9]Ibid. (1131a30–b15).   [10]ST II–II, Q. 61, A. 1.

as six is to four, since the proportion in each case is one and a half to one, and the greater number in each couplet is one-and-a-half times the lesser number. But the difference between the greater and lesser numbers in the two couplets is not quantitatively equal, since six exceeds four by two, and three exceeds two by one.

But in exchanges, things are rendered to individual persons because of things received from them. And this is most apparent in buying and selling, regarding which we first notice the character of commutation. And so the things exchanged need to be equal, so that one should restore to another as much as one is enriched by what belongs to the other. And then there is equality by an arithmetic mean, which we note by equal differences from the mean. For example, five is the mean between six and four, since six exceeds the mean by one, and the mean exceeds four by one. Therefore, if each party to an exchange started off with five, and one party received one of the other party's five, the one receiving will have six, and the other will be left with four. Therefore, there will be justice if both are brought back to the mean, so that the one with four receives one from the other with six, and the one with six gives one to the other with four, since both parties will then have five, which is the mean.

Reply Obj. 1. In other moral virtues, we understand the mean as one of reason, not a real mean. But we understand the mean in justice as a real mean. And so we understand the mean of justice in different ways according to real differences.

Reply Obj. 2. The general form of justice is equality, in which distributive and commutative justice agree. But there is equality in distributive justice by geometric proportionality, and equality in commutative justice by arithmetic proportionality.

Reply Obj. 3. In acting and being acted upon, the status of persons makes a real, quantitative difference. For example, there is a greater injustice if one strikes a ruler than if one strikes a private person. And so we consider the status of persons as such in distributive justice, and we consider the status of persons in commutative justice insofar as such status causes real differences.

Third Article
Do Distributive and Commutative Justice Have Different Subject Matter?

We thus proceed to the third inquiry. It seems that distributive and commutative justice have the same subject matter, for the following reasons:

Obj. 1. Different subject matter causes different virtues, as is evidently the case with moderation and courage. Therefore, if distributive and commutative justice have different subject matter, it seems that they are not included in the same virtue, namely, justice.

Obj. 2. The distribution of common goods, which belongs to distributive justice, consists of "riches or honors or whatever other things can be distributed among members of the political community," as the *Ethics* says.[11] And there are also exchanges of such things between one person and another, exchanges that belong to commutative justice. Therefore, distributive and commutative justice do not have different subject matter.

Obj. 3. If there be one subject matter of distributive justice and another of commutative justice because they differ specifically, there should be different subject matter wherever there is specific difference. But the Philosopher designates only one species of commutative justice,[12] which nonetheless has several kinds of subject matter. Therefore, it does not seem that these species of justice, distributive and commutative, have several kinds of subject matter.

On the contrary, the *Ethics* says that "one species of justice directs distributions, and another directs exchanges."[13]

I answer that, as I have said before,[14] justice concerns certain external actions, namely, distributions and exchanges. These actions concern the use of externals, whether things or persons or even deeds. Actions indeed concern the use of things, as when one either takes away or restores to another the other's property. And actions concern the use of persons, as when one does an injustice to the very person of a human being (e.g., by striking or insulting a person) or shows respect for a person. And actions concern the use of deeds, as when one justly requires a deed of another or performs a service to another. Therefore, if we should understand as the subject matter of distributive and commutative justice the things external actions use, the two species of justice have the same subject matter. For things can be both distributed from common goods to individuals and exchanged from one individual to another. And there are distributions of laborious tasks and payments for the tasks.

But if we should understand as the subject matter of both kinds of justice the chief actions themselves whereby we use persons, things, and deeds, then there is different subject matter in each. For distributive justice directs the distributions of common goods, and commutative justice directs the exchanges that we can observe between two persons.

And some of the latter actions are involuntary, and some voluntary. And actions are involuntary when one uses the possessions or the person or the

---

[11]Aristotle, *Ethics* V, 2 (1130b31–33).   [12]Ibid. (1131a1).
[13]Ibid. (1130b31–1131a1).   [14]ST II–II, Q. 58, AA. 8, 10.

deeds of another against the other's will. And this indeed sometimes happens secretly by fraud and sometimes openly by coercion. And in either case, the offense may be against the property or the proper person or the associate of another. In the case of offenses against the property of another, we call it theft if one takes it secretly, and robbery if one takes it openly.

And in the case of offenses against the proper person of another, the offense may regard either the very substance or reputation of the other. If the offense be against the substance of others, then one secretly harms others by deceitfully killing or striking or poisoning them, or one openly injures others by killing or imprisoning or striking or maiming them publicly. And if the offense be against the reputation of others, one indeed secretly harms others by false witness or detraction or the like, whereby one takes away the reputation of others, or one openly harms others by bringing charges against them in courts of law or shouting insults at them.

And if the offense be against an associate of others, one harms others in the person of their wives by adultery, usually in secret, or in the person of others' slaves when one induces the latter to leave their master. And these things can also be done openly. And like reasoning applies to other associated persons, and one can commit offenses against them in all the injurious ways that one can against the principal person. But adultery and inducing slaves to leave their masters are, strictly speaking, offenses against the wives and slaves. Nonetheless, inducing slaves to leave their masters is related to theft, since slaves are a form of property.

And we speak of voluntary exchanges when one voluntarily transfers one's property to another. And if one alienates one's property to another without the other incurring debt, as in the case of gifts, this is an act of generosity, not of justice. But voluntary transfers of property belong to justice insofar as they partake of the nature of debt, and this indeed happens in three ways. It happens in one way when one alienates one's property in exchange for other property, as in buying and selling.

Voluntary transfers of property partake of the nature of debt in a second way when one lends one's property to another, granting the use of the property to the other, with an obligation to return it. And if one indeed grants the use of one's property without compensation, we call such transfers usufruct regarding productive property, or simply borrowing and lending in the case of nonproductive property (e.g., money, dining utensils, and the like). And if one grants the use of one's property in return for compensation, we call such transfers leasing or renting.

In a third way, one transfers one's property to another, with the other incurring an obligation to return it, in order to preserve the property and not for the other's use, as in the case of deposits, or in order to guarantee fulfillment of an obligation, as when one pledges one's property as security for oneself or another.

And all such actions, whether voluntary or involuntary, have the same nature of obtaining the mean by equal recompense. And so all these actions belong to the same species of justice, namely, commutative justice.

Reply Objs. 1–3. The answer makes clear the replies to the objections.

4

Property

In ST II–II, Q. 66, Thomas explains that it is natural for human beings to possess material things (A. 1), indeed lawful for them to acquire and dispense material things, but they should be ready to share them with others in need (A. 2). He defines and distinguishes theft and robbery (AA. 3 and 4), maintains that theft is a sin (A. 5) and a mortal sin if the stolen goods have substantial value (A. 6), but holds that it is lawful to take another's property in case of need (A. 7). Robbery cannot be committed without sin (A. 8) and is a more serious sin than theft (A. 9).

In the selections from ST II–II, Q. 77, Thomas says that it is unlawful to sell goods for more than they are worth (A. 1), but that businessmen may aim to make a moderate profit for the support of their families (A. 4).

In ST II–II, Q. 78, Thomas says that interest-taking is a sin, whether the interest is money (A. 1) or any monetarily equivalent remuneration (A. 2). But lenders at interest are not obliged to return things acquired with the interest (A. 3), and borrowers may lawfully pay interest to lenders who unlawfully charge it (A. 4).

In ST I–II, Q. 118, Thomas says that it is a sin to wish to acquire or keep more that the proper amount of material goods (A. 1), that covetousness is contrary to generosity (A. 3), and that covetousness is a sin, indeed a capital sin (A. 7).

ST II–II
Question 66
On Theft and Robbery

FIRST ARTICLE
Is the Possession of External Goods Natural to Human Beings?

We thus proceed to the first inquiry. It seems that the possession of external goods is not natural to human beings, for the following reasons:

Obj. 1. No one should ascribe to oneself what belongs to God. But dominion over all creatures belongs uniquely to God, as Ps. 24:1 says: "The Lord's is the earth," etc. Therefore, the possession of goods is not natural to human beings.

Obj. 2. Basil, explaining the words of the rich man who in Lk. 12:18 said, "I shall gather all my harvest and my possessions," says: "Tell me, which goods are yours? Whence did you get them and bring them into existence?"[1] But human beings can appropriately claim that things they possess by nature are their own. Therefore, human beings do not by nature possess external goods.

Obj. 3. Ambrose says in his work *On the Trinity:* "Dominion denotes power."[2] But human beings have no power over external things, since they cannot alter the nature of such things. Therefore, the possession of external goods is not natural to human beings.

On the contrary, Ps. 8:6 says: "You [God] have put all things under their feet," that is, the feet of human beings.

I answer that we can consider external things in two ways. We can consider them in one way regarding their nature, which is subject only to God's power, which all things obey at his will, not to the power of human beings. We can consider external things in a second way regarding their use. And then human beings have dominion over external things from nature, since human beings can by their powers of reason and will make use of external things for their benefit, as things made for their sake, as it were. For less perfect things exist for the sake of more perfect things, as I have maintained before.[3] And the Philosopher by the latter argument proves in the *Politics* that the possession of external goods is natural to human beings.[4] And the natural dominion over other creatures, which belongs to human beings on account of their reason (in which the image of God consists), is evident in the very creation of human beings, as Gen. 1:26 says: "Let us make human beings in our likeness and image, and let them have dominion over the fish of the sea," etc.

Reply Obj. 1. God has the chief dominion over all things. And he in his providence has ordained some things for the material sustenance of human beings. And so human beings have dominion from nature regarding the power to use such things.

Reply Obj. 2. The rich man is criticized because he thought external goods belonged chiefly to him, as if he had not received them from another, namely, God.

Reply Obj. 3. The argument of this objection is valid about dominion over external goods regarding their nature, which indeed belongs only to God, as I have said.[5]

---

[1]*Homily 6*, on Lk. 12:18, n. 7 (PG 31:276).

[2]Actually, *On Faith* I, 1, n. 7 (PL 16:530).

[3]ST I–II, Q. 64, A. 1.   [4]*Politics* I, 3 (1256b7–8).

[5]In the body of the article.

SECOND ARTICLE
Are Individuals Permitted to Possess Property as Their Own?

We thus proceed to the second inquiry. It seems that individuals are not permitted to possess property as their own, for the following reasons:

Obj. 1. Everything contrary to the natural law is illicit. But all things are by the natural law common possessions, and individual ownership of possessions is indeed contrary to possession by the community. Therefore, it is illicit for human beings to appropriate external goods as their own.

Obj. 2. Basil, explaining the words of the rich man in Lk. 12:18, says: "As those who come to public events ahead of time would prevent those coming later from attending, by appropriating to themselves what is ordered to common use, so the rich think that common goods they seize before others belong to them."[6] But it is illicit to prevent others from possessing common goods. Therefore, it is illicit to appropriate common goods to oneself.

Obj. 3. Ambrose says,[7] and the *Decretum* holds[8]: "Let no one call one's own what is common property." But he calls external goods common property, as his prior remarks make clear. Therefore, it seems that no one is permitted to appropriate external goods to oneself.

On the contrary, Augustine says in his work *On Heresies*: "The 'Apostolics' have most arrogantly so designated themselves because they do not receive into their fellowship the married or those possessing their own property. (The Catholic Church likewise has very many monks and celibate clerics.)"[9] But these heretics hold this view because, cut off from the church, they think that the married and possessors of property, which they themselves are not, have no hope of salvation. Therefore, it is false to say that human beings are not permitted to possess their own property.

I answer that two things belong to human beings regarding external goods. One is the power to manage and dispense external goods. And human beings are permitted to possess them as their own in that regard. And this is necessary for human life for three reasons. First, indeed, the power to manage and dispense external goods is necessary for human life because individuals are more careful in managing goods that belong to them alone than goods that are common to all or many. This is so because individuals, shunning work, leave common property to the care of others, as happens when there are many servants.

---

[6]*Homily 6*, on Lk. 12:18, n. 7 (PG 31:276).

[7]*Sermon 81*, on Lk. 12:18 (PL 17:593–4).

[8]Gratian, *Decretum* I, dist. 47, c. 8.   [9]*On Heresies* 40 (PL 42:32).

Second, the power of individuals to manage and dispense external goods is necessary for human life because human affairs are conducted in a more orderly fashion if the requisite care in managing external goods be entrusted to individuals. On the other hand, there would be confusion if unspecified individuals were to manage everything.

Third, the power of individuals to manage and dispense external goods is necessary for human life because human beings content with their own property live in a condition of peace. And so we observe that quarrels arise rather frequently among those who possess goods in common and not individually.

But the use of external goods is the second thing that belongs to human beings regarding the goods. And human beings in that regard should not possess external goods as their own but as common possessions, namely, in such a way that they readily share the goods when others are in need. And so the Apostle says in 1 Tim. 6:17–8: "Teach the rich of this world to distribute and share readily."

Reply Obj. 1. The common possession of external goods is ascribed to the natural law, not because the natural law dictates that all such goods should be possessed in common, and nothing possessed as one's own, but because there is division of possessions by human agreement, which belongs to positive law, as I have said before,[10] rather than by the natural law. And so the individual ownership of possessions is not contrary to the natural law, although the inventiveness of human reason adds this to the natural law.

Reply Obj. 2. Those who come early to public events and prepare the way for others to attend would not act illicitly, but they act illicitly if they prevent others from attending. And likewise, the rich do not act improperly if they before others take possession of property that was in the beginning common and share the property with others. But the rich sin if they indiscriminately prevent others from using the property. And so Basil says in the same place: "Why are you rich and others beggars except in order that you gain the merit of dispensing your wealth well, and that others are rewarded for their patience?"[11]

Reply Obj. 3. When Ambrose says: "Let no one call one's own what is common property," he is speaking about individual ownership in regard to the use of external goods. And so he adds: "Those who spend too much are guilty of robbery."[12]

---

[10]ST I–II, Q. 57, AA. 2, 3. [11]See n. 6, supra.
[12]See n. 7, supra.

THIRD ARTICLE
Does Secretly Taking Another's
Property Belong to the Nature of Theft?

We thus proceed to the third inquiry. It seems that secretly taking another's property does not belong to the nature of theft, for the following reasons:

Obj. 1. What lessens a sin does not seem to belong to the sin's nature. But sinning in secret belongs to the diminution of sin, as, conversely, Is. 3:9 says about sin becoming more serious: "They like Sodom trumpeted and did not hide their sin." Therefore, the secret taking of another's property does not belong to the nature of theft.

Obj. 2. Ambrose says,[13] and the *Decretum* maintains[14]: "It is no less a crime to take from one who has than to deny to those who have not, if you can help them and have the means." Therefore, it is as much theft to refrain from giving property to a needy other as to take another's property.

Obj. 3. Human beings can secretly reclaim their own property (e.g., property on deposit or property unjustly taken) from others. Therefore, it does not belong to the nature of theft that one take another's property secretly.

On the contrary, Isidore says in his *Etymologies*: "We derive the word *thief* from the word *black* (i.e., dark),[15] because thieves operate at night."[16]

I answer that the nature of theft consists of a combination of three things. The first is characteristic of theft insofar as theft is contrary to justice, which renders to others what belongs to them. And so it is characteristic of theft that one takes something that belongs to somebody else.

And the second is characteristic of the nature of theft insofar as we distinguish theft from sins against the person like murder and adultery. And so it is characteristic of theft to regard possessions. For if one should take what belongs to another as a part of the other rather than as a possession (e.g., amputating the limb of another) or as an associated person (e.g., abducting the daughter or wife of another), such does not, strictly speaking, have the character of theft.

The third difference, namely, that one takes possession of another's property secretly, completes the nature of theft. And so the special nature of theft consists of taking another's property secretly.

Reply Obj. 1. Secrecy indeed sometimes causes sin. For example, secrecy causes sin if one uses secrecy in order to sin, as happens in fraud

---

[13]*Sermon 81*, on Lk. 12:18 (PL 17:593–4).

[14]Gratian, *Decretum* I, dist. 47, c. 8.

[15]The Latin word for thief is *fur*, and the Latin word for dark is *furvus*.

[16]*Etymologies* X, n. 107 (PL 82:378).

and deception. And secrecy in this way constitutes rather than diminishes the species of a sin. And such is the case with theft.

Secrecy is in another way the circumstance of a sin. And then secrecy lessens a sin both because it is a sign of shame, and because it removes scandal.

Reply Obj. 2. Keeping property belonging to another has the same nature of harm as taking another's property. And so we also understand keeping such property to be included in the sin of unjust taking.

Reply Obj. 3. Nothing prevents something belonging absolutely to one person from belonging to another in a particular respect. For example, entrusted goods indeed belong absolutely to depositors, but the goods in respect to their security belong to those entrusted with the goods. And stolen goods belong to thieves in respect to the goods' detention, not absolutely.

FOURTH ARTICLE
Are Theft and Robbery Specifically Different Sins?

We thus proceed to the fourth inquiry. It seems that theft and robbery are not specifically different sins, for the following reasons:

Obj. 1. Theft and robbery differ by whether they are done secretly or openly. For theft signifies secret taking, and robbery coercive and open taking. But other kinds of sins do not differ specifically by whether they are committed secretly or openly. Therefore, theft and robbery do not differ specifically.

Obj. 2. Ends specify moral actions, as I have said before.[17] But theft and robbery have the same end, namely, possession of another's goods. Therefore, theft and robbery do not differ specifically.

Obj. 3. As one steals material things in order to possess them, so one abducts women in order to take pleasure with them. And so also Isidore says in his *Etymologies* that "we say that an abductor corrupts a woman, and that an abducted woman is corrupted."[18] But we call it abduction whether one carries off an abducted woman publicly or secretly. Therefore, we say that one carries off the possessions of another whether one does so publicly or secretly. Therefore, theft and robbery do not differ.

On the contrary, the Philosopher in the *Ethics* distinguishes theft from robbery, designating theft as secret and robbery as coercive.[19]

I answer that theft and robbery are sins contrary to justice, since their perpetrators commit injustice against others. And "no one suffers

---

[17]*ST* I–II: Q. 1, A. 3; Q. 18, A. 6. [18]*Etymologies* X, n. 237 (PL 82:392).
[19]*Ethics* V, 2 (1131a6–9).

injustice willingly," as the *Ethics* proves.[20] And so theft and robbery have the nature of sin because the taking of goods is involuntary regarding those from whom the goods are taken. But we speak of things being involuntary in two ways, namely, by reason of ignorance or by reason of coercion, as the *Ethics* maintains.[21] And so robbery has one sinful character, and theft another. And so they differ specifically.

Reply Obj. 1. We do not note the sinful character of other kinds of sin by reason of things being involuntary, as we do regarding the sins contrary to justice. And so there are different species of sin where things are involuntary in essentially different ways.

Reply Obj. 2. The remote ends of robbery and theft are the same, but this does not suffice to make robbery and theft specifically the same, since the two sins have different proximate ends. For robbers want to take things using their power, while thieves want to take things using their cleverness.

Reply Obj. 3. The abduction of a woman cannot be secret regarding the woman who is abducted. And so also the character of abduction still remains regarding the women against whom such violence is committed even if the abduction should be hidden from the others from whom she is abducted.

FIFTH ARTICLE
Is Theft Always a Sin?

We thus proceed to the fifth inquiry. It seems that theft is not always a sin, for the following reasons:

Obj. 1. God commands no sin, for Sir. 15:21 says: "He [God] commanded no one to act wickedly." But God commanded theft, for Ex. 12:35–6 says: "The children of Israel did as the Lord had commanded Moses, and they despoiled the Egyptians." Therefore, theft is not always a sin.

Obj. 2. Those who find things that do not belong to them seem to commit theft if they retain those things. But this seems to be permitted by natural justice, as the jurists say.[22] Therefore, it seems that theft is not always a sin.

Obj. 3. Those who take things that belong to them do not seem to sin, since they do not act against justice or take away its reciprocity. But one commits theft even if one should secretly take one's property in the care or custody of another. Therefore, it seems that theft is not always a sin.

---

[20]Ibid., 11 (1138a12).   [21]Ibid., III, 1 (1009b35–1110a1).
[22]See the reply to obj. 2 and its notes (nn. 23–6, 28)

On the contrary, Ex. 20:15 says: "Thou shalt not steal."

I answer that if one should consider the nature of theft, one would find that it has two aspects of sin. First, theft is indeed sinful because it is contrary to justice, which renders to all persons what is their due. And then theft is contrary to justice because it consists of taking another's goods. Second, theft is sinful because of the deception or fraud that a thief commits when he takes possession of another's property secretly and almost treacherously. And so every theft is clearly a sin.

Reply Obj. 1. It is not theft for someone to take the goods of another, whether secretly or openly, in execution of a court order, since a judge has authorized the former to take the goods. And so it was much less theft when the children of Israel took the spoils of the Egyptians at the command of the Lord, who decreed this in compensation for the afflictions that the Egyptians without cause inflicted on the Israelites. And so Wis. 10:19 says pointedly: "The just took the spoils of the wicked."

Reply Obj. 2. We should make distinctions about found things. For there are some things that were never in the possession of anyone (e.g., precious stones and jewels found on the seashore), and finders are allowed to keep them.[23] And the argument is the same regarding long buried treasures that belong to no one, unless civil laws require the finder to give half to the owner of the field, if the treasure happens to lie in the field of another.[24] And so Mt. 13:44, in the Gospel parable on the finding of treasure in a field, says that the finder bought the field, as if to have the right to possess the whole treasure.

And there are some things found near the possessions of others. And then one does not commit theft if one should take such things, intending not to keep them but to return them to their owner, who does not consider them abandoned. And likewise, finders do not commit theft in keeping things for themselves if the things should have been abandoned, and the finders so believe.[25] In all other cases, the finder of such things does commit the sin of theft.[26] And so Augustine says in a homily,[27] and the *Decretum* maintains[28]: "If you have found and not returned something, you have stolen it."

Reply Obj. 3. Those who covertly reclaim their goods on deposit with another, burden the one with whom they deposited the goods, since the latter is obliged to return the goods or demonstrate that the goods are unharmed. And so they clearly sin and are obliged to relieve the burden of the one with whom they deposited the goods.

---

[23]Cf. Justinian, *Digest* I, title 8, c. 3.   [24]Cf. Justinian, *Institutes* II, title 1, n. 39.
[25]Cf. ibid., II, title 1, n. 47.   [26]Justinian, *Digest* XLI, title 1, c. 8.
[27]*Sermon 178*, c. 8 (PL 38:965).   [28]Gratian, *Decretum* II, cause 14, q. 5, c. 6.

But those who covertly reclaim their goods in the custody of another unjustly indeed do not sin because they burden the one holding the goods, and so they are not obliged to restore anything or make any recompense. Still, they sin against justice in general when they usurp for themselves the right to reclaim their goods without recourse to legal procedures. And so they are obliged to make satisfaction to God and to endeavor to allay any scandal to neighbor if such has arisen from their behavior.

SIXTH ARTICLE
Is Theft a Mortal Sin?

We thus proceed to the sixth inquiry. It seems that theft is not a mortal sin, for the following reasons:

Obj. 1. Prov. 6:30 says: "There is no great sin if one has committed theft." But every mortal sin is a great sin. Therefore, theft is not a mortal sin.

Obj. 2. Mortal sin deserves the punishment of death. But the Old Law inflicts the punishment of indemnity, not the punishment of death, for theft, as Ex. 22:1 says: "If one has stolen an ox or a sheep, one shall repay five oxen for each one stolen, and four sheep for each one stolen." Therefore, theft is not a mortal sin.

Obj. 3. One can commit theft in small as well as large matters. But it seems inappropriate that one be punished by eternal death for the theft of a small thing (e.g., a needle or a pen). Therefore, theft is not a mortal sin.

On the contrary, God's judgment condemns no one except for mortal sin. But God condemns persons for theft, as Zech. 5:3 says: "This is the curse that pours over the face of the earth, that every thief is condemned as it is written on the scroll." Therefore, theft is a mortal sin.

I answer that, as I have said before,[29] mortal sin is contrary to charity, which brings spiritual life to the soul. And charity indeed consists chiefly of love of God and secondarily of love of neighbor, to which wishing and doing good to neighbor belong. But human beings in committing theft inflict harm on their neighbor in the neighbor's goods, and human society would collapse if human beings were to steal from one another promiscuously. And so theft, because contrary to charity, is a mortal sin.

Reply Obj. 1. The cited text says that theft is not a great sin for two reasons. First, indeed, theft is not a great sin because of a necessity that induces someone to steal, and such necessity lessens or totally eliminates moral fault, as I shall show later.[30] And so the text immediately adds: "For the thief steals to satisfy his hungry spirit." Second, the text says theft is not a great sin in comparison to the guilt incurred by adultery, which is

---

[29]ST. I–II, Q. 72, A.5; II II, Q. 59, A. 4.   [30]ST II–II, Q. 66, A 7

punished by death.[31] And so Prov. 6:31–2 adds regarding the thief: "The thief will repay sevenfold, but the adulterer will lose his soul."

Reply Obj. 2. The punishments of this life are more medicinal than retributive, since retribution against sinners is reserved to God's righteous judgment. And so judgment in this life inflicts the punishment of death only for mortal sins that cause irreparable harm or have a terrible deformity, not for every mortal sin. And so present judgment does not inflict the punishment of death for theft, which causes reparable loss, unless a grave circumstance makes the theft more serious. For example, such is evidently the case with sacrilege, that is, the theft of something sacred; with peculation, that is, the theft of common property, as Augustine makes clear in his *Commentary on the Gospel of John*[32]; with abduction, that is, the theft of a human being, for which one is punished by death, as Ex. 21:16 makes clear.

Reply Obj. 3. Reason understands slight matters as if they are nothing. And so human beings do not consider themselves harmed regarding very little things, and those who take such things can presume that the taking is not contrary to the will of those who own the things. And persons can be excused from mortal sin inasmuch as they take very little things covertly. But if they should intend to steal and cause harm to neighbor, there can be mortal sin even regarding such very little things, just as there can be by consent only in a plan to do evil.

SEVENTH ARTICLE
May One Lawfully Steal out of Necessity?

We thus proceed to the seventh inquiry. It seems that one is not permitted to steal out of necessity, for the following reasons:

Obj. 1. Penances are imposed only on sinners. But a decretal on thefts says: "If one should out of the necessity of hunger or lack of clothing steal food, clothing, or beast, the person shall do penance for three weeks."[33] Therefore, one may not lawfully steal out of necessity.

Obj. 2. The Philosopher says in the *Ethics* that "some things by their very name involve wickedness," and he includes theft therein.[34] But things evil as such cannot become good because of a good end. Therefore, no one can lawfully steal in order to alleviate one's necessity.

Obj. 3. Human beings should love their neighbor as themselves. But one may not lawfully steal in order to assist a neighbor by giving the

---

[31]Cf. Lev. 20:10; Dt. 22:22.

[32]*Commentary on the Gospel of John*, on Jn. 12:6, tr. 50, n. 10 (PL 35:1762).

[33]Gregory IX, *Decretals* V, title 18, c. 3.   [34]*Ethics* II, 6 (1107a9–17).

neighbor alms, as Augustine says in his work *Against Lying.*[35] Therefore, one also may not lawfully steal to alleviate one's own necessity.

On the contrary, all things are common property in cases of necessity. And so it does not seem to be a sin if one takes the property of another, since necessity has made the property common.

I answer that prescriptions of human law cannot derogate from natural or divine law. But the natural order established by divine providence has ordered inferior things to alleviate the necessity of human beings. And so the division and appropriation of material things, which proceeds from human law, does not preclude that such things should alleviate the necessity of human beings. And so the natural law requires that superfluous things in one's possession be used for the sustenance of the poor. And so Ambrose says,[36] and the *Decretum* maintains[37]: "It is the bread of the hungry that you withhold; it is the garments of the naked that you hide away; the money you bury in the ground is the ransom and freedom of the unfortunate." But because many persons are in need, and the same things cannot assist everybody, the dispensing of one's own goods is committed to each individual, so that each may out of them assist those in need.

Still, if the necessity is so pressing and clear that one has an immediate need of things at hand (e.g., when personal danger threatens, and there is no other way to avoid it), then one may lawfully alleviate one's necessity with the goods of another, whether one takes the goods openly or secretly. Nor does this, properly speaking, have the character of theft or robbery.

Reply Obj. 1. The decretal is talking about cases in which there is no pressing necessity.

Reply Obj. 2. Using the property of another taken in a case of extreme necessity does not have the character of theft, properly speaking. This is because such necessity makes one's own what one takes to support one's life.

Reply Obj. 3. One can also in cases of like necessity secretly take the property of another in order to assist a neighbor in such need.

EIGHTH ARTICLE
Can One Commit Robbery without Sin?

We thus proceed to the eighth inquiry. It seems that one can commit robbery without sin, for the following reasons:

---

[35]*Against Lying* 7, n. 18 (PL 40:528).

[36]*Sermon 81*, on Lk. 12:18 (PL 17:593–4).

[37]Gratian, *Decretum* I, dist. 47, c. 8.

Obj. 1. Warriors take spoils by force of arms, and this seems to belong to the nature of robbery, as I have said before.[38] But warriors are permitted to take spoils from the enemy, for Ambrose says in his work *On Abraham*: "When a conqueror has acquired spoils of war, it befits military discipline that everything be set aside for the king,"[39] namely, for him to distribute. Therefore, robbery is lawful in some cases.

Obj. 2. One is permitted to take from others property that does not belong to them. But property in the possession of unbelievers does not belong to them. For Augustine says in a letter to a Donatist: "You call yours things that you do not justly possess, and the laws of earthly kings require that you forfeit them."[40] Therefore, it seems that believers could lawfully rob from unbelievers.

Obj. 3. Earthly rulers forcibly exact many goods and services from their subjects, and this seems to partake of the nature of robbery. But it is grievous to say that rulers sin in this regard, since almost all rulers would then be condemned. Therefore, robbery is lawful in some cases.

On the contrary, one can offer sacrifices and oblations to God from things lawfully acquired. But one cannot do so from the fruits of robbery, as Is. 61:8 says: "I, the Lord, love justice and hate robbery in connection with sacrifices." Therefore, one may not lawfully take anything by robbery.

I answer that robbery signifies the use of force and coercion to take from others property that belongs to them, and this is contrary to justice. But no human being can exercise coercion except by public authority. And so those who forcibly take things from others, if the former be private persons not exercising public authority, act unlawfully and commit robbery, as robbers evidently do.

But public authority is committed to rulers in order that they may safeguard justice. And so they are permitted to use force and coercion only in the course of justice, whether in wars against enemies or in punishing civilian criminals. And property taken by such force does not have the nature of robbery, since the taking is not contrary to justice. On the other hand, if, contrary to justice, some in the exercise of public authority forcibly take the property of others, such persons act unlawfully and commit robbery and are obliged to make restitution.

Reply Obj. 1. We need to make a distinction about the spoils of war. For if those who despoil the enemy wage just war, things forcibly acquired in the war become theirs. And this does not have the character of robbery. And so they are not obliged to make restitution. But those engaging in just

---

[38]ST II–II, Q. 66, A. 4.   [39]*On Abraham* I, 3, n. 17 (PL 14:427).
[40]*Letter 93*, to the Donatist Vincent, c. 12, n. 50 (PL 33:345).

war could, in taking spoils, sin by covetousness or wicked intention, namely, if they wage war chiefly for the spoils and not for the sake of justice. For Augustine says in his sermon on the Lord's words that "it is a sin to wage war for the sake of booty."[41]

On the other hand, if those taking spoils should be engaged in an unjust war, they commit robbery and are obliged to make restitution.

Reply Obj. 2. Some unbelievers unjustly possess their property insofar as the laws of earthly rulers command forfeiture of the property. And so public, not private, authority can forcibly take the property from those unbelievers.

Reply Obj. 3. If rulers exact from their subjects what is due them in justice in order to maintain the common good, even if the rulers use force, there is no robbery. But if rulers unduly exact things by force, it is robbery. And so Augustine says in *The City of God*: "If justice is taken away, what are kingdoms but massive robberies? And what are robberies but petty kingdoms?"[42] And Ez. 22:27 says: "Her [Jerusalem's] rulers are in her midst like wolves ravishing their prey." And so also rulers, like robbers, are obliged to make restitution. And the more dangerously and the more extensively rulers act against public justice, of which they are constituted the guardians, the more seriously do they sin than robbers.

NINTH ARTICLE
Is Theft a More Serious Sin than Robbery?

We thus proceed to the ninth inquiry. It seems that theft is a more serious sin than robbery, for the following reasons:

Obj. 1. Theft has fraud and deception in addition to the taking of property that belongs to another, and robbery does not. But fraud and deception as such have the nature of sin, as I have maintained before.[43] Therefore, theft is a more serious sin than robbery.

Obj. 2. Shame is fear about a wicked act, as the *Ethics* says.[44] But human beings are more ashamed about theft than about robbery. Therefore, it seems that theft is a more wicked sin than robbery.

Obj. 3. The more people a sin harms, the more serious it seems to be. But theft can inflict harm on both the mighty and the lowly, while robbery can inflict harm only on the weak, over whom force can be exercised. Therefore, it seems that theft is a more serious sin than robbery.

On the contrary, laws punish robbery more severely than theft.

---

[41]*Sermon 82*, on the Lord's words, n. 1 (PL 39:1904).

[42]*The City of God* IV, 4 (PL 41:115).   [43]ST II–II, Q. 55, AA. 4, 5.

[44]Aristotle, *Ethics* IV, 9 (1128b11–2, 22–3).

I answer that, as I have said before,[45] robbery and theft have the nature of sin because of the unwillingness of those from whom things are taken, unwillingness through ignorance in the case of theft, and unwillingness through force in the case of robbery. But force makes things more involuntary than ignorance does, since force is more directly contrary to the will than ignorance is. And so robbery is a more serious sin than theft.

And there is another reason, since robbery both inflicts loss on another regarding the other's goods and borders on insult and injury to the other's person. And the latter outweighs the fraud and deception that belong to theft.

Reply Obj. 1. And so the reply to obj. 1 is clear.

Reply Obj. 2. Human beings who cling to material things boast more about external power, which robbery evidences, than about internal power, which sin destroys. And so they are less ashamed about robbery than about theft.

Reply Obj. 3. Although theft can harm more people than robbery can, robbery can inflict greater harms than theft can. And so robbery is also for this reason more detestable.

Question 77
On Fraud in Buying and Selling

[This question is divided into four articles, two of which are translated here.]

First Article
Can One Lawfully Sell Goods for More than They Are Worth?

We thus proceed to the first inquiry. It seems that one can lawfully sell goods for more than they are worth, for the following reasons:

Obj. 1. Civil laws specify justice in the exchanges of human life. But these laws allow buyers and sellers to deceive one another,[1] which indeed happens by sellers selling goods for more than they are worth, and by buyers buying goods for less than they are worth. Therefore, it is lawful to sell goods for more than they are worth.

Obj. 2. Common human practices seem to be natural and no sin. But Augustine relates in his work *On the Trinity* that everybody accepted the comment of a certain jester: "You want to buy cheaply and sell dearly."[2] And the saying of Prov. 20:14, "Every buyer says, 'I am ruined, I am

---

[45]ST II–II, Q. 66, A. 4.

[1]Justinian, *Code* IV, title 44, laws 8, 15.   [2]*On the Trinity* XIII, 3 (PL 42:1017).

ruined,' and will gloat when he has walked off," agrees with the jester's comment. Therefore, one may lawfully sell goods more dearly and buy goods more cheaply than they are worth.

Obj. 3. It seems lawful for one to do by mutual agreement what one should do by requisite virtue. But the Philosopher says in the *Ethics* that in the case of friendships of utility, those who have received benefits from friends should make proportional recompense to the friends,[3] and the benefits received sometimes indeed exceed the value of the goods given. For example, one may have great need of a particular thing, whether to avoid danger or to gain an advantage. Therefore, in sales contracts, one may lawfully sell goods for more than they are worth.

On the contrary, Mt. 7:12 says: "Do to others what you wish others to do for you." But no one wishes that others sell goods to oneself more dearly than the goods are worth. Therefore, no one should sell goods to others more dearly than the goods are worth.

I answer that it is completely sinful to use fraud in order to sell goods for more than their just price, since sellers thereby deceive, and cause loss to, their neighbors. And so also Cicero says in his work *On Duties*: "There should be no deception in contractual affairs; sellers will not set up false bidders, nor buyers suborn those who bid against them."[4]

But absent fraud, we can speak about buying and selling in two ways. We can speak about buying and selling in one way absolutely. And buying and selling in this respect seems to have been established for the common benefit of both parties, namely, each party needs something belonging to the other, as the Philosopher makes clear in the *Politics*.[5] But things established for the common benefit of both parties should not burden one party more than the other. And so the equality of the goods exchanged should be the basis of contracts between the parties. But we measure the worth of goods useful to human beings by the price paid for them, and money was invented for that purpose, as the *Ethics* says.[6] And so if either the price exceeds the worth of the goods, or if, conversely, the goods exceed the price, the equality required by justice is absent. And so selling goods more dearly or buying goods more cheaply than they are worth is in itself unjust and illicit.

We can speak of buying and selling in a second way insofar as the buying and selling accidentally benefits one party and disadvantages the other. For example, such would be the case if one party has great need of a particular thing, and the other would suffer without it. And the just price in

---

[3]*Ethics* VIII, 13 (1163a16–23).   [4]*On Duties* III, 15.

[5]*Politics* I, 3 (1257a6–9).   [6]Aristotle, *Ethics* V, 5 (1133a29–31).

such a case will be related both to the goods that are sold and the loss that sellers incur by the sale. And so one could sell such goods for more than they are worth in themselves, although not for more than they are worth to the owner.

And if the buyer benefits greatly from the goods received from the seller, and if the seller suffers no loss by being without the goods, the latter should not raise the price. The seller should not raise the price because the benefit accruing to the buyer does not come from the seller but results from the condition of the buyer, and no one can sell to another what is not one's own, although one could charge another for the loss one suffers. But buyers who are greatly benefited from the goods received from sellers can of their own free will pay the sellers something extra, and this belongs to the buyer's virtue.

Reply Obj. 1. As I have said before,[7] human laws are enacted for the whole people, among whom there are many who lack virtue, and not only for the virtuous. And so human law could not prohibit everything contrary to virtue. And it is enough for human law to prohibit things destructive of human society and to consider other matters as licit because it does not punish them, not because it would approve them. Therefore, the law considers buying and selling as licit and does not punish it if, without fraud, the seller overcharges for his goods, or the buyer underpays for them, unless the difference be too much, for even human law then requires restitution. For example, human law requires restitution if one should be cheated by more than half of the amount of the just price.[8] But divine law lets nothing contrary to virtue go unpunished. And so divine law reckons buying and selling illicit whenever buyers or sellers do not observe the equality required by justice. And those who gain more than they should are obliged to recompense those who have suffered more loss than they should, if the loss be significant. And I make this qualification because the just price of goods sometimes consists of a rough estimate and is not exactly fixed, so that a slight addition or subtraction does not seem to take away the equality required by justice.

Reply Obj. 2. Augustine says in the same place: "The jester, whether by reflecting about himself or by his experience of others, believed that everybody wishes to buy cheaply and sell dearly. But since this is indeed sinful, everyone has the power to acquire the justice that resists and conquers this inclination."[9] And he gives the example of a person who paid a slight price for a book because of the seller's ignorance of the just price. And so such a common desire is clearly sinful, not natural. And so it is

---

[7]ST I–II, Q. 96, A. 2.   [8]Justinian, *Code* IV, title 44, law 8.   [9]See n. 2, supra.

common to the many people who walk on the broad road of sin.

Reply Obj. 3. We chiefly consider the equality of goods regarding commutative justice. But we consider the equality of utility in friendships of utility. And so one should in such friendships recompense another in proportion to the benefit one receives. But in buying, one should recompense the seller in proportion to the value of the goods bought.

FOURTH ARTICLE

**Is It Lawful in Business to Sell Goods
for More than One Paid for Them?**

We thus proceed to the fourth inquiry. It seems that it is not lawful to sell goods for more than one paid for them, for the following reasons:

Obj. 1. On Mt. 21:5, Chrysostom says: "Those who buy goods in order to sell them, entire and unaltered, at a profit, are the sellers cast out of the temple of God."[10] And Cassidorus, commenting on Ps. 71:15, "Since I do not know scholarly ways," or "business" according to another version,[11] says the same: "What else is business," he says, "than wanting to buy goods more cheaply and to sell them more dearly?"[12] And he adds: "The Lord cast such merchants out of the temple." But persons are cast out of the temple only because of some sin. Therefore, such business is sinful.

Obj. 2. It is contrary to justice for anyone to sell goods for more than they are worth or to buy them for less than they are worth, as is clear from what I have said before.[13] But businessmen who sell goods for more than they paid for them must have either bought the goods for less than they are worth or sold the goods for more than they are worth. Therefore, businessmen cannot do this without committing sin.

Obj. 3. Jerome says: "Shun like a plague a businessman cleric, who from being poor has become rich, and from being a nobody has become a celebrity."[14] But business seems to have been prohibited to clerics only because of its sinfulness. Therefore, it is sinful for businessmen to buy goods more cheaply and sell them more dearly.

On the contrary, Augustine on Ps. 71:15, "Since I do not know scholarly ways," says: "The businessman greedy to acquire blasphemes over his losses, lies and perjures himself over the prices of goods. But these sins belong to the person, not to the profession, which can be carried on

---

[10]Pseudo-Chrysostom, *Incomplete Work on the Gospel of Matthew*, homily 38 (PG 56:840).   [11]The Septuagint.

[12]*Expositions on the Psalms*, on Ps. 71:15 (PL 70:500–1).

[13]ST II–II, Q. 77, A. 1.   [14]*Letter 52*, to Nepotian, n. 5 (PL 22:531).

without those sins."[15] Therefore, business as such is not unlawful.

I answer that it is proper for businessmen to engage earnestly in trade. And there are two ways of trading goods, as the Philosopher says in the *Politics.*[16] One way is indeed quite natural and necessary, namely, that people exchange goods for other goods, or goods for money, to satisfy the needs of life. And such exchanges are not, strictly speaking, proper to businessmen. Rather, such exchanges belong to household managers or statesmen, who have charge of providing households or political communities with the goods necessary to sustain life. The second kind of exchange is one of money for money, or goods for money, in order to make a profit, not in order to satisfy the needs of life. And this business indeed seems to belong strictly to businessmen.

And according to the Philosopher,[17] the first kind of exchange is praiseworthy, since it is devoted to satisfying natural needs. But he rightly condemns the second kind of exchange, since it as such is devoted to satisfying the desire for profit, and such desire knows no bounds and always strives for more. And so business, absolutely speaking, is wicked, since it does not essentially signify a worthy or necessary objective.

But profit, the aim of business, although it does not essentially signify anything worthy or necessary, does not essentially signify anything vicious or contrary to virtue. And so nothing prevents gain from being ordered to a necessary or even worthy end. And then business becomes lawful. For example, one may order a moderate business profit to support one's family or even to help the needy. Or one may engage in business for public advantage, namely, lest one's country lack necessary goods, and seek profit as payment for one's labor, not as an end.

Reply Obj. 1. We should understand the words of Chrysostom about business insofar as a businessman constitutes the ultimate end in profit, and this seems chiefly to be the case when one sells unaltered goods more dearly. For if one should sell altered goods more dearly, one seems to receive pay for one's labor. And one could also lawfully strive for the profit for the sake of a necessary or worthy end and not as the ultimate end, as I have said.[18]

Reply Obj. 2. Not everybody who sells goods more dearly than the person paid for them is a businessman. Rather, only one who buys goods in order to sell them more dearly is a businessman. And if one buys goods in order to possess them and not in order to sell them, and should want

---

[15]*Narrations on the Psalms*, on Ps. 71, c. 1, n. 17 (PL 36:886).

[16]*Politics* I, 3 (1257a19–b10).   [17]Ibid. (1258a38–b8).

[18]In the body of the article.

later for some reason to sell them, such a person is not a businessman even though he sells the goods more dearly than he paid for them. For one can lawfully do this, either because one has improved the goods, or because a different place or time has affected the price of the goods, or because of the danger that one incurs in moving the goods from one place to another or in having another do so. And neither the buying nor the selling involved is unjust.

Reply Obj. 3. Clerics should abstain both from things that as such are evil and from things that have the appearance of evil. And the latter indeed happens in business both because business is ordered to earthly gain, which clerics should despise, and because businessmen commit frequent sins, since "businessmen are only with difficulty drawn away from sins of the lips," as Sir. 26:28 says. And there is another reason, in that business engages the spirit too much in worldly cares and so draws it away from spiritual cares. And so the Apostle says in 2 Tim. 2:4: "No one fighting for God entangles oneself in worldly businesses."

Nevertheless, clerics may lawfully engage in the first kind of exchange, which is ordered to satisfying the needs of life, by buying or selling goods.

Question 78
On the Sin of Interest-Taking

FIRST ARTICLE
Is It a Sin to Take Interest for Money Lent?

We thus proceed to the first inquiry. It seems that it is not a sin to take interest for money lent, for the following reasons:

Obj. 1. No one sins in following the example of Christ. But the Lord says of himself in Lk. 19:23: "At my coming, I might have exacted it," namely, the money lent, "with interest." Therefore, it is no sin to take interest for lending money.

Obj. 2. Ps. 19:8 says that "the law of the Lord is pure," namely, in that it forbids sin. But the divine law allows some interest-taking, as Dt. 23:19–20 says: "You shall not lend money nor produce nor any other thing to your fellow countryman at interest, but you may to a foreigner." And what is more, the divine law even promises a reward for observing the law, as Dt. 28:12 says: "You will lend to many peoples, and you yourselves will borrow from no one." Therefore, taking interest is no sin.

Obj. 3. Civil laws specify justice in human affairs. But civil laws allow interest-taking. Therefore, interest-taking does not seem to be unlawful.

Obj. 4. The evangelical counsels do not bind one under sin. But Lk. 6:35 posits among the counsels: "Lend, looking for nothing in return." Therefore, interest-taking is not a sin.

Obj. 5. Receiving payment for something one is not obliged to do does not seem as such to be a sin. But one in the possession of money is not always obliged to lend it to a neighbor. Therefore, it is sometimes lawful for a person to accept payment for lending money.

Obj. 6. Silver coins do not differ specifically from silver vessels. But it is lawful to accept payment for silver vessels one lends. Therefore, it is also lawful to accept payment for silver coins one lends. Therefore, interest-taking as such is not a sin.

Obj. 7. A person can lawfully receive property that its owner freely gives to the person. But one who contracts a loan, freely agrees to pay interest. Therefore, the one who lends can lawfully accept interest.

On the contrary, Ex. 22:25 says: "If you should lend money to the poor people of mine who dwell with you, you shall not harass them like extortioners nor oppress them with interest."

I answer that interest-taking for money lent is in itself unjust, since this is to sell something that does not exist, and clearly constitutes inequality, which is contrary to justice. And to prove this, we should note that there are some things whose use consists of their consumption. For example, we consume wine when we use it to drink, and we consume wheat when we use it as food. And so regarding such things, we should not reckon the value of their use separately from the value of the things themselves. Rather, we give up the things to whomever we grant their use. And so lending in such cases transfers ownership. Therefore, if one were to want to sell wine and the use of wine as two separate things, one would be selling the same thing twice, that is, selling something that does not exist. And so the seller would obviously commit a sin of injustice. And by like reasoning, one who lends wine or wheat, seeking double payment for oneself, indeed one equal to the thing lent and the other for the thing's use, which we call interest, commits injustice.

But there are some things whose use does not consist of their very consumption. For example, one uses houses by dwelling in them, not by destroying them. And so regarding such things, one can grant another either the things or their use. For example, one may hand over ownership of a house to another but retain use of the house for a specified period of time. Or, conversely, one may grant use of a house to another but retain ownership of the house. And so human beings can lawfully both accept payments for the use of their homes and reclaim the homes at the expiration of the leases, as in the case of landlords leasing and tenants renting homes.

But as the Philosopher says in the *Ethics*[1] and the *Politics*,[2] human beings invented money chiefly to facilitate exchanges, and so the special and chief use of money is its very consumption or alienation as it is spent in exchanges. And so accepting payment for the use of money, which we call interest, is as such unlawful. And as human beings are obliged to make restitution for other things unjustly acquired, so also are they for money received as interest.

Reply Obj. 1. We understand the interest mentioned in the cited text metaphorically to mean dividends from spiritual goods, which God demands from us because he wants us to grow in the goods received from him. And this is for our profit, not his.

Reply Obj. 2. God prohibited the Jews from taking interest from their brothers, namely, their fellow Jews, and we are given to understand by this that interest-taking from any human being is absolutely evil. For we ought to consider every human being as our neighbor and brother, especially in the evangelical way of living, to which all are called. And so, without qualification, Ps. 15:5 praises "those who do not lend their money at interest," and Ez. 18:17 praises "those who do not accept interest." And God did not allow the Jews to take interest from foreigners as if the practice was lawful. Rather, he allowed the Jews to take interest from foreigners in order to avoid an evil, namely, lest the Jews out of greed, to which they were given, take interest from their fellow Jews, who worship the true God.

And we broadly understand the lending to foreigners promised the Jews as a reward in the cited text, "You will lend to many peoples," etc., as lending in general. Just so, Sir. 29:7 says: "Many refused to lend" (i.e., to lend in general) but "not out of malice." Therefore, God promises the Jews as a reward an abundance of wealth so that they may lend to others.

Reply Obj. 3. Human laws leave some sins unpunished because of the conditions of imperfect human beings, regarding whom many benefits would be prevented if all sins were to be strictly prohibited, and punishments for the sins were to be applied. And so human law allows interest-taking lest benefits for many be prevented, and not as if judging interest-taking to be in accord with justice. And so the civil law says, "By neither natural nor civil reason should things consumed in their use have a distinct usufruct," and "The Senate did not, nor could it, create a usufruct of such things, although it established a usufruct, as it were,"[3] namely, allowed interest-taking. And the Philosopher, led by natural reason, says in the *Politics* that "the acquisition of money by taking

---

[1]*Ethics* V, 5 (1133a20–1).   [2]*Politics* I, 3 (1257a35–41).
[3]Justinian, *Institutes* II, title 4, n. 2.

interest is especially contrary to nature."[4]

Reply Obj. 4. Human beings are not always obliged to lend, and so Christ in that respect includes lending with the counsels. But it falls under the nature of a precept that human beings should not seek profits from loans.

And Christ may call lending a counsel in contrast to the opinion of the Pharisees, who thought that any interest on loans was lawful, just as he counsels love of enemies in contrast to their opinion.

Or Christ is speaking in the citation about expecting things from human beings, not about lenders expecting profit. For we should lend and do good deeds because of hope in God, not because of hope in our fellow human beings.

Reply Obj. 5. Those under no obligation to lend can receive recompense for what they have done, and they should demand no more than that. But lenders are recompensed in accord with the equality required by justice if borrowers repay as much as they have borrowed. And so if lenders demand more for the use and enjoyment of things that have no other use than consumption of the things' substance, they demand payment for something that does not exist. And so the demand is unjust.

Reply Obj. 6. The chief use of silver vessels is not their very consumption, and so one can lawfully sell their use and retain ownership of them. But the chief use of silver money is to be transferred from one owner to another in exchanges. And so one may not lawfully sell its use as well as wanting repayment of the money lent.

But we should note that silver vessels could have a secondary use as exchanges. And it would not be lawful to sell such use of them. And likewise, there can be a secondary use of silver money, as, for example, if one were to lend silver coins for exhibition or for deposit as security. And human beings can lawfully charge for such use.

Reply Obj. 7. Those who pay interest do not pay it freely, absolutely speaking. Rather, they do so under some necessity, since they need to borrow money, which the lenders are unwilling to lend without receiving interest.

SECOND ARTICLE
Can One Seek Any Other Advantage for Money Lent?

We thus proceed to the second inquiry. It seems that one can seek some other advantage for money lent, for the following reasons:

Obj. 1. Persons can lawfully protect themselves against losses. But

---

[4]*Politics* I, 3 (1256b7–8).

persons sometimes suffer loss because they lend money. Therefore, they may lawfully seek, or even require, something more than the money lent in order to cover the risk of loss.

Obj. 2. Everyone is in honor obliged "to recompense those who have done them a favor," as the *Ethics* says.[5] But those who lend money to others in need do them a favor. And so also borrowers should be grateful. Therefore, a natural obligation obliges the borrowers to make some recompense to lenders. But it does not seem unlawful to commit oneself to what the natural law obliges one. Therefore, it does not seem unlawful if those lending money require recompense from borrowers.

Obj. 3. As there is "monetary remuneration," so there are "remuneration by praise" and "remuneration by service," as a gloss on Is. 33:15, "Blessed are those who tear their hands away from every bribe," says.[6] But it is lawful for one to accept service or praise from another to whom one has lent money. Therefore, by like reasoning, it is lawful for one to accept any other remuneration.

Obj. 4. There is the same relation of one gift to another and of one loan to another. But it is lawful for a person to receive money from another for money given to the other. Therefore, it is lawful for a person to accept the recompense of a loan from another for money lent to the other.

Obj. 5. Those who transfer ownership of money by lending it, alienate it more than those who invest it with merchants or craftsmen. But one may lawfully accept profit from money invested with merchants or craftsmen. Therefore, one may lawfully receive profit from money lent.

Obj. 6. Lenders can obtain security for money they lend, as when borrowers give their farms or dwellings to lenders as security, and lenders could sell use of the security. Therefore, lenders may lawfully profit from money lent.

Obj. 7. By reason of loans, persons may sometimes sell their goods more dearly or buy others' goods more cheaply, or increase the price of their goods in return for giving buyers a longer time to repay the loans, or lower the price of the goods in return for buyers repaying the loans earlier. In all of the above cases, recompense seems to be made for loans of money and not clearly unlawful. Therefore, it seems that one may lawfully look for, or even demand, an advantage from money lent.

On the contrary, among other things required of a just man, Ez. 18:17 says: "He will not exact interest or extra recompense."

I answer that, as the Philosopher says in the *Ethics*,[7] we consider as

---

[5]Aristotle, *Ethics* V, 5 (1133a4–5).   [6]*Glossa interlinearis*, on Is. 33:15.

money "things whose value money can measure." And those who by tacit or express contract accept money for the loan of money or of anything else consumed in its very use, sin against justice, as I have said.[8] And just so, therefore, those who should by tacit or express contract accept anything else whose value money can measure, likewise incur sin. But a lender does not sin if the lender should accept such a thing as a free gift, not as something required by either a tacit or express obligation. This is so because the lender could have accepted a free gift before the lender lent money, and the lender is in no worse condition by lending money.

On the other hand, a lender can lawfully demand in return for a loan the recompense of things not measured by money, for example, the friendship and love of the lender, or some such thing.

Reply Obj. 1. Lenders may without sin enter contracts with borrowers to recompense the lenders for losses that they would incur of things to which they are entitled, since such recompense is to avoid loss, not to sell the use of money. And borrowers may by taking loans avoid greater loss than lenders of the money may incur. And so borrowers out of their gains compensate lenders' losses.

But lenders may not make contracts with borrowers to recompense the lenders for putative losses of monetary profit, since one should not sell what one does not have and can be prevented in many ways from having.

Reply Obj. 2. One can make recompense for benefits in two ways. One can indeed make recompense in one way to satisfy a debt of justice, and one may be obligated to such recompense by a fixed contract. And we measure this debt by how much benefit one receives. And so those who borrow money or any such thing whose use consists of its consumption are not obliged to repay more than they borrowed. And so to oblige them to repay more is contrary to justice.

One is obliged to make recompense for benefits in a second way to satisfy a debt of friendship, in which one weighs the affection of the benefactor in conferring the benefit more than the size of the benefit conferred. And such a debt involves no legal obligation, which introduces a coercive element that takes away the free character of the recompense.

Reply Obj. 3. If a lender by reason of money lent should look for or demand the recompense of remuneration by service or praise as the obligation of a tacit or express contract, this is the same as if the lender were to look for or demand monetary remuneration. This is so because money can measure service and words of praise, as is evident in the case of those

---

[7]*Ethics* IV, 1 (1119b26–7).   [8]*ST* II–II, Q. 78, A. 1.

who sell their services or speech. But if a borrower gives remuneration by service or speech out of friendship, which money cannot measure, and not out of contractual obligation, the lender may lawfully accept and demand and look for such remuneration.

Reply Obj. 4. Lenders may not sell money for more than the sum lent, which borrowers are to repay, nor should lenders demand or look for anything more in recompense than friendly affection, which money does not measure, and which can give rise to freely willed loans. But an obligation to grant a future loan is inconsistent with demanding or looking for the affection of friendship, since money could also measure such an obligation. And so a borrower may lawfully lend something else to a lender at the time the lender lends money to the borrower, but the lender may not obligate the borrower to grant a future loan.

Reply Obj. 5. Lenders of money transfer ownership of the money to borrowers. And so the borrowers possess the money at their own risk and are obliged to repay all of it. And so lenders should not demand more. But those who invest their money with merchants or craftsmen by way of a partnership do not transfer ownership of their money to the merchants or craftsmen. Rather, investors retain ownership of their invested money, so that merchants carry on their business, and craftsmen their craft, with risk to the investors. And so investors may lawfully seek to share the profits from the business, as the profits partially belong to them.

Reply Obj. 6. If borrowers give as security for the money lent them things whose use money can measure, lenders should calculate use of the things toward the repayment of what they have lent. Otherwise, if lenders should want the free use of the things in addition to repayment, it is just as if they were to accept money for their loans. And this is to take interest, unless the things were perhaps such as friends usually grant the use of without charge, as is clearly the case with borrowed books.

Reply Obj. 7. Persons evidently take interest if they sell their goods on credit more dearly than the goods' just price, since such credit has the nature of a loan. And so everything demanded in exchange for such credit beyond the just price is like a charge on the loan, which belongs essentially to interest-taking.

Likewise, if buyers should want to buy goods by prepaying more cheaply than the goods' just price, this is the sin of interest-taking, since such prepayment has the nature of a loan, the charge for which is the reduction on the just price of the goods purchased. But if sellers should want to offer reductions on the just price in order to get their money sooner, they do not commit the sin of interest-taking.

THIRD ARTICLE
Are Persons Obliged to Return All of Their Profits from Money Obtained as Interest?

We thus proceed to the third inquiry. It seems that persons are obliged to return all of their profits from money obtained as interest, for the following reasons:

Obj. 1. The Apostle says in Rom. 11:16: "If the root is holy, so are the branches." Therefore, by like reasoning, if the root is poisoned, so are the branches. But the root of profits from money obtained as interest was interest-taking. Therefore, everything acquired from money obtained as interest is interest-taking. Therefore, one is obliged to return every such thing.

Obj. 2. A decretal on interest-taking says: "Property accruing from interest-taking should be sold, and the proceeds turned over to those from whom they were extorted."[9] Therefore, by like reasoning, everything else accruing from money obtained as interest should be returned.

Obj. 3. The goods people buy with money obtained as interest belong to them by reason of the money they paid for the goods. Therefore, they do not have a greater right to the goods they purchased than they have to the money they used to pay for the goods. But people are obliged to return money obtained as interest. Therefore, they are also obliged to return things they acquired with such money.

On the contrary, one can lawfully keep what one has lawfully acquired. But one sometimes lawfully acquires things with money obtained as interest. Therefore, one can lawfully keep such things.

I answer that, as I have said before,[10] there are some things whose use consists of their very consumption, things that the laws allow no separate right to use and enjoy.[11] And so if lenders should have extorted such things (e.g., money, wheat, wine, and the like) by taking interest, they are obliged to return only what they took, since anything they obtain out of such things is the fruit of their human effort, not the fruit of the things. A possible exception is if a borrower, in losing part of his property, should suffer loss by the lender's retention of the property, since the lender is then obliged to recompense the harm to the borrower.

And there are some things whose use does not consist of their consumption (e.g., homes and farms and the like), and there is a separate right to enjoy and use such things. And so if lenders should have extorted the home or farm of another, they are obliged to return both the home or

---

[9]Gregory IX, *Decretals* V, title 19, c. 5.   [10]ST II–II, Q. 78, A. 1.
[11]See n. 3, supra.

farm and the fruits derived therefrom, since the latter are the fruits of things owned by the other, and so due to the other.

Reply Obj. 1. A root has not only the nature of matter, as money obtained as interest does, but it also has somewhat the nature of an efficient cause, since it brings nourishment. And so there is no analogy.

Reply Obj. 2. Property acquired from interest-taking belongs to those who bought the property, not to those who paid the interest. But those who paid the interest have a claim on such property or other goods of the interest-taker. And so the law does not command that the property be ascribed to those who paid the interest, since the property is perhaps worth more than the interest they paid. Rather, the law commands that the property be sold, and the proceeds be repaid to the borrower, namely, by the amount of the interest paid.

Reply Obj. 3. Things acquired from interest money indeed belong to those acquiring them, with the interest money as the acquisition's instrumental cause, but with the acquirers' own efforts as the acquisition's chief cause. And so those who acquire things from interest money have more right to the things obtained from the interest money than they do to the interest money itself.

FOURTH ARTICLE
May One Lawfully Borrow Money Subject to the Payment of Interest?

We thus proceed to the fourth inquiry. It seems one may not lawfully borrow money subject to the payment of interest, for the following reasons:

Obj. 1. The Apostle says in Rom. 1:32: "Both those who commit sins, and those who approve of others committing sins, deserve to die." But those who borrow money at interest approve the sin of interest-takers and offer them an occasion of sin. Therefore, the borrowers of money at interest themselves also sin.

Obj. 2. For no earthly advantage should one offer another any occasion of sin, since this belongs to the nature of intentional or intrinsic scandal, which is always a sin, as I have said before.[12] But those who seek to borrow at interest expressly offer lenders an occasion of sin. Therefore, no earthly advantage excuses borrowers at interest from sin.

Obj. 3. There seems to be no less occasional necessity to deposit one's money with lenders who take interest than to borrow at interest from them. But depositing money with lenders who take interest seems to be completely unlawful, as it would be unlawful to deposit one's sword with

---

[12]ST II–II, Q. 43, A. 2.

a madman, to hand over a maiden to a libertine, or to give food to a glutton. Therefore, it is also unlawful to borrow at interest from lenders.

On the contrary, those who suffer injury, do not sin, as the Philosopher says in the *Ethics*.[13] And so justice is not a mean between two vices, as he says in the same work.[14] But those who lend at interest sin insofar as they cause injustice to borrowers at interest. Therefore, borrowers at interest do not sin.

I answer that it is in no way lawful to induce human beings to sin, but it is lawful to use another's sin for good, since even God uses all sins for some good by drawing good out of every evil, as Augustine says in his *Enchiridion*.[15] And so when Publicola asked him whether it would be lawful to use the oath of a man who swore by false gods—something obviously sinful because it gives divine reverence to false gods, he gave this reply: "Those who for good rather than evil use the truthfulness of another who swears by false gods associate themselves with the other's praiseworthy promise to tell the truth, not with the other's sin of swearing by false gods."[16] But one would sin if one were to induce another to swear by false gods.

So also in the matter under discussion, we should say that it is in no way lawful to induce lenders to lend at interest. But it is lawful to borrow at interest from those who are ready to lend at interest and make a practice of doing so, for the sake of some good, namely, to alleviate the need of the borrower or the need of another. Just so, one who falls into the hands of robbers may lawfully reveal his goods, in the taking of which the robbers sin, in order not to be killed. An example is that of the ten men who said to Ishmael, "Don't kill us, since we have stores in our fields," as Jer. 41:8 says.

Reply Obj. 1. Borrowers at interest make use of the sin of lenders at interest but do not approve their sin. And borrowers approve the lenders' lending, which is good, not the lenders' acceptance of interest.

Reply Obj. 2. Borrowers of money at interest offer lenders an opportunity to lend, not the opportunity for them to take interest, and lenders at interest themselves, out of the wickedness of their hearts, seize the opportunity to sin. And so there is passive scandal by the lenders at interest, and there is no active scandal by would-be borrowers at interest. And yet a would-be borrower in need should not refrain from borrowing at interest because of such passive scandal, since the latter results from the lenders' wickedness, not the public's weakness or ignorance.

---

[13]*Ethics* V, 11 (1138a34–b1). [14]Ibid., 5 (1133b32–1134a1).
[15]*Enchiridion* 11 (PL 40:236). [16]*Letter 47*, to Publicola, n. 2 (PL 33:184).

Reply Obj. 3. If one were to entrust one's money to a lender of money at interest who has no other sources of money to lend, or to entrust one's money to a lender of money at interest with the intention that the lender thereby profit more handsomely, the depositor would be giving the lender the material with which to sin. And so also the depositor would be participating in the sin. But if, in order to keep one's money safer, one should entrust it to a lender of money at interest who has other sources of money to lend, the depositor uses the sinner for good and does not himself sin.

Question 118
On Covetousness

[This question is divided into eight articles, three of which are translated here.]

First Article
Is Covetousness a Sin?

We thus proceed to the first inquiry. It seems that covetousness is not a sin, for the following reasons:

Obj. 1. We call covetousness love of money, namely, in that covetousness consists of the desire for money, by which we can understand all external goods. But desiring external goods is not a sin, since human beings by nature desire such things both because external things are subject to human beings, and because they sustain human life (for which reason we also refer to external goods as the substance of a human person). Therefore, covetousness is not a sin.

Obj. 2. Every sin is either against God or against neighbor or against oneself, as I have maintained before.[1] But covetousness is not, strictly speaking, a sin against God, since covetousness is neither contrary to religion nor contrary to the theological virtues, which direct human beings toward God. Nor is covetousness a sin against oneself, since the latter kind of sin, properly speaking, belongs to gluttony and sexual lust, about which the Apostle says in 1 Cor. 6:18: "Fornicators sin against their own body." Likewise, covetousness seems to be no sin against neighbor, since human beings by keeping their own property commit no injury against others. Therefore, covetousness is no sin.

Obj. 3. Things that come from nature are not sins. But covetousness results from old age and any disability, as the Philosopher says in the *Ethics.*[2] Therefore, covetousness is not a sin.

---

[1]ST I–II, Q. 72, A. 4.   [2]*Ethics* IV, 1 (1121b13–16).

On the contrary, Heb. 13:5 says: "Let your way of life be without avarice and satisfied with what you have."

I answer that in everything in which good consists of a proper measure, evil necessarily results by having more or less than that measure. And in every means to an end, good consists of the proportion of the means to the end, since means are necessarily commensurate to ends (e.g., medicine to health), as the Philosopher makes clear in the *Politics*.[3] And external goods have the nature of utility for our end, as I have said.[4] And so the human good in their regard necessarily consists of a proportion, namely, when human beings seek to possess external goods in the measure that they are necessary for their state of life. And so sin consists of seeking more than this measure, namely, when one wishes either to acquire or keep more than the proper measure. And this belongs to the nature of covetousness, which is defined as "the immoderate desire to possess."[5] And so covetousness is clearly a sin.

Reply Obj. 1. The desire for external things is natural to human beings insofar as those things are for the sake of the human end. And so such desire is without sin insofar as it stays within the measure understood from the nature of the human end. But covetousness exceeds this measure. And so covetousness is a sin.

Reply Obj. 2. Covetousness can signify lack of moderation regarding external things in two ways. Covetousness signifies lack of moderation in one way directly, regarding the acquisition or retention of external things, namely, that human beings acquire or keep more of them than they ought. And in this way, there is sin directly against neighbor, since one human being cannot have too many external riches without another having too little, as many cannot simultaneously possess earthly goods.

Covetousness signifies lack of moderation in a second way regarding internal desires that one has for riches, as, for example, that one immoderately loves or desires riches, or immoderately takes pleasure in them. And then human beings sin against themselves, since their desires are thereby misdirected. (But their bodies are not thereby disordered, as their bodies would be by sins of the flesh.)

And so there is sin against God, as all mortal sins are, since human beings by mortal sin contemn the eternal good for the sake of an earthly good.

Reply Obj. 3. Reason, which is the governing power in human nature, should rule natural inclinations. And so the elderly, although they more covetously seek assistance because of their natural weakness, as all the

---

[3]*Politics* 1, 3 (1257b25–30).   [4]ST: I–II, Q. 2, A. 1; II–II, Q. 117, A. 3.
[5]Hugh of St. Victor, *On the Sacraments* II, part 13, c. 1 (PL 176:526).

poor seek to have their need alleviated, are not excused from sin if they exceed the proper measure of reason regarding riches.

THIRD ARTICLE
Is Covetousness Contrary to Generosity?

We thus proceed to the third inquiry. It seems that covetousness is not contrary to generosity, for the following reasons:

Obj. 1. On Mt. 5:6, "Blessed are those who hunger and thirst for justice," Chrysostom says that there are two kinds of justice, one general and the other special, and that covetousness is contrary to the latter justice.[6] And the Philosopher says the same in the *Ethics.*[7] Therefore, covetousness is not contrary to the virtue of generosity.

Obj. 2. The sin of covetousness consists of human beings going beyond the measure regarding possessions. But justice establishes such a measure. Therefore, covetousness is directly contrary to justice, not to the virtue of generosity.

Obj. 3. Generosity is a virtue in between two contrary vices, as the Philosopher makes clear in the *Ethics.*[8] But covetousness has no juxtaposed contrary vice, as the Philosopher makes clear in the *Ethics.*[9] Therefore, covetousness is not contrary to generosity.

On the contrary, Eccl. 5:10 says: "The covetous are not satisfied with the money they have, and lovers of riches will enjoy no fruit from their riches." But not being satisfied with one's money and inordinately loving one's riches are contrary to generosity, which adheres to the mean in desiring riches. Therefore, covetousness is contrary to generosity.

I answer that: covetousness in two ways signifies lack of moderation regarding riches. Covetousness signifies lack of moderation in one way directly, regarding the very acquisition and retention of riches, namely, that one acquires money beyond one's due by taking or keeping the goods of another. And then covetousness is contrary to justice. And Ez. 22:27 understands covetousness in this sense when it says: "Her [Jerusalem's] rulers dwell in her like wolves preying on the people in order to shed blood and to pursue profit greedily."

Covetousness in a second way signifies lack of moderation regarding internal desires for riches, as, for example, when one loves or desires riches too much, or takes too much pleasure in them, even if one does not

---

[6]*Homilies on the Gospel of Matthew*, homily 15, n. 3 (PG 57:227).
[7]*Ethics*: V, 1 (1129b27–9); V, 2 (1130a14–6).
[8]Ibid.: II, 7 (1107b8–16); IV, 1 (1119b22–8).
[9]Ibid., IV, 1 (1121b1–3).

want to steal the goods of another. And covetousness in this way is contrary to generosity, which moderates such desires, as I have said.[10] And 2 Cor. 9:5 so understands covetousness: "Let them [the brethren] prepare for this promised blessing as if ready for a blessing and not as if for covetousness." And a gloss on that text adds: "Namely, lest they regret what they have given and give little."[11]

Reply Obj. 1. Chrysostom and the Philosopher are speaking about covetousness in the first way. But the Philosopher calls covetousness in the second way lack of generosity.[12]

Reply Obj. 2. Justice, properly speaking, establishes the measure to be observed as a matter of legal obligation in acquiring and retaining riches, namely, that human beings should not take or keep the property of another. But generosity, indeed, chiefly establishes the measure of reason regarding internal desires for possessions, and so regarding the external acquisition, retention, and spending of money insofar as such actions result from such internal desires. Generosity establishes this measure by looking to the nature of moral obligation, which one considers by the rule of reason, and not to the nature of legal obligation.

Reply Obj. 3. Covetousness as contrary to justice has no juxtaposed contrary vice, since such covetousness consists of having more than one ought to have in justice, and having less than one ought to have, the contrary, has the nature of punishment rather than sin. But covetousness as contrary to generosity has the juxtaposed contrary vice of prodigality.

Seventh Article
Is Covetousness a Capital Sin?

We thus proceed to the seventh inquiry. It seems that covetousness is not a capital sin, for the following reasons:

Obj. 1. Covetousness is contrary to generosity as the mean and to prodigality as the other extreme. But generosity is not a chief virtue, nor is prodigality a capital sin. Therefore, we should also not designate covetousness a capital sin.

Obj. 2. As I have said before,[13] we call sins capital sins if they have chief ends to which the ends of other sins are ordered. But such does not belong to covetousness, since riches have the nature of a means to an end, not of an end, as the *Ethics* says.[14] Therefore, covetousness is not a capital sin.

---

[10]ST II–II, Q. 117: A. 2, *ad* 1; A. 3, *ad* 3; A. 6.

[11]Peter Lombard, *Glossa*, on 2 Cor. 9:5 (PL 192:62).

[12]*Ethics* II, 7 (1107b13–6).   [13]ST I–II, Q. 84, AA. 3, 4.

[14]Aristotle, *Ethics* I, 5 (1096a5–10).

Obj. 3. Gregory says in his work *Morals*: "Covetousness sometimes arises out of pride, sometimes out of fear. For example, some, when they think they lack things necessary for their expenses, let their minds turn to coveting. And others are incited to covet other people's property when they desire to seem more powerful."[15] Therefore, covetousness is the product of other sins rather than itself a capital sin with respect to other sins.

On the contrary, Gregory in his work *Morals* includes covetousness in the list of capital sins.[16]

I answer that, as I have said before,[17] we call sins capital if other sins arise from them by reason of the capital sins' ends, since human beings proceed to do many things, whether good or evil, because they will very desirable ends. But the most desirable end is blessedness or happiness, which is the ultimate end of human life, as I have said before.[18] And so the more things partake of the conditions of happiness, the more desirable they are. And one of the conditions of happiness is that one be self-sufficient. Otherwise, happiness as the ultimate end would not satisfy the desire for it. But riches especially promise self-sufficiency, as Boethius says in his work *On the Consolation of Philosophy*.[19] And the reason why, as the Philosopher says in the *Ethics*,[20] is that "we use money as a unit of exchange to buy every kind of material thing." And Eccl. 10:19 says that "everything is at the service of money." And so covetousness, which consists of the desire for money, is a capital sin.

Reply Obj. 1. Reason accomplishes virtue, and the inclinations of sense appetites accomplish vice. But reason does not chiefly belong to the same genus as sense appetites. And so the chief vices need not be contrary to the chief virtues. And so, although generosity is not a chief virtue, since it does not regard a chief good of reason, covetousness is nonetheless a chief vice, since it regards money, which has a leading role regarding material goods, for the reason I mentioned.[21]

And prodigality is not ordered to any chiefly desirable end. Rather, prodigality seems to result from lack of reasoning. And so the Philosopher says in the *Ethics* that a prodigal person is called a fool rather than a knave.[22]

---

[15]*Morals* XV, 25, n. 30 (PL 75:1096).   [16]Ibid., XXXI, 45, n. 88 (PL 76:621).
[17]See n. 13, supra.   [18]ST I–II, Q. 1, A. 8, *On the contrary*.
[19]*On the Consolation of Philosophy* III, prose 3 (PL 63:732).
[20]*Ethics* V, 5 (1133b10–14).   [21]In the body of the article.
[22]*Ethics* IV, 1 (1121a25–27).

Reply Obj. 2. Money is indeed ordered to other things as its end, but it in one respect includes all material things virtually insofar as it is useful for acquiring them. And so it has an analogy to happiness, as I have said.[23]

Reply Obj. 3. Nothing prevents a capital sin from sometimes arising from other sins, as I have said, provided that it itself generally and frequently gives rise to other sins.[24]

---

[23]In the body of the article.

[24]ST II–II, Q. 36, A. 4, *ad* 1.

5

War and Killing

In ST II–II, Q. 40, A. 1, Thomas asserts that waging war can be justified if three conditions are satisfied: (1) that legitimate authority makes the decision to wage war; (2) that there is a just cause to wage war; (3) that those waging war have a right intention, namely, to wage only for the sake of justice.

In ST II–II, Q. 64, Thomas holds that it is never lawful to kill an innocent human being (A. 6), that it is lawful for private persons to kill another in necessary self-defense of their lives but unlawful for the persons to intend the resulting death (A. 7), and that one killing another accidentally is not guilty of homicide, that is, murder or manslaughter (A. 8).

ST II–II
Question 40
On War

[This question is divided into four articles, one of which is translated here.]

FIRST ARTICLE
Is It Always Sinful to Wage War?

We thus proceed to the first inquiry. It seems that it is always sinful to wage war, for the following reasons:

Obj. 1. Punishment is inflicted only for sin. But the Lord declares that those who wage war will be punished, as Mt. 26:52 says: "Those who take to the sword will perish by the sword." Therefore, all wars are unlawful.

Obj. 2. Everything contrary to a divine precept is a sin. But waging war is contrary to a divine precept, since Mt. 5:39 says: "I tell you not to resist evil," and Rom. 12:19 says: "Do not defend yourselves, dearly beloved, but leave it to [God's] wrath." Therefore, it is always sinful to wage war.

Obj. 3. Only sin is contrary to a virtuous act. But war is contrary to peace. Therefore, war is always a sin.

Obj. 4. Every exercise regarding something lawful is lawful, as is clearly the case with scientific exercises. But the church prohibits the warlike exercises in tournaments, since the church denies those who die in such contests Christian burial. Therefore, war seems to be absolutely sinful.

On the contrary, Augustine says in a sermon on the centurion's servant: "If Christian teaching were altogether to condemn war, the soldiers in the

Gospel who sought salutary advice [Lk. 3:14] would have been told to cast aside their arms and abandon military service altogether. But Christ told them: 'Do violence to no one, and be content with your pay.' And if Christ commanded them to be satisfied with their pay, he did not forbid military service."[1]

I answer that three things are required for a war to be just. Indeed, the first requirement is that the ruler at whose command the war is to be waged have the lawful authority to do so. For it belongs to no private citizen to initiate war, since private persons can pursue vindication of their rights through the decisions of their superiors. Likewise, it belongs to no private citizen to initiate war, because no private citizen can call on the people to wage war, which has to be done in wars. Rather, since the care of the commonweal has been committed to rulers, it belongs to them to protect the commonweal of the city or kingdom or province subject to them. And they lawfully use physical weapons to defend the commonweal against domestic rebels when they punish malefactors, as the Apostle says in Rom. 13:4: "He [the ruler] does not carry a sword without cause, since he is God's servant, an avenger to execute wrath on the evildoer." Just so, it also belongs to rulers to use weapons of war to protect the commonweal against foreign enemies. And Ps. 82:4 tells rulers: "Rescue the poor and free the needy from the hands of sinners." And so Augustine says in his work *Against Faustus*: "The natural order conducive to peace among mortals requires that the legitimate authority to undertake war, and deliberation regarding war, be in the hands of rulers."[2]

Second, there needs to be a just cause to wage war, namely, that the enemy deserve to have war waged against it because of some wrong it has inflicted. And so Augustine says in his *Questions on the Heptateuch*: "We usually define just wars as those that avenge wrongs, when peoples or political communities need to be punished either because they have failed to rectify wrongs committed by their subjects, or because they have failed to restore property unjustly seized."[3]

Third, those waging war need to have a right intention, namely, an intention to promote good or avoid evil. And so Augustine says: "For true worshipers of God, wars waged with zeal for peace and not out of desire for gain or out of cruelty, wars waged to restrain the wicked and assist the good, are also conducive of peace."[4] But even if legitimate authority

---

[1]*Letter 138*, to Marcellinus, c. 2, n. 15 (PL 33:531).

[2]*Against Faustus* XXII, 75 (PL 42:448).

[3]*Questions on the Heptateuch*, q. 10, on Jos. 8:2 (PL 34:781).

[4]Actually, Gratian, *Decretum* II, causa 23, q. 1, c. 6.

declares war, and the cause is just, wars may be unlawful because they are waged with a wicked intention. For Augustine says in his work _Against Faustus_: "Desire to harm, vengeful cruelty, insatiate and implacable animus, savagery in renewing combat, lust for dominance, and the like are justly condemned in the matter of waging war."[5]

Reply Obj. 1. Augustine says in his work _Against Faustus_: "They take to the sword who take up arms against the life of another without any superior or legitimate authority either commanding or allowing it."[6] But those who use the sword by the authority of a ruler or judge, if they be private citizens, or out of zeal for justice and by the authority of God, as it were, if they be public officials, do not themselves "take to" the sword. Rather, they "use" the sword committed to them by another. And so they do not deserve punishment.

Still, even those who use the sword sinfully are not always slain by the sword, although they always perish by their own sword, since they are eternally punished for their sinful use of the sword unless they repent.

Reply Obj. 2. As Augustine says in his work _On the Lord's Sermon on the Mount_,[7] human beings should always observe such precepts in readiness of spirit, namely, that they be ready, if necessary, not to resist and not to defend themselves. But one sometimes should act otherwise for the sake of the common good, and also for the good of those against whom one is fighting. And so Augustine says in a letter to Marcellinus: "We should also do many things to those whom we punish with a kindly severity against their will. For they are beneficially vanquished who are snatched from the licentiousness of sin, since nothing is more miserable than the happiness of sinners, which feeds a punishable licentiousness and, like an internal enemy, strengthens an evil will."[8]

Reply Obj. 3. Even those who wage just war strive for peace. And so they are only contrary to the evil peace that the Lord "did not come to send upon the earth," as Mt. 10:34 says. And so Augustine says in a letter to Boniface: "We do not seek peace in order to wage war. Rather, we wage war in order to achieve peace. Therefore, be peacemakers in waging war, so that you may in winning bring those against whom you war to the benefit of peace."[9]

Reply Obj. 4. Not all military exercises by human beings are forbidden. Rather, only disordered and dangerous military exercises that give rise to

---

[5]_Against Faustus_ XXII, 74 (PL 42:447).   [6]Ibid., 70 (PL 42:444).

[7]_On the Lord's Sermon on the Mount_ I, 19, nn. 58–9 (PL 34:1260).

[8]_Letter 138_, to Marcellinus, c. 2, n. 14 (PL 33:531).

[9]_Letter 189_, to Boniface, n. 6 (PL 33:856).

slayings and plunderings are forbidden. And the ancients took part in military exercises without such risks. And so the ancients called them "military exercises" or "bloodless wars," as Jerome makes clear in one of his letters.[10]

Question 64
On Homicide

[This question is divided into eight articles, three of which are translated here.]

SIXTH ARTICLE
Is It Ever Lawful to Kill an Innocent Person?

We thus proceed to the sixth inquiry. It seems that it is sometimes lawful to kill an innocent person, for the following reasons:

Obj. 1. Sin does not manifest fear of God. On the contrary, "fear of the Lord drives away sin," as Sir. 1:27 says. But Abraham is praised for having feared God, since he was willing to kill his innocent son.[1] Therefore, one may without sin kill an innocent person.

Obj. 2. Of sins committed against neighbor, the more serious the harm inflicted on the person against whom one sins, the more serious seems to be the sin. But killing a sinner harms the sinner more than killing an innocent person harms the innocent person, who by death goes from the wretchedness of this life to heavenly glory. Therefore, since it is sometimes lawful to kill a sinner, much more is it lawful to kill an innocent or righteous person.

Obj. 3. Things done in accord with the order of justice are not sins. But the order of justice sometimes compels one to kill an innocent person. For example, judges, who are bound to judge according to the evidence, condemn to death those accused by false witnesses, although the judges know the accused to be innocent. And the same is true about an executioner who, obeying a judge, kills an unjustly condemned man. Therefore, one may without sin kill an innocent person.

On the contrary, Ex. 23:7 says: "You shall not kill any innocent or righteous person."

I answer that we can consider an individual human being in two ways: in one way as such; in a second way in relation to something else. Considering human beings as such, it is indeed never lawful to kill

---

[10]Actually, Vegetius, *Institutes of Military Affairs* I, 9–28; II, 23.
[1]Gen. 22:12.

anyone, since, in the case of every human being, even a sinner, we should love the nature that God created, and that killing destroys. But as I have said before,[2] killing sinners becomes lawful in relation to the common good, which sin corrupts. On the other hand, the life of the just preserves and promotes the common good, since the just are the most important members of the community. And so it is never lawful to kill an innocent person.

Reply Obj. 1. God has dominion over life and death, since both sinners and the righteous die by his ordinance. And so a person who kills an innocent at God's command does not sin, just as God, whose will such a person carries out, does not. And such a person in obeying God's commands manifests fear of him.

Reply Obj. 2. In weighing the seriousness of sin, we should consider the intrinsic rather than the accidental. And so one who kills a righteous person commits a more serious sin than one who kills a sinner. First, this is indeed so because those who kill a righteous person harm one whom they should love more, and so act more against charity. Second, it is so because they inflict injury on one who less deserves to be injured, and so act more against justice. Third, it is so because they deprive the community of a greater good. Fourth, it is so because they thereby contemn God more, as Lk. 10:16 says: "Those who despise you, despise me [Christ]." But it is incidental to killing that God brings a righteous person to glory.

Reply Obj. 3. If a judge knows that one accused by false witnesses is innocent, the judge should examine the witnesses more closely in order to find a way to acquit the innocent person, as the prophet Daniel did.[3] But if the judge cannot acquit the person, the judge should remit the person to a higher court. And if the judge cannot do this, the judge does not sin in passing judgment according to the evidence, since those who accused the innocent person, not the judge, kill the accused.

And the official assigned to carry out a judge's order to execute an innocent person should not obey the order if the sentence contains flagrant error. Otherwise, the executioners who killed the martyrs would be excused of moral fault. But if the sentence contains no evident injustice, the official does not sin in carrying out the order, since the official has no right to dispute the judgment of a superior. Nor does the official kill the innocent person. Rather, the judge, whom the official serves, does so.

---

[2] ST II–II, Q. 64, A. 2   [3] Dan. 13:51–9 (Septuagint).

SEVENTH ARTICLE
Is It Lawful for a Person to Kill Another in Self-Defense?

We thus proceed to the seventh inquiry. It seems that it is not lawful for anyone to kill another in self-defense, for the following reasons:

Obj. 1. Augustine says in a letter to Publicola: "I do not agree with the advice that one may kill another lest one be killed by the other, except perhaps in the case of a soldier or public official, who is legally authorized and does so for the sake of others and not to save himself, provided that the person slain deserves to be."[4] But one who kills another in self-defense does so lest the other kill oneself. Therefore, this seems to be unlawful.

Obj. 2. Augustine says in his work *On Free Choice*: "How in the sight of divine providence are they free of sin who are stained with human slaughter for the sake of such contemptible things?"[5] But he calls things contemptible "that human beings can lose against their will," as is evident from what he said immediately before.[6] And corporeal life is one of these things. Therefore, it is unlawful for anyone to kill a human being to save one's corporeal life.

Obj. 3. Pope Nicholas I says,[7] and the *Decretum* maintains[8]: "You inquire regarding the clerics about whom you consulted us, namely, those who killed a pagan in self-defense, whether they could after repentance later return to their former station or rise to a higher station. Know that we admit no occasion nor grant any permission to them to kill any human being under any circumstance." But clerics and laypersons alike are obliged to observe moral precepts. Therefore, it is also unlawful for laypersons to kill anyone in self-defense.

Obj. 4. Homicide is a more serious sin than adultery or ordinary fornication. But it is unlawful for anyone to commit adultery or ordinary fornication or any other mortal sin to save one's life, since one should prefer one's spiritual life to one's corporeal life. Therefore, it is unlawful for anyone to kill another in self-defense in order to save one's life.

Obj. 5. If a tree is rotten, so is its fruit, as Mt. 7:17–8 says. But self-defense itself seems to be unlawful, as Rom. 12.19 says: "Do not defend yourselves, dearly beloved." Therefore, killing a human being in self-defense is unlawful.

On the contrary, Ex. 22:2 says: "If a thief should break into or dig under one's home and be wounded and die, the defender who inflicted the wound will not be guilty of the thief's blood." But it is much more lawful

---

[4]*Letter 47*, to Publicola, n. 5 (PL 33:186).

[5]*On Free Choice* I, 5, n. 13 (PL 32:1228).   [6]Ibid.

[7]*Letter 138*, to Osbald (PL 119:1131).   [8]Gratian, *Decretum* I, dist. 50, c. 6.

to defend one's life than to defend one's home. Therefore, neither is one who should kill another in self-defense guilty of murder.

I answer that nothing prevents one action having two effects, only one of which is intended, and the other of which is unintended. But as is clear from what I have said before,[9] what one intends specifies moral actions, not what one does not intend, since the latter result is incidental. Therefore, one's action in defending oneself can have two effects: saving one's life and slaying the aggressor. And so such acts of self-defense, as one intends by them to preserve one's life, do not have the character of being unlawful, since it is natural for everything to keep itself in existence as far as possible.

But an action originating from a good intention can be rendered unlawful if the action should be disproportionate to the end. And so it will be unlawful to use greater force than necessary to defend one's life. And it will be lawful in self-defense to resist force in due moderation, since the laws "permit one to resist force with force in the measure of blameless self-defense."[10] Nor is it necessary for salvation that human beings omit acts of moderate self-defense in order to avoid killing another, since they have a higher obligation to safeguard their own lives than the life of another.

Nonetheless, it is only lawful for public authority to kill human beings, and in that case only for the common good, as is evident from what I have said before.[11] Therefore, it is unlawful for human beings other than those holding public authority to intend to kill an aggressor in the course of self-defense. And those holding public authority, intending to kill human beings in the course of self-defense, relate such killing to the public good. The latter is evident in the case of soldiers warring against enemies and in the case of police fighting against robbers, although even these sin if they are motivated by private animosity.

Reply Obj. 1. We should understand the cited authority of Augustine to apply to the case of one who intends to kill another in order to avoid death.

Reply Obj. 2. And we should also understand the cited authority of Augustine quoted from his work *On Free Choice* to apply to such a case. And so he significantly adds "for the sake of these things," meaning "with such an intention." And this makes clear the reply to the second objection.

Reply Obj. 3. Acts of homicide, even if they be without sin, as in the case of judges who justly condemn persons to death, result in clerics

---

[9]ST I–II, Q. 72, A. 1; II–II, Q. 43, A. 3.

[10]Gregory IX, *Decretals* V, title 12, c. 18.

[11]ST II–II, Q. 64, A. 3.

incurring the canonical penalty of irregularity. And so clerics, even if they kill someone in self-defense, incur irregularity, although they intended only to defend themselves, not to kill.

Reply Obj. 4. Acts of fornication or adultery are not necessarily ordered to saving one's life, as are acts that sometimes result in homicide.

Reply Obj. 5. The cited text forbids self-defense that is vengeful. And so a gloss says: "Do not defend yourselves, that is, do not strike back against your enemy."[12]

EIGHTH ARTICLE
Is One Who Accidentally Kills Another Guilty of Homicide?

We thus proceed to the eighth inquiry. It seems that one who accidentally kills another is guilty of homicide, for the following reasons:

Obj. 1. We read in Gen. 4:23–4 that Lamech, thinking he was killing a wild beast, killed a human being, and he was considered guilty of homicide. Therefore, those who kill another accidentally incur the guilt of homicide.

Obj. 2. Ex. 21:22–3 says: "If one should strike a pregnant woman and cause a miscarriage, if her death should result, will repay life for life." But this can happen without the one who strikes the woman intending to kill her. Therefore, accidental homicide incurs the guilt of homicide.

Obj. 3. The *Decretum* contains several canons that prescribe penalties for accidental homicides.[13] But only sins deserve punishment. Therefore, those who kill another accidentally incur the sin of homicide.

On the contrary, Augustine says in a letter to Publicola: "Let not things that we do for a good and lawful purpose be imputed to us if anything evil thereby happens to another unintentionally."[14] But homicide may sometimes accidentally happen as a result of people doing things for good purposes. Therefore, such accidental homicides should not be imputed as sins.

I answer that, as the Philosopher says in the *Physics*,[15] chance is a cause that produces an effect unintentionally. And so accidental things are, strictly speaking, neither intended nor voluntary. And because every sin is voluntary, as Augustine says,[16] it follows logically that accidental things as such are not sins. But what is not actually willed or intended may be willed and intended incidentally, insofar as we call accidental a cause that

---

[12]Peter Lombard, *Glossa*, on Rom. 12:19 (PL 191:1502).

[13]Gratian, *Decretum* I, dist. 50, cc. 4–8.

[14]*Letter 47*, to Publicola, n. 5 (PL 33:187).   [15]*Physics* II, 6 (197b18–22).

[16]*On True Religion* 14, n. 27 (PL 34:133).

removes something that prevents an effect. And so those who do not remove things that result in homicide, if they should remove them, will be guilty of voluntary homicide in one respect.

And the latter may happen in two ways. It may happen in one way if one causes homicide in the course of unlawful activity, which one ought to avoid. It may happen in a second way if one does not take proper care. And so, according to the laws,[17] if a person be engaged in lawful activity and exercise proper care, and homicide thereby result, the person is not guilty of homicide. But if a person is engaged in unlawful activity or engaged in lawful activity without exercising proper care, the person does not escape the guilt of homicide if one's activity should result in the death of a human being.

Reply Obj. 1. Lamech did not take sufficient care to avoid homicide. And so he did not escape the guilt of homicide.

Reply Obj. 2. Those who strike a pregnant woman act unlawfully. And so they do not escape the guilt of homicide if either the woman or the ensouled fetus dies as a result, especially if death would clearly result from such a blow.

Reply Obj. 3. The canons impose penalties on those who kill accidentally when engaged in unlawful activities or not exercising proper care.

---

[17]Gratian, *Decretum* I, dist. 50, cc. 48, 49.

6

Obedience and Rebellion

In ST II–II, Thomas holds: that the natural law and the divine law oblige human beings to obey other human beings (A. 1); that obedience of superiors is part of justice (A. 2); that the theological virtue of charity is greater than the natural moral virtue of obedience (A. 3); that God should be obeyed in all things (A. 4); that subjects should obey human superiors only insofar as the former are subject to the latter, and insofar as the latter command nothing contrary to what God commands (A. 5); that Christians are obliged to obey secular rulers (A. 6).

In ST II–II, Q. 60, A. 6, Thomas says that subjects are not obliged to obey laws or legal judgments unsanctioned by public authority, but he also there (ad 3) upholds the authority of spiritual superiors (bishops and pope) to issue commands in temporal affairs regarding matters subject to them. On other comments by him on church-state relations, see selections from the CS in Chapter 7.

In ST II–II, Q, 42, A. 2, Thomas bluntly calls any rebellion a mortal sin but excludes resistance against tyrants from his definition of rebellion. For a more detailed treatment by him on resistance of tyrants, see On Kingship I, 6, in Chapter 8.

ST II–II
Question 104
On Obedience

FIRST ARTICLE
Is One Human Being Obliged to Obey Another?

We thus proceed to the first inquiry. It seems that one human being is not obliged to obey another, for the following reasons:

Obj. 1. One should not do anything contrary to what God has ordained. But God has ordained that human beings rule themselves by their own practical reason, as Sir. 15:14 says: "God established human beings at the beginning and left them in the hands of their own practical reason." Therefore, one human being is not obliged to obey another.

Obj. 2. If one person were obliged to obey another, the will of the latter would necessarily constitute the rule of the former's action. But only the divine will, which is always correct, is the rule of human action. Therefore, human beings are obliged to obey no one but God.

Obj. 3. The more freely rendered the service, the more acceptable it is to God. But what human beings do out of obligation is not freely rendered. Therefore, if human beings were strictly obliged to obey others regarding performance of good deeds, good deeds done out of obedience would by that very fact be rendered less acceptable to God. Therefore, human beings are not obliged to obey other human beings.

On the contrary, Heb. 13:17 says: "Obey your superiors and be subject to them."

I answer that as natural powers cause the activities of things of nature, so also the human will causes human activities. But it was fitting that higher things of nature, by reason of the preeminent natural powers God bestowed on them, move lower things of nature. And so also it is fitting in regard to human affairs that superiors by their will, by reason of the power of authority ordained by God, move inferiors to their activities. But to cause things by reason and will is to command. And so as lower things of nature need to be subject to the causal influence of higher things of nature by reason of the natural order God established, so also regarding human affairs, inferiors are obliged by the order of natural and divine law to obey their superiors.

Reply Obj. 1. God left human beings in the hands of their practical reason because the free choice of their will and not necessity of nature, as in the case of irrational creatures, determines what they are to do, and not because it would be lawful for human beings to do whatever they wish. And as one should act by one's practical reason in doing other things, so also one should act in obeying superiors. For Gregory says in his work *Morals*: "When we humbly submit to the bidding of another, we conquer our inner selves."[1]

Reply Obj. 2. The divine rule is the primary will, and that rule directs all rational wills. But one rational will approximates the divine will more than another regarding the order God has established. And so the will of one human being issuing a command can be, as it were, a secondary rule for the will of another human being obeying the command.

Reply Obj. 3. We can deem things freely willed in two ways. We can consider things freely willed in one way regarding the deeds themselves, namely, that human beings are not obliged to do them. We can consider things freely willed in a second way regarding those who perform the deeds, namely, that they do them of their own free will. But deeds are rendered virtuous and praiseworthy and meritorious precisely because they are done willingly. And so, although obedience is obligatory, its merit is

---

[1]*Morals* XXXV, 14, n. 28 (PL 76:765).

not on that account diminished if one should obey with a ready will. And this is especially true about obeying God, who sees both external deeds and the internal will.

SECOND ARTICLE
Is Obedience a Special Virtue?

We thus proceed to the second inquiry. It seems that obedience is not a special virtue, for the following reasons:

Obj. 1. Disobedience is contrary to obedience. But disobedience is sin in general, for Ambrose says that sin is "disobedience of the divine law."[2] Therefore, obedience is virtue in general, not a special virtue.

Obj. 2. Every special virtue is either a theological virtue or a moral virtue. But obedience is not a theological virtue, since it is not part of faith or hope or charity. Likewise, it is not a moral virtue, since it is not the mean between too much and too little. For example, the more obedient one is, the more one is praised. Therefore, obedience is not a special virtue.

Obj. 3. Gregory says in his work *Morals*: "The less obedience regards oneself, the more meritorious and praiseworthy it is."[3] But the more every special virtue regards oneself, the more it is praised, since virtue requires one to exercise one's will and choice, as the *Ethics* says.[4] Therefore, obedience is not a special virtue.

Obj. 4. Virtues differ specifically by their objects. But the object of obedience seems to be the command of a superior, and the commands of superiors seem to vary in as many ways as there are different grades of superiors. Therefore, obedience is virtue in general, including many special virtues.

On the contrary, some designate obedience part of justice,[5] as I have said before.[6]

I answer that we define special virtues in relation to all good deeds that have a special praiseworthy character, since it belongs strictly to virtue "to make deeds good."[7] But the divinely established order of things obliges us to obey superiors, as I have shown.[8] And so obeying superiors is good, since good consists of a "mode, species, and order" of being, as Augustine says in his work *On the Nature of Good*.[9] And such an act has a special praiseworthy character from its special object.

---

[2]*On Paradise* 8, n. 39 (PL 14:292).   [3]*Morals* XXXV, 14, n. 30 (PL 76:766).
[4]Aristotle, *Ethics* II, 4 (1105a31–b5).
[5]E.g., William of Auvergne, *On Virtues and Morals* 12.
[6]ST II–II, Q. 80, A.1, obj. 3.   [7]Aristotle, *Ethics* II, 6 (1106a15–23).
[8]ST II–II, Q. 104, A. 1.   [9]*On the Nature of Good* 3 (PL 42:553).

For although inferiors should evidence many things to their superiors, one of these things, the obligation of inferiors to obey the commands of superiors, is special. And so obedience is a special virtue, and its special object is a superior's tacit or express command. For the will of a superior, howsoever the superior makes it known, is a tacit command, and the more one understands the will of a superior and by obeying it anticipates an express command, the readier the obedience seems.

Reply Obj. 1. Nothing prevents two special aspects regarding two special virtues from both being present in one and the same material object. For example, soldiers in defending a king's fort perform courageous acts by standing fast in the face of the danger of death for the sake of a good end and acts of justice by rendering proper service to their lord. Therefore, the aspect of command, which obedience regards, accompanies some but not all acts of every virtue, since not all virtuous acts fall under precept, as I have maintained before.[10] Likewise, some things pertaining to no other virtue sometimes fall under precept, as is evident in the case of things that are evil only because they are prohibited.

Therefore, obedience, if we should understand it in the strict sense as intentionally regarding the formal aspect of command, will be a special virtue, and disobedience a special sin. In this respect, obedience will require that one perform acts of justice or another virtue with the intention of carrying out a superior's command, and disobedience will require that one actually contemn a superior's command.

But if we should understand obedience broadly as carrying out anything that can fall under precept, and disobedience as failing to do so, with whatever intention, then obedience will be virtue in general, and disobedience will be sin in general.

Reply Obj. 2. Obedience is not a theological virtue, since its intrinsic object is not God. Rather, its intrinsic object is the command of any superior, whether the command be expressed or implied, that is, merely a word indicating a religious superior's will, which a subject readily obeys, as Tit. 3:1 says: "Remind them to obey at a superior's word."

But obedience is a moral virtue, since it is part of justice, and a mean between too much and too little. And we do not consider excess of obedience regarding how much obedience there is, but regarding other circumstances, namely, as one obeys either someone that one should not, or in matters that one should not, just as I have said before about religion.[11]

---

[10]ST I–II: Q. 96, A. 3; Q. 100, A. 2.
[11]ST II–II, Q. 81, A. 5, *ad* 3.

And we can say in the case of justice that there is excess in one who keeps the property of another, and deficiency in one whose property is not returned, as the Philosopher says in the *Ethics*.[12] Just so, obedience is a mean between the excess we note regarding those who withhold proper obedience to a superior, since such persons excessively follow their own will, and the deficiency we note regarding superiors whom disobedient subjects do not obey. And so obedience in this respect will not be a mean between two evils, as I have said before about justice.[13]

Reply Obj. 3. Obedience, just like any virtue, should have a ready will for its proper object and not for the contrary. But the proper object of obedience is a superior's command, which indeed comes from the will of another. And so obedience renders the will of human beings ready to carry out the will of another, namely, of the one issuing a command.

And if subjects will to carry out the things commanded for their own sake, even apart from the aspect of command, as happens in favorable matters, subjects then strive for the commanded things by their own will and seem to carry out the command because of their own will and not because of the command. But if subjects in no way intrinsically will the things commanded, which are, absolutely speaking, contrary to their will, as happens in difficult matters, then it is completely evident that subjects carry out the commanded things only because of the command. And so Gregory says in his work *Morals* that "obedience that partially regards oneself in favorable matters is lesser or nothing,"[14] namely, in that such a subject's will seems chiefly to strive to carry out a superior's command in order to acquire what the subject wills, not in order to carry out the command. "But," says Gregory,[15] "obedience in hard or difficult matters is greater," since a subject's will strives only to carry out the command.

Still, we should understand this regarding external appearances. But in the judgment of God, who searches hearts, obedience even in favorable matters, obedience partially regarding oneself, may not be less praiseworthy on that account if, namely, an obedient subject's will should strive no less eagerly to carry out a superior's command.

Reply Obj. 4. Reverence directly regards the excellence of a person, and so there are different kinds of reverence in relation to different aspects of excellence. And obedience regards a command from a preeminent person and so belongs to one and the same aspect of excellence. But since one should obey a superior's command because of reverence for the superior's

---

[12]*Ethics* V, 4 (1132a10–2, b11–2).   [13]ST II–II, Q. 58, A. 10, *ad* 2.
[14]*Morals* XXXV, 14, n. 30 (PL 76:766).   [15]Ibid.

person, all obedience consequently belongs to the same species, although the causes giving rise to obedience differ specifically.

THIRD ARTICLE
Is Obedience the Greatest Virtue?

We thus proceed to the third inquiry. It seems that obedience is the greatest virtue, for the following reasons:

Obj. 1. 1 Sam. 15:22 says: "Obedience is better than sacrifice." But offering sacrifices belongs to religion, which is the most powerful moral virtue, as is evident from what I have said before.[16] Therefore, obedience is the most powerful virtue.

Obj. 2. Gregory says in his work *Morals*: "Obedience is the only virtue that sows other virtues in our mind and preserves them when planted."[17] But causes are more powerful than their effects. Therefore, obedience is more powerful than all the other virtues.

Obj. 3. Gregory says in his work *Morals*: "Obedience never causes evil, although it sometimes obliges us to postpone good deeds."[18] But we postpone things only for better things. Therefore, obedience, for which we postpone the good deeds of other virtues, is better than other virtues.

On the contrary, obedience is praiseworthy because it is the product of charity. For Gregory says in his work *Morals*: "We should observe obedience with affectionate love, not servile fear; with love of justice, not fear of punishment."[19] Therefore, charity is a more powerful virtue than obedience.

I answer that, as sin consists of human beings adhering to transitory goods and contemning God, so, contrariwise, the merit of virtuous acts consists of human beings adhering to God and contemning created goods. But ends are more powerful than means. Therefore, if one should contemn created goods in order to adhere to God, one's virtue is more praiseworthy because one adheres to God than because one contemns earthly goods. And so the virtues whereby one adheres to God as such, namely, the theological virtues, are more powerful than the moral virtues, whereby one contemns earthly things in order to adhere to God.

And regarding moral virtues, the more one contemns things in order to adhere to God, the more powerful the virtue. But there are three kinds of human goods that human beings can contemn for the sake of God. The lowest kind are external goods; the middle kind are goods of the body; the highest kind are goods of the soul, the chief of which is the will, namely,

---

[16]ST II–II, Q. 81, A. 6.   [17]*Morals* XXXV, 14, n. 28 (PL 76:765).
[18]Ibid., n. 29 (PL 76:766).   [19]Ibid., n. 32 (PL 76:768).

insofar as human beings use all other goods by means of the will. And so, absolutely speaking, the virtue of obedience, which contemns one's own will for the sake of God, is more praiseworthy than other moral virtues, which contemn other particular goods for the sake of God. And so Gregory says in his work *Morals*: "We rightly prefer obedience to sacrifices, since sacrifices offer up the flesh of another, but obedience offers up one's own will."[20]

And so also all other virtuous deeds are meritorious with God because they are done in order to obey God's will. For example, if one were even to undergo martyrdom or to give away all one's possessions to the poor, such deeds could only be meritorious if they were ordered to fulfilling God's will, which rightly belongs to obedience. Just so, neither could such deeds be meritorious if one were to do them without charity, which cannot exist apart from obedience. For 1 Jn. 2:4–5 says: "Those who say they know God but do not keep his commandments are liars. And love of God is truly perfect in those who keep his words." And this is so because friendship causes friends to know and will the same thing.[21]

Reply Obj. 1. Reverence, which shows respect and honor to superiors, generates obedience. And in this regard, different virtues include obedience, although obedience, absolutely speaking, as regards the aspect of command, is a special virtue. Therefore, insofar as reverence of religious superiors generates obedience, the former virtue includes the latter in that respect. And insofar as reverence of parents generates obedience, filial piety includes obedience in that respect. And insofar as reverence of God generates obedience, the latter virtue is included in religion and belongs to devotion, which is the chief act of religion. And so obeying God is in this respect more praiseworthy than offering sacrifices. And obeying God is also more praiseworthy because "the flesh of another is offered in sacrifices, but obedience offers up one's own will," as Gregory says.[22]

But specifically regarding the case about which Samuel was speaking, it would have been better if Saul had obeyed God than if he, contrary to God's command, had offered the fat animals of the Amalekites in sacrifice.[23]

Reply Obj. 2. All virtuous acts belong to obedience insofar as they are done in response to commands. Therefore, Gregory says that obedience sows all the virtues in our mind and preserves them insofar as virtuous acts operate causally or dispositively to generate and preserve virtues.

But there are two reasons why it does not follow that obedience, absolutely speaking, has priority over all the other virtues. The first

---

[20]Ibid., n. 28 (PL 76:765).   [21]Cf. Cicero, *On Friendship* 17.
[22]*Morals* XXXV, 14, n. 28 (PL 76:765).   [23]1 Sam. 15:23, 26.

reason, indeed, is because one can perform virtuous acts without advert-ing to the aspect of command, even though the acts fall under a command. And so if a virtue be one whose object by nature has priority over a com-mand, we say that such a virtue by nature has priority over obedience. For example, this is clearly the case regarding the virtue of faith, which makes the supremacy of God's authority known to us, and this authority gives him the power to command. The second reason is because the infusion of grace and virtues can precede, even temporally, every kind of virtuous act. And so obedience has neither temporal nor natural priority over all the other virtues.

Reply Obj. 3. There are two kinds of good. One is the kind that human beings are necessarily obliged to do (e.g., to love God and suchlike). And human beings should never omit such goods for the sake of obedience. But the other kind human beings are not necessarily obliged to do. And human beings should sometimes omit such good deeds for the sake of obedience, which they are necessarily obliged to observe, since they should not commit sin in order to do good deeds. And yet, as Gregory says in the same place: "Those who prohibit their subjects any one good, need to allow them many others, lest the spirit of obedient subjects completely wither if it be starved by the complete denial of all goods."[24] And so obe-dience and other goods can recompense the loss of one good.

FOURTH ARTICLE
Should One Obey God in All Things?

We thus proceed to the fourth inquiry. It seems that one should not obey God in all things, for the following reasons:

Obj. 1. Mt. 9:30–1 says that the Lord commanded two blind men he had cured: " 'Tell no one.' But they, going away, broadcast the story about him throughout the region." And yet the Gospel does not blame them for that. Therefore, it seems that we are not obliged to obey God in all things.

Obj. 2. No one is obliged to do anything contrary to virtue. But some of God's commands are contrary to virtue. For example, God com-manded Abraham to kill his innocent son (Gen. 22:2) and the Jews to steal property of the Egyptians (Ex. 11:2), which commands are contrary to justice, and Hosea to take an adulterous wife (Hos. 1:2; 3:1), which command is contrary to chastity. Therefore, one should not obey God in all things.

Obj. 3. Those who obey God conform their wills to his even in the object willed. But we are not obliged to conform our will to God's

---

[24]*Morals* XXXV, 14, n. 29 (PL 76:766).

regarding everything in the object willed, as I have maintained before.[25] Therefore, human beings are not obliged to obey God in all things.

On the contrary, Ex. 24:7 says: "We shall do all the things the Lord has spoken, and we shall obey him."

I answer that as I have said before,[26] the commands of superiors move obedient subjects to act, as natural agents cause things of nature to move. But as God is the primary cause of the movement of everything moved physically, so also is he the primary cause of the movement of all wills, as is evident from what I have said before.[27] And so as natural necessity subjects all things of nature to God's causal activity, so also a requirement of justice obliges all created wills to obey his commands.

Reply Obj. 1. The Lord did not tell the blind men to keep quiet about the miracle as if intending the force of God's command to oblige them. Rather, as Gregory says in his work *Morals,*[28] "He gave an example to his servants to imitate him, that they themselves should desire to keep their virtues hidden. And yet the disciples, contrary to their desire, would become celebrated in order that others profit by their example."

Reply Obj. 2. God does not act contrary to nature, since "the nature of everything is what God causes in it," as a gloss on Rom. 11:24 says.[29] Rather, God causes some things contrary to the ordinary course of nature. Just so, God cannot command anything contrary to virtue, since the virtue and rectitude of a human will consist chiefly of it being conformed to God's will and obeying his commands, although the commands are contrary to the usual way of virtue. Accordingly, therefore, God's command to Abraham to kill his innocent son was not contrary to justice, since God is the author of life and death.

Likewise, God's command to the Jews to take the property of the Egyptians was not contrary to justice, since all property belongs to him, and he gives it to whomever he wants.

Likewise, God's command to Hosea to take an adulterous wife was not contrary to chastity, since God himself ordains human generation, and the means of sexual union of man and woman that God appoints is a fit means.

And so the aforementioned individuals evidently did not sin either in obeying God or in willing to obey him.

Reply Obj. 3. Although human beings are not always obliged to will what God wills, they are nonetheless obliged to will what God wants them to will. But God's commands make the latter most known to human

---

[25]ST I–II, Q. 19, A. 10.   [26]ST II–II, Q. 104, A. 1.   [27]ST I–II, Q. 9, A. 6
[28]*Morals* XIX, 23, n. 36 (PL 76:120).   [29]*Glossa ordinaria*, on Rom. 11:24 (PL 114:508); Peter Lombard, *Glossa* (PL 191:1488).

beings. And so human beings are obliged to obey his commands in all things.

FIFTH ARTICLE
Are Subjects Obliged to Obey Their Superiors in All Things?

We thus proceed to the fifth inquiry. It seems that subjects are obliged to obey their superiors in all things, for the following reasons:

Obj. 1. The Apostle says in Col. 3:20: "Children, obey your parents in everything." And v. 22 adds: "Slaves, obey your earthly masters in all things." Therefore, by like reasoning, other subjects should obey their religious superiors in all things.

Obj. 2. Religious superiors are intermediaries between God and subjects, as Dt. 5:5 says: "I [Moses] was a go-between and intermediary between God and you at that time, to declare his words to you." But there are intermediaries only between two ends. Therefore, we should regard religious superiors' commands as God's commands. And so also the Apostle says in Gal. 4:14: "You received me as an angel of God, as Christ Jesus." And he says in 1 Th. 2:13: "When you received the word of God that you heard from us, you received it as the word of God, as it truly is, and not as human words." Therefore, as human beings should obey God in all things, so also should they obey religious superiors in all things.

Obj. 3. As religious by their profession vow poverty and chastity, so also do they vow obedience. But religious are obliged to observe chastity and poverty in all respects. Therefore, they should likewise obey religious superiors in all things.

On the contrary, Acts 5:29 says: "One should obey God rather than human beings." But the commands of religious superiors are sometimes contrary to God's commands. Therefore, one should not obey religious superiors in all things.

I answer that, as I have said,[30] as the power of natural agents necessarily causes change in things of nature, a requirement of justice causes obedient subjects to act at the command of superiors. But there are two ways in which natural agents may fail to cause things of nature to change. Such may happen in one way because the stronger power of another cause prevents change. For example, fire does not burn wood if the stronger power of water should keep the wood from burning. It may happen in a second way because of a deficient relation of the changeable thing to the cause of change, since the changeable thing is subject to the cause in one but not all respects. For example, liquids are sometimes subject to the

---

[30]ST II–II, Q. 104, AA. 1, 4.

process of heating as to being heated but not as to being vaporized or destroyed.

And there are likewise two ways in which subjects may not be obliged to obey superiors in all things. This can happen in one way because of the command of a higher power. For example, a gloss on Rom. 13:2, "Those who resist bring damnation on themselves," says: "If a provincial official should command something, is it not obvious that you should do nothing if the command runs counter to a command of the governor? Also, if the governor himself should command one thing, and the emperor another, is it not obvious that you should obey the emperor and disobey the governor? Therefore, if the emperor should command one thing, and God another, you should obey God and disobey the emperor."[31]

Subjects are not obliged to obey superiors in a second way if their superiors command things regarding which the subjects are not subject to the superiors. For example, Seneca says in his work *On Benefits*: "One errs if one thinks that a slave's status involves the whole human being. A slave's better part is excluded from a master's control. Slaves' bodies are subject and ascribed to their masters, but slaves' inner selves indeed belong to themselves."[32] And so human beings are obliged to obey only God, not human beings, regarding things that belong to interior acts of the will.

And human beings are obliged to obey human beings regarding external deeds that require the use of the body to perform. But human beings are obliged to obey only God, not human beings, even regarding such things insofar as the things belong to the body's nature (e.g., things proper to sustaining the body and to begetting offspring), since all human beings are by nature equal. And so slaves are not obliged to obey their masters, nor children their parents, in regard to contracting marriage or observing virginity, or such like.

But regarding things that pertain to the disposition of their activities and of human affairs, subjects are obliged to obey their superiors insofar as the latter are constituted such. For example, soldiers are obliged to obey their commanders in military matters, slaves their masters in performing servile tasks, children their parents in matters of life training and household chores, and the like.

Reply Obj. 1. We should understand the words of the Apostle, "in everything," to refer to things proper to the legitimate authority of parents or masters.

---

[31]Peter Lombard, *Glossa*, on Rom. 13:2 (PL 191:1505).
[32]*On Benefits* III, 20.

Reply Obj. 2. Human beings are absolutely subject to God regarding all things, both internal and external. And so human beings are obliged to obey God in all things. But human beings are subject to their superiors regarding particular things in fixed ways, not regarding all things. And regarding those particular things, superiors are intermediaries between God and their subjects. And regarding other things, human beings are directly subject to God, who instructs them by the natural law or Scripture.

Reply Obj. 3. Religious promise obedience regarding observance of their congregation's rule, which subjects them to their religious superiors. And so religious are obliged to obey their religious superiors only regarding matters that may belong to observance of the rule. And this is enough obedience for salvation. But if religious should wish also to obey in other matters, this will belong to greater perfection, provided that the things be not contrary to God's command or profession of the rule, since the latter obedience is unlawful.

Therefore, we distinguish three kinds of obedience: one kind sufficient for salvation, namely, obedience regarding obligatory matters; a second, perfect kind, namely, obedience regarding all lawful matters; a third, indiscriminate kind, namely, obedience even regarding unlawful matters.

SIXTH ARTICLE
Are Christians Obliged to Obey Secular Authorities?

We thus proceed to the sixth inquiry. It seems that Christians are not obliged to obey secular authorities, for the following reasons:

Obj. 1. A gloss on Mt. 17:26, "Therefore, the sons are free," says: "If the sons of a reigning king are free in every kingdom, then the sons of the king to whom all kingdoms are subject should be free in every kingdom."[33] But faith in Christ constitutes Christians sons of God, as Jn. 1:12 says: "He gave the power to become sons of God to those who believe in his name." Therefore, Christians are not obliged to obey secular authorities.

Obj. 2. Rom. 7:4 says: "The body of Christ made you dead to the law," and the text is speaking about the divine law of the Old Testament. But human law, which subjects human beings to secular authorities, is a lesser law than the divine law of the Old Testament. Therefore, much more are human beings, by being constituted members of the body of Christ, freed from the law of subjection that binds them to secular rulers.

---

[33]*Glossa ordinaria*, on Mt. 17:25 (PL 114:145).

Obj. 3. Human beings are not obliged to obey robbers, who use force against them. But Augustine says in *The City of God*: "If justice is absent, what are kingdoms but large-scale robberies?"[34] Therefore, since the secular power of rulers is very often unjustly exercised or unjustly usurped, it seems that Christians need not obey secular rulers.

On the contrary, Tit. 3:1 says: "Warn them to be subject to rulers and authorities." And 1 Pet. 2:13–4 says: "For the sake of God, be subject to every human creature, whether to kings as supreme rulers or to governors as the rulers' deputies."

I answer that faith in Christ is the source and cause of justice, as Rom. 3:22 speaks of "the righteousness of God through faith in Jesus Christ." And so faith in Christ confirms rather than takes away the order of justice. But the order of justice requires that subjects obey their superiors, since stability in human affairs could not otherwise be maintained. And so faith in Christ does not excuse the faithful from being obliged to obey secular rulers.

Reply Obj. 1. As I have said before,[35] the servitude that subjects one human being to another belongs to the body, not to the soul, which remains free. But now, in the condition of this life, the grace of Christ frees us from deficiencies of the soul, not from those of the body, as the Apostle makes clear about himself in Rom. 7:25: "I serve God's law with my reason, but I serve the law of sin with my flesh." And so those whom grace makes children of God are freed from the spiritual servitude of sin but not from bodily servitude, which holds them bound to their earthly masters, as a gloss on 1 Tim. 6:1, "Let all under the yoke of slavery," etc., says.[36]

Reply Obj. 2. The Old Law prefigures the New Testament and so had to cease when the truth of the New Testament came into force. But there is no comparison between the Old Law and human law, which subjects human beings to other human beings. And yet the divine law also obliges human beings to obey human beings.

Reply Obj. 3. Human beings are obliged to obey secular rulers insofar as the order of justice requires. And so if secular rulers have usurped power and have no just authority, or if secular rulers command unjust things, subjects are not obliged to obey them, except, perhaps incidentally, in order to avoid scandal or danger.

---

[34]*The City of God* IV, 4 (PL 41:115).

[35]ST II–II, Q. 104, A. 5.

[36]*Glossa ordinaria*, on 1 Tim. 6:1 (PL 114:631); Peter Lombard, *Glossa* (PL 192:375).

Question 60
On Legal Judgment

[This question is divided into six articles, one of which is translated here.]

SIXTH ARTICLE
Does Usurpation Render Legal Judgments Unjust?

We thus proceed to the sixth inquiry. It seems that usurpation does not render legal judgments unjust, for the following reasons:

Obj. 1. Justice is a rectitude regarding things to be done. But truth loses nothing by reason of those who happen to utter it. Rather, truth suffers by reason of those who should but do not accept it. Therefore, justice likewise loses nothing by reason of the person who determines what is just, which belongs to the nature of legal judgment.

Obj. 2. It belongs to legal judgment to punish sins. But we read that some are praised for having punished sins, although they had no legal authority over those they punished. For example, Ex. 2:11–2 praises Moses for killing an Egyptian. And Num. 25:7–14 praises Phinehas, the son of Eleazar, for killing Zimbri, the son of Salu, about which Ps. 106:31 says: "And it was reckoned to him [Phinehas] as righteousness." Therefore, usurpation of judicial power does not partake of injustice.

Obj. 3. We distinguish spiritual power from earthly power. But religious superiors holding spiritual power sometimes interpose themselves regarding matters that belong to earthly power. Therefore, usurped judicial power is not unlawful.

Obj. 4. As lawful authority is required to render proper legal judgments, so also are just and wise judges, as is evident from what I have said before.[1] But we do not say that legal judgments are unjust if judges lacking habitual justice or knowledge of the law happen to be the ones who pass judgment. Therefore, neither will legal judgments by usurpers, who lack lawful authority, be always unjust.

On the contrary, Rom. 14:4 says: "Who are you to judge the servant of another?"

I answer that since judges should render judgments according to written laws, as I have said,[2] they in a way interpret the words of the laws by applying the words to particular cases. But since it belongs to the same authority to interpret laws and to establish laws, as only public authority can establish laws, so also only public authority, which indeed extends to

---

[1]ST II–II, Q. 60, A. 1, *ad* 1 and 3; A. 2.   [2]Ibid., A. 5.

those subject to the community, can render legal judgments. And so as it would be unjust for anyone to force another to observe laws not sanctioned by public authority, so also is it unjust for anyone to force others to carry out legal judgments not sanctioned by public authority.

Reply Obj. 1. Uttering truths signifies no compulsion on hearers to accept them. Rather, individual hearers are free to accept or reject the statements, as they choose. But legal judgments signify a form of compulsion. And so it is unjust for anyone not holding public authority to render legal judgments regarding others.

Reply Obj. 2. Moses seems to have killed the Egyptian under the inspiration of God's authority, so to speak, as Acts 7:25 indicates: "By striking the Egyptian, Moses thought that his brethren understood that the Lord would deliver Israel by Moses' hand." Or one can say that Moses killed the Egyptian in defense of the victim, with the due moderation of blameless defense. And so Ambrose says in his work *On Duties* that "those who do not avert injury to a companion when they can are implicated in the sin as much as those who inflict the injury," and he introduces the example of Moses killing the Egyptian.[3]

Or one can say, as Augustine does in his work *Questions on the Heptateuch,*[4] that "as the fertility of useless plants deserves praise before their seeds bear fruit, so the deed of Moses was indeed sinful but produced a sign of great fertility," namely, as the deed was the sign of the power whereby he was about to deliver the people.

And we should say that Phinehas, moved by zeal for God, acted under divine inspiration. Or we should say that Phinehas did it because he, although not yet the high priest, was nonetheless the son of the high priest and enjoyed the same power to render legal judgments as the other priests God empowered.[5]

Reply Obj. 3. Secular power is subject to spiritual power as the body is subject to the soul. And so the power of legal judgment is not usurped if a spiritual superior interposes himself about earthly affairs regarding matters in which secular power is subject to him, or that secular power relinquishes to him.[6]

---

[3]*On Duties* I, 36, n. 178 (PL 16:75).   [4]*Questions on the Heptateuch*, q. 2, on Ex. 2:12 (PL 34:597).   [5]Cf. Ex. 22:20; Lev. 20; Dt. 13 and 17.

[6]Cf. ST II–II, Q. 147, A. 3: "As it belongs to secular rulers to prescribe legal regulations specifying the natural law with regard to matters that pertain to the common benefit in earthly affairs, so also does it belong to church superiors to prescribe by legal regulations things that pertain to the common benefit of the faithful in spiritual goods."

Reply Obj. 4. Habitual knowledge and habitual justice are perfections of individual persons. And so it is not by reason of their lack that people call a legal judgment usurped, but because the latter lacks public authority, from which it has the power to compel.

Question 42
On Rebellion

[This question is divided into two articles, one of which is translated here.]

SECOND ARTICLE
Is Rebellion Always a Mortal Sin?

We thus proceed to the second inquiry. It seems that rebellion is not always a mortal sin, for the following reasons:

Obj. 1. Rebellion signifies "a military insurrection," as a gloss on 2 Cor. 12:20 makes clear.[1] But war is not always a mortal sin and sometimes just and lawful, as I have maintained before.[2] Therefore, much more can there be rebellion without mortal sin.

Obj. 2. Rebellion is a form of discord, as I have said.[3] But there can be discord without mortal sin, and sometimes without any sin. Therefore, there can also be rebellion without mortal sin or any sin.

Obj. 3. We praise those who deliver a people from the power of a tyrant. But this cannot be easily done without a popular insurrection if some of the people strive to maintain the tyrant, and others strive to unseat him. Therefore, there can be rebellion without sin.

On the contrary, the Apostle in 2 Cor. 12:20 prohibits rebellion along with other sins that are mortal. Therefore, rebellion is a mortal sin.

I answer that, as I have said,[4] rebellion is contrary to the unity of citizens (i.e., the people) of a political community or kingdom. But Augustine says in *The City of God* that wise persons define the people as "a popular assembly legally constituted and bound by common interest, not any popular assembly."[5] And so the unity contrary to rebellion is evidently one of law and common interest. Therefore, rebellion is obviously contrary to both justice and the common good. And so rebellion is by its nature a mortal sin and more serious insofar as the common

---

[1]Peter Lombard, *Glossa*, on 2 Cor. 12:20 (PL 192:89).

[2]ST II–II: Q. 40, A. 1; Q. 41, A. 1.   [3]Ibid., Q. 42, A. 1, *ad* 3.

[4]Ibid., A. 1.   [5]*The City of God* II, 21, n. 2 (PL 41:67).

good, which rebellion subverts, surpasses private goods, which private disputes subvert.

And the leaders of rebellions indeed first and chiefly incur the sin of rebellion, and they sin most seriously. Second, supporters of rebellion who disturb the common good also incur the sin of rebellion. But we should not call those resisting the rebels and defending the common good seditious, just as we do not call those defending themselves brawlers, as I have said before.[6]

Reply Obj. 1. Lawful war is waged for the benefit of the community, as I have said before.[7] But rebellion is waged against the common good of the people. And so rebellion is always a mortal sin.

Reply Obj. 2. Discord from what is not clearly good can occur without sin. But discord from what is clearly good cannot happen without sin. And rebellion, which is contrary to the unity of the people, something clearly good, is the latter kind of discord.

Reply Obj. 3. Tyrannical governance is unjust, since it is ordered to the private good of the ruler, not to the common good, as the Philosopher makes clear in the *Politics*[8] and the *Ethics*.[9] And so disturbance of such governance does not have the character of rebellion, except, perhaps, in cases where the tyrant's governance is so inordinately disturbed that the subject people suffer greater harm from the resulting disturbance than from the tyrant's governance. Rather, tyrants, who by seeking greater domination incite discontent and rebellion in the people subject to them, are the rebels. For governance is tyrannical when ordered to the ruler's own good to the detriment of the people.

---

[6]ST II–II, Q. 41, A. 1.   [7]Ibid., Q. 40, A. 1.
[8]*Politics* III, 5 (1279b6–10).   [9]*Ethics* VIII, 10 (1160b8–12).

7

Tolerance and Church–State Relations

In ST II–II, Q. 10, Thomas endorses very limited tolerance of unbelievers. They should not be compelled to embrace the faith, but they should be compelled not to hinder the faith (A. 8). Jewish rites should be tolerated, but the rites of other unbelievers should not (A. 11).

In Q. 11, Thomas approves complete intolerance of public heresy. Public authorities are urged to put persistent heretics to death (A. 3).

In the two selections from the CS on church–state relations, Thomas recognizes the autonomy of the secular power in matters pertaining to civic well-being (except in the Papal States, where the pope has secular power) but subjects the secular power to the spiritual power in matters pertaining to the salvation of souls. See also ST II–II, Q. 104, A. 6, and ST II–II, Q. 60, ad 3, in Chapter 6.

ST II–II
Question 10
On Unbelief in General

[This question is divided into twelve articles, two of which are translated here.]

EIGHTH ARTICLE
Should Unbelievers Be Compelled to Embrace the Faith?

We thus proceed to the eighth inquiry. It seems that unbelievers should not be compelled to embrace the faith, for the following reasons:

Obj. 1. Mt. 13:28–9 says that the servants of the master of a household in whose field weeds were sown asked him: "Do you want us to go and gather up the weeds?" And he replied: "No, lest you in gathering the weeds perhaps pull up the grain as well." And Chrysostom comments on the text: "The Lord in saying this forbad killing heretics. It is indeed unfitting to kill them, since, to do so, you would need to kill many saints at the same time."[1] Therefore, it seems by like reasoning that no unbelievers should be compelled to embrace the faith.

---

[1] *Homilies on the Gospel of Matthew*, homily 46, nn. 1, 2 (PG 58:477).

Obj. 2. The *Decretum* says: "The holy synod commanded, secondly, that no Jews be forced to embrace the faith."[2] Therefore, no other unbeliever should by like reasoning be forced to embrace the faith.

Obj. 3. Augustine says that unwilling persons, moreover, can "believe only if they want to."[3] But the will cannot be compelled. Therefore, it seems that unbelievers should not be compelled to embrace the faith.

Obj. 4. Ez. 18:23, 32 says in the person of God: "I do not wish the death of sinners." But we should conform our will to God's, as I have said before.[4] Therefore, we should also not wish to kill unbelievers.

On the contrary, Lk. 14:23 says: "Go out into the roads and byways and force them to enter, in order that my house may be filled." But human beings by faith enter God's house, that is, the church. Therefore, some should be compelled to embrace the faith.

I answer that there are some unbelievers who never embraced the faith (e.g., pagans and Jews). And such unbelievers should never be compelled to embrace the faith, to believe, since belief is proper to the individual's own will. But the faithful should compel them, if possible, not to hinder the faith, whether by blasphemies or wicked influences or open persecution. And so the Christian faithful often wage war against unbelievers in order to compel the latter not to hinder the faith, not indeed to compel them to embrace the faith, since unbelievers would remain free to decide whether they wanted to believe even if the faithful were to conquer them and hold them captive.

And there are other unbelievers who once accepted and professed the faith (e.g., heretics or any kind of apostates). And we should compel such unbelievers, even by physical force, to fulfill what they promised and to hold fast to what they once accepted.

Reply Obj. 1. Some have understood the scriptural text to prohibit the killing of heretics, although not indeed their excommunication, as the cited text of Chrysostom makes clear. And Augustine says of himself in his letter to Vincent: "My opinion at first was that no one should be compelled into Christian unity, that unbelievers should be brought into that unity by exhortation and fought by discussion. But the examples cited by those arguing against that opinion, not their words of refutation, won me over. For fear of the laws was so helpful that many said: 'Thanks be to the Lord, who freed us from our chains.'"[5] Therefore, the meaning of

---

[2]Gratian, *Decretum* I, dist. 45, c. 5.

[3]*Commentary on the Gospel of John*, on 6:44, tr. 26, n. 2 (PL 35:1607).

[4]ST I–II, Q. 19, AA. 9, 10.

[5]*Letter 93*, to the Donatist Vincent, c. 5, nn. 17, 18 (PL 33:329–30).

the Lord's statement (Mt. 13:30), "Let both the weeds and the grain grow until the harvest," is clear by what he adds: "Lest in gathering the weeds, you perhaps pull up the grain as well." And as Augustine says against Parmenian: "This shows sufficiently that rigorous discipline flourishes when fear of pulling up the grain does not exist, that is, when the sin of each is so known and appears so despicable to all that there are either absolutely no defenders of the sin or no defenders who could give rise to schism."[6]

Reply Obj. 2. Jews should never be compelled to embrace the faith if they have never accepted it. But if they have, "it is fitting that they of necessity be compelled to maintain the faith," as the same Chapter Five says.

Reply Obj. 3. As "making vows to God is a matter of free will, but observing them a matter of obligation,"[7] so accepting the faith is a matter of free will, but maintaining it once accepted a matter of obligation. And so heretics should be compelled to maintain the faith. For Augustine says in a letter to Count Boniface: "Why are they accustomed to exclaim: 'One is free to believe or not. Whom did Christ force to believe?'? Let them recognize in the case of Paul one whom Christ first compelled and then instructed."[8]

Reply Obj. 4. Augustine says in the same letter to Count Boniface: "None of us wishes any heretic to perish. But the house of David would not otherwise have deserved to enjoy peace unless his son Absalom were to have been crushed in the war Absalom waged against him. Thus does the Catholic Church, when it gains some in losing others, ease the sorrow of her maternal heart in liberating so many people."[9]

ELEVENTH ARTICLE
Should the Religious Rites of Unbelievers Be Tolerated?

We thus proceed to the eleventh inquiry. It seems that the religious rites of unbelievers should not be tolerated, for the following reasons:

Obj. 1. Unbelievers evidently sin when they observe their religious rites. But those who do not prevent sin when they could, seem to consent to sin, as a gloss on Rom. 1:32, "Both those who do evil and those who consent to others doing evil," etc., maintains.[10] Therefore, those who tolerate the religious rites of unbelievers sin.

---

[6]*Response to the Letter of Parmenian* III, 2, n. 13 (PL 43:92).

[7]Peter Lombard, *Glossa*, on Ps. 76:11 (PL 191:709).

[8]*Letter 185*, to Count Boniface, c. 6, n. 22 (PL 33:803).

[9]Ibid., c. 8, n. 32 (PL 33:807).

[10]*Glossa ordinaria*, on Rom. 1:32 (PL 114:474); Peter Lombard, *Glossa* (PL 191:1336).

Obj. 2. Jewish religious rites are related to idolatry, for a gloss on Gal. 5:1, "Do not again become subject to the yoke of servitude," says: "The servitude of the [Old] Law is as heavy as that of idolatry."[11] But no one would maintain that some should be permitted to practice idolatry. Rather, Christian rulers first closed, then destroyed, pagan temples, as Augustine relates in *The City of God*.[12] Therefore, Jewish religious rites should also not be tolerated.

Obj. 3. The sin of unbelief is the greatest, as I have said before.[13] But civil law does not tolerate and punishes other sins (e.g., adultery, theft, and such like). Therefore, civil law should also not tolerate the religious rites of unbelievers.

On the contrary, Gregory in a decretal says regarding the Jews: "Let them be legally free to observe and celebrate their holy days, as they and their ancestors have for so long observed and celebrated them in worship up to now."[14]

I answer that human governance derives from God's and should be modeled on his. But God, although all-powerful and supremely good, nonetheless allows some evils to take place in the universe, evils that he could prevent, lest greater goods be lost if the evils were removed, or lest still worse evils result. Therefore, likewise in human governance, rulers rightly tolerate certain evils lest certain goods be prevented, or even worse evils incurred. Just so, Augustine says in his work *On Order*: "Do away with prostitutes in human society, and you will stir up all sorts of things out of sexual lust."[15] Therefore, although unbelievers sin regarding their religious rites, rulers can tolerate the rites either to bring about good from them or to avoid evil.

And Jews observe their religious rites, which in former times prefigured the true faith that we profess. And so Jews observing their religious rites produce good, namely, that our enemies bear witness to our faith, and that their rites represent to us in figures, as it were, what we believe. And so Jews are allowed to practice their religious rites.

But rulers should in no way tolerate the religious rites of other unbelievers, who contribute no truth or benefit, except, perhaps, in order to avoid such evils as possible resulting scandal or discontent, or in order to avoid preventing the salvation of those who will, little by little, be converted to the faith if they are tolerated in this way. For example, the

---

[11]Peter Lombard, *Glossa*, on Gal. 5:1 (PL 192:152).

[12]*The City of God* XVIII, 54, n. 1 (PL 41:620).   [13]ST II–II, Q. 10, A. 3.

[14]Actually, Gratian, *Decretum* I, dist. 45, c. 3.

[15]*On Order* II, 4, n. 12 (PL 32:1000).

church has at times tolerated the religious rites of heretics and pagans for the latter reason when there were very many unbelievers.

Reply Objs. 1–3. The foregoing makes clear the reply to the objections.

Question 11
On Heresy

[This question is divided into four articles, one of which is translated here.]

THIRD ARTICLE
Should Heretics Be Tolerated?

We thus proceed to the third inquiry. It seems that heretics should be tolerated, for the following reasons:

Obj. 1. The Apostle says in 2 Tim. 2:24–6: "Servants of God should be meek, modestly correcting those who resist the truth, so that God may at any moment grant them repentance to know the truth, and that they may escape the snares of the devil." But if we do not tolerate heretics and hand them over to death, we take away the opportunity for them to repent. Therefore, such seems to be contrary to the Apostle's command.

Obj. 2. Things necessary in the church should be tolerated. But there need to be heretics in the church, for the Apostle says in 1 Cor. 11:19: "Heresies need to exist in order that the upright also be manifested among you." Therefore, it seems that heretics should be tolerated.

Obj. 3. The Lord commanded his servants in Mt. 13:30 that they allow the weeds to grow until harvest time, that is, the end of the world, as v. 39 explains. But the weeds signify heretics, as the saints explain.[1] Therefore, heretics should be tolerated.

On the contrary, the Apostle says in Tit. 3:10–1: "After correcting heretics once or twice, avoid them, for you know that such persons are wicked."

I answer that we should consider two points regarding heretics: one, indeed, regarding themselves; the other regarding the church. Regarding themselves, they by their sins indeed deserved to be both separated from the church by excommunication and excluded from the world by death. For it is a more serious crime to corrupt the faith, which gives life to the soul, than to counterfeit money, which supports earthly life. And so if secular rulers justly put counterfeiters and other felons immediately to

---

[1]E.g., Chrysostom, *Homilies on the Gospel of Matthew*, homily 46, n. 1 (PG 58:475).

death, much more could heretics be both excommunicated and justly killed immediately upon conviction of heresy.

But the church is merciful in order to convert those in error. And so the church condemns heretics only after admonishing them once or twice, as the Apostle teaches,[2] not immediately. And later, if heretics should still persist, the church, despairing of their conversion, provides for the salvation of others by separating the heretics from the church by excommunication and in addition relinquishes them to the judgment of secular courts, to separate them from the world by death. For Jerome says,[3] and the *Decretum* maintains[4]: "Rotten flesh should be cut off, and mangy sheep should be driven out of the sheepfolds, lest the whole house (the mass, the material substance, the animals) catch fire, be corrupted, rot, perish. Arius was a tiny spark in Alexandria, but his flame set fire to the whole world because he was not immediately suppressed."

Reply Obj. 1. That heretics be admonished once or twice belongs to the recommended modesty. But if heretics are unwilling to repent, we should then consider them wicked, as the cited authority of the Apostle makes clear.

Reply Obj. 2. The benefit that heresies produce, namely, that they commend the constancy of the faithful, as the Apostle says,[5] and that we cut away sloth by more carefully contemplating the sacred Scriptures, as Augustine says, is contrary to the aim of heretics. Rather, they intend to corrupt the faith, which result is most harmful. And so we should regard what they intrinsically intend, so as to exclude them, rather than regard what is contrary to their intention, so as to support them.

Reply Obj. 3. The *Decretum* holds: "Excommunication and inflicting death are different things. For persons are excommunicated 'in order that their spirit be saved on the day of the Lord,' as the Apostle says[6]."[7]

And if death should completely exterminate heretics, this is likewise compatible with the cited command of the Lord. For we should understand this command to apply to cases where we cannot pull up the weeds without pulling up the grain, as I said before when I was treating of unbelievers in general.[8]

---

[2] Tit. 3:10–1, quoted in the section *On the contrary.*

[3] *Commentary on Galatians* III, on 5:9 (PL 26: 403).

[4] Gratian, *Decretum* II, cause 24, q. 3, c. 16.

[5] *Commentary on Genesis, against the Manicheans* I, 1, n. 2 (PL 34:173).

[6] 1 Cor. 5:5.

[7] Gratian, *Decretum* II, cause 24, q. 3, c. 37.

[8] ST II–II, Q. 10, A. 8, *ad* 1.

CS II
Distinction 44
On the Relation of the Spiritual Power to the Secular Power

Explanation of the Text

Text. "We should consider next whether we have the power to sin from God or ourselves," etc.

Obj. 4. The spiritual power is higher than the secular power. Therefore, if we should obey the greater power more, a spiritual superior could always release his subjects from the obligation to obey the secular power. But this conclusion is false.

Reply Obj. 4. Both the spiritual power and the secular power derive from God's power. And so the secular power is subject to the spiritual power insofar as God has subjected the former to the latter, namely, in matters pertaining to the salvation of souls. And so we should obey the spiritual power rather than the secular power in such matters. But in matters pertaining to civic welfare, we should obey the secular power rather than the spiritual power, as Mt. 22:21 says: "Render to Caesar the things that are Caesar's." A possible exception is when the secular power is joined to the spiritual power. Such is the case of the pope, who holds the supremacy of both powers, namely, the spiritual and the temporal, by the disposition of him who is priest and king according to the order of Melchizedek, of him who is the king of kings and the lord of lords, whose power is not taken away, and whose kingdom is eternally indestructible. Amen.

CS IV
Distinction 37
On the Church's Power to Command the Secular Power

Explanation of the Text

Text. "God's holy church . . . has no sword except the spiritual sword."

Comment. On the contrary, Bernard says to Pope Eugene III that the church has both swords.[1] And we should say that the church has the spiritual sword only regarding what it can accomplish by itself, but the church in addition has the temporal sword regarding what it can command, since the temporal sword should be unsheathed at the church's bidding, as Bernard says.

---

[1] Bernard of Clairvaux, *On Contemplation* IV, 3 (PL 182:775).

8

Practical Wisdom and Statecraft

In ST II–II, Q. 47, Thomas argues that practical wisdom includes political wisdom, the wisdom involved in governance (A. 10), and that political wisdom differs specifically from the wisdom involved in an individual's personal life (A. 11).

In ST II–II, Q. 50, Thomas argues that kingly (monarchical) wisdom in governance is a special kind of practical wisdom, the wisdom to govern, and the archetype of the wisdom in other forms of governance (A. 1), and that subjects need a related specific kind of wisdom, the wisdom to direct themselves to obey their rulers (A. 2).

In the selections from the treatise On Kingship, *Thomas explains why it is natural for human beings to live in political communities (I, 1), and how to prevent kings from becoming tyrants and what to do with kings who do (I, 6). To complement the treatment of tyranny here, see ST I–II, Q. 105, A. 1, in chapter 2. The latter selection, written later, complements the former.*

ST II–II
Question 47
On Practical Wisdom as Such

[This question is divided into sixteen articles, two of which are translated here.]

TENTH ARTICLE
Does Practical Wisdom Include the Governance of Peoples?

We thus proceed to the tenth inquiry. It seems that practical wisdom extends only to governance of oneself, not to the governance of peoples, for the following reasons:

Obj. 1. The Philosopher says in the *Ethics* that virtue related to the common good is justice.[1] But practical wisdom differs from justice. Therefore, practical wisdom is not related to the common good.

Obj. 2. Those who seek and act for their own good seem to be practically wise. But those who seek communal goods often neglect their own. Therefore, the latter are not practically wise.

---

[1] *Ethics* V, 1 (1129b17–9).

Obj. 3. We contradistinguish practical wisdom from moderation and courage. But we seem to speak of moderation and courage only in relation to one's own good. Therefore, we should also speak of practical wisdom in the same way.

On the contrary, the Lord says in Mt. 24:45: "Who, do you think, are the faithful and prudent servants whom the Lord will place in charge of his household?"

I answer that the Philosopher says in the *Ethics* that certain thinkers held that practical wisdom extends only to one's own good, not the common good.[2] And they said this because they thought it necessary for human beings to seek nothing but their own good. But this opinion is contrary to charity, which "does not seek one's own benefit," as 1 Cor. 13:5 says. And so also the Apostle says about himself in 1 Cor. 10:33: "Not seeking my own benefit but seeking what benefits many, that they be saved." The opinion is also contrary to right reason, which esteems the common good as superior to one's own.

Therefore, since it belongs to practical reason to deliberate rightly, judge, and command regarding the means to attain our requisite end, practical wisdom is evidently related both to the private good of individuals and to the common good of the people.

Reply Obj. 1. The Philosopher in the cited text is speaking about moral virtue. And as we call all moral virtue related to the common good legal justice, so we call practical wisdom related to the common good political wisdom. Thus political wisdom is related to legal justice as practical wisdom, absolutely speaking, is related to moral virtue.

Reply Obj. 2. Those who seek the common good of the people also consequently seek their own good. This is true for two reasons. The first reason, indeed, is because there can be no good of one's own apart from the common good, whether the common good of a household or a city or a kingdom. And so also Valerius Maximus says that the Romans of old "preferred to be poor in a wealthy regime than wealthy in a poor one."[3] The second reason is because human beings, since they are parts of households and political communities, need to contemplate what is good for themselves by what is practically wise regarding the good of the people. For we understand the right disposition of parts in relation to the whole of which they are parts, since, as Augustine says in his *Confessions*,[4] "every part unbefitting the whole of which it is a part is base."

---

[2]Ibid., VI, 8 (1142a1–2).   [3]*Memorable Deeds and Sayings* IV, 4.
[4]*Confessions* III, 8, n. 15 (PL 32:689).

Reply Obj. 3. Even moderation and courage can be related to the common good, and so laws command things regarding acts of those virtues, as the *Ethics* says.[5] But practical wisdom and justice, which belong to the rational part of the soul, can be more related to the common good, since universal things belong directly to that part of the soul, as individual things belong directly to the sentient part of the soul.

ELEVENTH ARTICLE
Is Practical Wisdom Regarding One's Own Good Specifically the Same as Practical Wisdom Including the Common Good?

We thus proceed to the eleventh inquiry. It seems that practical wisdom regarding one's own good is specifically the same as practical wisdom including the common good, for the following reasons:

Obj. 1. The Philosopher says in the *Ethics* that "we consider political wisdom and practical wisdom the same but not the same as such."[6]

Obj. 2. The Philosopher says in the *Politics* that "good persons and good rulers have the same virtue."[7] But political wisdom belongs most to rulers, who have such virtue as master builders have theirs. Therefore, since practical wisdom is the virtue of good persons, it seems that practical wisdom and political wisdom are the same characteristic disposition.

Obj. 3. Things ordered one to another do not differentiate habits specifically or substantially. But one's own good, which belongs to practical wisdom in an absolute sense, is ordered to the common good, which belongs to political wisdom. Therefore, political wisdom and practical wisdom differ neither specifically nor substantially as habits.

On the contrary, political wisdom, which is ordered to the common good of a political community, and household management, which regards matters pertaining to the common good of a household or a family, and personal management, which regards matters pertaining to the good of only one person, are different fields of expert knowledge. Therefore, by like argument, practical wisdoms also differ specifically by these different subject matters.

I answer that, as I have said before,[8] we distinguish species of habits by differences we note regarding the formal aspect of the habits' objects. But we note the formal aspect of every means in relation to its end, as is clear from what I have said before.[9] And so relations to different ends necessarily distinguish species of habits. But the proper good of individuals and

---

[5]Aristotle, *Ethics* V, 1 (1129b19–25).   [6]Ibid., VI, 7 (1141b23–4).
[7]*Politics* III, 2 (1277a20–1).   [8]ST II–II, Q. 47, A. 5; I–II, Q. 54, A. 2, *ad* 1.
[9]ST I–II: Q. 1, introduction; Q. 102, A. 1.

the good of families and the good of cities and kingdoms are different ends. And so the differences between these ends also of necessity specifically distinguish different kinds of practical wisdom. One kind is practical wisdom in an absolute sense, which is ordered to one's own good; a second kind is household practical wisdom, which is ordered to the common good of a household or family; a third kind is political practical wisdom, which is ordered to the common good of a city or kingdom.

Reply Obj. 1. The Philosopher means to say that political wisdom is the same as practical wisdom ordered to the common good, and not that political wisdom is the same as any practical wisdom regarding the habit's substance. And he indeed calls political wisdom practical by reason of the general nature of practical wisdom, namely, as political wisdom consists of right reasoning about actions, and he calls political wisdom political by reason of being ordered to the common good.

Reply Obj. 2. The Philosopher in the same text says that "it belongs to good persons to be fit to rule well and to be ruled well."[10] And so the virtue of a good person includes the virtue of a ruler. But the virtue of rulers and that of subjects differ specifically, just as the virtue of men and that of women do, as he says in the same text.[11]

Reply Obj. 3. Even different ends ordered one to another distinguish species of habits. For example, the ends of knights, soldiers, and citizens differ specifically even though their ends are ordered one to another. And likewise, the good of individuals, although ordered to the good of the people, does not prevent such different ends causing their respective habits to differ specifically. But the habit ordered to the ultimate end is consequently more important and commands the other habits.

Question 50
On the Constitutive Parts of Practical Wisdom

[This question is divided into four articles, two of which are translated here.]

FIRST ARTICLE
Should We Designate Kingly Wisdom in Governance a Species of Practical Wisdom?

We thus proceed to the first inquiry. It seems that we should not designate kingly wisdom in governance a species of practical wisdom, for the following reasons:

---

[10]*Politics* III, 4 (1277b13–5).   [11]Ibid. (1277b20–1).

Obj. 1. Kingly wisdom in governing is ordered to maintaining justice, since the *Ethics* says that "the ruler is the guardian of justice."[1] Therefore, kingly wisdom in governing belongs to justice rather than to practical wisdom.

Obj. 2. The Philosopher says in the *Politics* that a kingdom is one of six kinds of regime.[2] But we do not understand the other five kinds of regime, namely, aristocracy, polity (also called timocracy), tyranny, oligarchy, and democracy, to signify species of practical wisdom. Therefore, neither should we understand kingdom to signify kingly wisdom in governance as a species of practical wisdom.

Obj. 3. Lawmaking belongs both to kings and other rulers and even to the people, as Isidore makes clear.[3] But the Philosopher in the *Ethics* designates lawmaking part of practical wisdom.[4] Therefore, it is inappropriate to substitute kingly wisdom in governance for lawmaking.

On the contrary, the Philosopher says in the *Politics* that "practical wisdom is the special virtue of rulers."[5] Therefore, there should be a special practical wisdom consisting of kingly wisdom in governance.

I answer that, as is clear from what I have said before,[6] ruling and commanding belong to practical wisdom, and so there is the special character of practical wisdom wherever there is the special character of governance and command in human affairs. But those responsible for ruling both themselves and the perfect community of a city or kingdom clearly have the special and complete character of governance. For the more extensive governance is, extending to many matters and achieving a higher end, the nearer perfect governance is. And so practical wisdom in its special and most complete character belongs to kings, who have authority to rule cities or kingdoms. And so we designate kingly wisdom in governance a species of practical wisdom.

Reply Obj. 1. Everything proper to moral virtue belongs to practical wisdom to direct. And so also we posit the right reasoning of practical wisdom in the definition of moral virtue, as I have said before.[7] And so also carrying out justice, since justice is ordered to the common good and belongs to the office of king, needs the guidance of practical wisdom. And so those two virtues, practical wisdom and justice, belong most to kings, as Jer. 23:5 says: "The king will rule and be wise, and he will decide cases and execute justice on the earth." But because direction belongs more to kings, and execution more to subjects, we designate kingly wisdom in

---

[1]Aristotle, *Ethics* V, 6 (1134b1–2).   [2]*Politics* III, 5 (1279a32–b10).
[3]*Etymologies* II, 10, n. 1 (PL 82:130); V, 10 (PL 82:200).
[4]*Ethics* VI, 8 (1141b25–9).   [5]*Politics* III, 4 (1277b25–6).
[6]ST II–II, Q. 47, AA 8, 12.
[7]ST II–II, Q. 47, A. 5, obj. 1; I–II, Q. 58, A. 2, *ad* 4.

governance a species of practical wisdom, which directs justice, rather than a species of justice, which executes practical wisdom.

Reply Obj. 2. Kingdom is the best regime, as the *Ethics* says.[8] And so we should designate kingdoms rather than other regimes as the political species of practical wisdom. But we should designate kingdoms as the political species of practical wisdom so as to include under kingdoms all the other good regimes, but not the bad regimes, which are contrary to virtue and so do not belong to practical wisdom.

Reply Obj. 3. The Philosopher designates kingly wisdom in governance from the chief activity of kings, namely, lawmaking. And although lawmaking belongs to rulers other than kings, it belongs to the others only insofar as they partake of kingly governance.

SECOND ARTICLE
Do We Appropriately Designate
Political Wisdom Part of Practical Wisdom?

We thus proceed to the second inquiry. It seems that we do not designate political wisdom part of practical wisdom, for the following reasons:

Obj. 1. Kingly wisdom in governing is part of political practical wisdom, as I have said.[9] But we should not contradistinguish parts from the whole of which they are parts. Therefore, we should not designate political wisdom a separate species of practical wisdom.

Obj. 2. Different objects distinguish different species of habit. But what kings need to command, and what subjects need to execute, have the same object. Therefore, we should not designate political wisdom, insofar as it belongs to subjects, a different species of practical wisdom from kingly wisdom in governing.

Obj. 3. Every subject is an individual person. But every individual person can direct himself or herself adequately by practical wisdom in general. Therefore, we should not designate another species of practical wisdom, a species called political.

On the contrary, the Philosopher says in the *Ethics*: "The part of practical wisdom that regards the political community is indeed the architectonic practical wisdom of lawmaking, but the part that regards individual situations has the general name *political wisdom*."[10]

---

[8]Aristotle, *Ethics* VIII, 10 (1160a35–6).   [9]ST II–II, Q. 48.

[10]*Ethics* VI, 7 (1141b24–9). Aristotle refers to the separate functions in Greek city-states of establishing basic laws and of applying those laws to individual cases. City founders did the former, and citizens in general assembly did the latter. We make a similar distinction in modern times, for example, between zoning

I answer that masters by their commands induce their slaves[11] to act, and rulers their subjects. But masters and rulers do so otherwise than causes induce irrational and inanimate things to act. For irrational and inanimate things, since they do not enjoy mastery of their activity by the exercise of free choice, do not induce themselves to act. Rather, other things induce them to act. And so their right governance resides only in the other things causing their actions, not in themselves. But other human beings by issuing commands induce slaves or any human subjects to act in such a way that the slaves or subjects proceed to act by the exercise of free choice. And so slaves and subjects need to have a right governance whereby they direct themselves to obey those in charge. And the species of practical wisdom called political belongs to this right governance.

Reply Obj. 1. As I have said,[12] kingly wisdom in governing is the most complete kind of practical wisdom. And so the practical wisdom of subjects, which falls short of the practical wisdom of kings in governing, keeps the general name of practical wisdom that we call political. Just so, in logic, convertible terms that do not signify the essence of something keep the general name *logical property.*

Reply Obj. 2. Different aspects of objects specifically differentiate habits, as is evident from what I have said before.[13] But kings indeed consider the same prospective actions from a more universal aspect than subjects do when they obey, since many subjects in carrying out various duties obey the same king. And so kingly wisdom in governing is related to the political wisdom of which we are speaking as a master builder's skill is related to the skills of construction workers.

Reply Obj. 3. Human beings direct themselves in relation to their own good by practical wisdom in general, but in relation to the common good by the political wisdom of which we are speaking.

On Kingship, to the King of Cyprus, Book I

Chapter One
What the Name *King* Signifies

We need at the outset of our work to explain what one should understand by the word *king.* And regarding all things ordered to an end, in

---

laws and zoning variances, although select boards rather than town meetings provide for the latter.   [11]See Glossary, s.v. *Slavery.*

[12]ST II–II, Q. 50, A. 1.   [13]ST II–II, Q. 47, A. 5; I–II, Q. 54, A. 2.

which things there may be this or that way of proceeding, something needs to give the direction whereby they arrive straightaway to the requisite end. For example, ships, which the force of various winds may toss in different directions, would not arrive at their destination unless the efforts of pilots were to guide the ships to port. And human beings have an end to the attainment of which their whole lives and actions are ordered, since those who act intelligently evidently act for the sake of an end. But human beings may advance in different ways toward their intended end, which the very diversity of human endeavors and activities makes clear. Therefore, human beings need something that directs them to their end.

And nature implants in all human beings the light of reason, which directs them in their activities toward their end. And if it were appropriate for human beings to live solitary, like many animals, they would indeed need no other direction to their end. Rather, each would be king unto self under God, the supreme king, since the light of reason divinely bestowed on each would direct individual human beings themselves in their actions. But human beings are by their nature social and political, living in community even more than every other animal. And natural necessity indeed makes this evident. For nature has in the case of other animals provided food, fur covering, means of defense (e.g., teeth, horns, claws, or at least fleetness for flight). But human beings have been constituted with none of these things provided by nature. Rather, human beings have instead been provided with reason, which enables them to provide all these things for themselves by the work of their hands. But a single human being does not suffice to provide all these things, since single human beings by themselves could not adequately make their way through life. Therefore, it is natural for human beings to live in community with many.

Moreover, nature has implanted in other animals indigenous structures regarding everything useful or harmful for them. For example, sheep by nature recognize wolves as enemies. Some animals by their naturally indigenous structure even recognize the medicinal plants and other things necessary to sustain their lives. But human beings by nature know only in a general way the things necessary to sustain their lives, so that they can arrive at knowledge of particular necessary things for human life by their power to reason from the first principles of nature. And individual human beings cannot attain all such things by their own reason. Therefore, human beings need to live in community, so that they assist one another, with different human beings engaged in discovering different things by reason (e.g., one in medicine, others in this or that).

This is made most clearly evident by the fact that human beings have the characteristic ability to use speech, whereby human beings can completely express their ideas to one another. Other animals indeed communicate their emotions in a general way (e.g., dogs express their anger by barking, and other animals their emotions in different ways). Therefore, human beings can communicate with one another more than any other animals we see living communally, such as cranes and ants and bees, can. Therefore, Solomon, contemplating this, says in Eccl. 4:9: "Two human beings are better than one, since they have the enrichment of mutual association."

Therefore, if human beings by nature live in association with many others, all of them need to have some power to govern them. For if there are many human beings, and they provide for their own individual interests, the people would split into different factions unless there were also to exist a power to provide for what belongs to the common good. Just so, even the body of a human being or any animal would disintegrate unless there were to exist a general regulative power in the body to strive for the common good of all the body's members. And Solomon, contemplating this, said in Prov. 11:14: "The people will be destroyed if there is no ruler."

And this happens in accord with reason. For what belongs to individuals, and what is common to all, are not the same. Human beings indeed differ by what is proper to each one and are united by what is common to all. But there are different causes of different things. Therefore, besides what causes individual human beings to act for their own good, there needs to be a power that causes them to act for the common good of the community. And so also regarding all things ordered to one thing, we find a power that governs other things. For example, in the universe of material substances, primary material substances, namely, heavenly bodies, govern other material substances by an order of God's providence,[1] and rational creatures by his order govern the use of all material substances. Also, in each human being, the soul governs the body, and reason governs the irascible and concupiscible parts of the soul. And likewise, one chief bodily member, whether the heart or the head, moves all the others. Therefore, every people needs to have a power that rules.

And regarding some things ordered to an end, there may be a right or wrong way of proceeding. And so also a people may be governed rightly or wrongly. And a people is governed rightly when it is guided to a suitable end, and wrongly when it is guided to an unsuitable end. And the end suitable to a community of free persons is different from the end suitable for a community of slaves, since free persons are their own agents, and slaves belong to others. Therefore, if a ruler should direct a community of

---

[1]Thomas is alluding to the Aristotelian theory that heavenly bodies like the sun and the moon cause the activity of earthly material things.

free persons for the common good of the people, there will be a right and just regime, as befits free persons. And if the governance of a ruler be ordered to the private good of the ruler and not for the common good of the people, there will be an unjust and wicked regime. And so also the Lord, speaking through Ezekiel, threatens such rulers in Ez. 34:2: "Woe to the shepherds of Israel who have fed themselves" so as to gain their own advantage. "Are not shepherds to feed their flock?" Shepherds of the flock should indeed seek the good of their flock, and every ruler the good of the people subject to him.

Therefore, if there be an unjust regime in the hands of only one person who seeks from the regime his own advantage, not the good of the people subject to him, we call such a ruler a tyrant, a name derived from strength, namely, in that he crushes by his power and does not rule by justice. And so also the ancients called all powerful persons tyrants. And if there be an unjust regime in the hands of several persons, not one, we call it oligarchy (i.e., rule by the few) if it is indeed in the hands of a few persons. This is a case where a few persons crush the people for the sake of riches, and it differs from tyranny only by the plurality of rulers. And if a wicked regime is in the hands of many, we call it democracy (i.e., rule of the people). This is a case where the mass of common citizens crush the rich by the power of their number. For then even the whole people will be as if a single tyrant.

And likewise, we also need to distinguish just regimes. For if a just regime is in the hands of many people, we call it by the general name *polity* (e.g., when a large number of warriors rule in a city or province). And if a just regime is in the hands of a few persons, who are also virtuous, we call it aristocracy (i.e., the best rule or rule by the best, whom we call aristocrats for that reason). And if a just regime is in the hands of only one person, we properly call that person king. And so the Lord says through Ezekiel in Ez. 37:24: "My servant David will be king over them, and there will be one shepherd of all of them." And this clearly shows that it belongs to the idea of a king that there is one person who rules, and that he is a shepherd who seeks the common good of the people and not his own individual good.

And because it belongs to human beings to live in a community, since they are insufficient to secure the necessities of life for themselves if they should remain solitary, the unity of the people is necessarily more complete the more intrinsically self-sufficient it will be to provide the necessities of life. There is indeed a sufficiency of life in one family comprising one household, namely, regarding natural acts of nutrition and procreation and such like. And there is a sufficiency of life in a district, namely, regarding things proper to one occupation. And there is a sufficiency of life in a city, that is, a perfect community, namely, regarding all the necessities of life, but still more in a province because of the need to wage war and afford mutual assistance against enemies. And so we refer to those who rule perfect communities, that is, cities or provinces, as kings in the fullest sense. And we call those who rule households fathers of families, not kings, although fathers are analogous to kings, and we for that reason sometimes call kings fathers of their peoples.

Therefore, it is clear from what I have said that a king is a single person who governs the people of a city or province for the sake of the common good. And so Solomon says in Eccl. 5:8: "The king rules all the territory subject to him."

Chapter Six
How to Prevent Kings Lapsing into Tyranny

Therefore, since we should choose a regime under one ruler, which is the best regime, and he may lapse into tyranny, which is the worst regime, as is clear from what I have said before,[2] we should work diligently to protect the people from kings lapsing into tyranny.

And first of all, it is necessary that those responsible elevate to kingship men of such character that makes it unlikely that they will lapse into tyranny. And so Samuel, commending God's providence regarding the establishment of a king [of Israel], says in 1 Sam. 13:14: "The Lord sought for himself a man after his own heart, and the Lord commanded him to be the leader of his people." Second, governance of the kingdom should be so arranged that there is no opportunity for a king in power to become a tyrant. At the same time that a king is installed, his power should be so moderated that he cannot easily lapse into tyranny. And we indeed will need to consider subsequently how such things are accomplished. And third, provision should be made for how to be able to deal with tyranny if a king were to lapse into it.

And it is indeed more advantageous to tolerate a lesser tyranny for a time, if there has been no excessive tyranny, than by undertaking action against the tyrant to bring on many worse dangers than the tyranny itself. For example, it may be that those who undertake action against the tyrant cannot prevail, and then the enraged tyrant may become more cruel. And if one could prevail against the tyrant, the worst kind of disagreements among the people very often arises, whether during the insurrection against the tyrant or after his deposition, when the people divide into factions regarding the constitution of the regime. It also sometimes happens

---

[2] *On Kingship* I, 3.

that after the people expel the tyrant with someone's assistance, the latter, once in power, becomes a tyrant. And fearing to suffer from a third party what he himself did to the first tyrant, the second tyrant crushes his subjects with still worse slavery. For it regularly so happens in the case of tyranny that a subsequent tyrant becomes worse than his predecessor when the subsequent tyrant does not abandon the previous wrongs and himself even plans new severities out of the malice of his heart. And so at the time when everyone in Syracuse desired the death of Dionysius, an elderly woman prayed over and over that he would be unharmed and outlive her. And after the tyrant learned about this, he asked her why she did so. Then the woman said: "When I was a girl, we had an oppressive tyrant, and I wished for another ruler. And after the tyrant was killed, a harsher one succeeded the latter shortly afterwards, and I thought that it would be a great blessing if the successor's rule would also be terminated. We then had a still harsher ruler, yourself. And so if you were removed, a worse tyrant will replace you."[3]

And if an excessive tyranny should be intolerable, some thought that it was for virtuous, courageous men to kill the tyrant and expose themselves to the danger of death in order to liberate the people. And we also have an example of this in the Old Testament. For Jgs. 3:15–5 relates how a certain Ehud killed Eglon, king of Moab, who was oppressing the people of God with a harsh slavery, by thrusting a dagger into the king's thigh,[4] and Ehud was made a judge of the people. But such conduct is not in accord with apostolic teaching. For Peter teaches us in 1 Pet. 2: 18–9 "to be reverently submissive both to good and gentle rulers and to those who are overbearing. For it is a favor if one unjustly suffering misfortunes should undergo them out of regard for God." And so when many Roman emperors were tyrannically persecuting the Christian faith, and a large number of both nobles and commoners were being converted to the faith, the faithful are praised for not resisting and for patiently undergoing death for Christ, although they were equipped to resist. This is clearly evident in the case of the dedicated Theban legion.[5] And we should judge that Ehud killed an enemy rather than a ruler of the people, although a tyrant. And so also we read in the Old Testament (2 Kgs. 14:5–6) that the killers of Joash, king of Judah, were put to death, although Joash had departed from worship of God, but that their children were spared according to the Law's prescription.

---

[3]On this story, cf. Valerius Maximus, *Memorable Deeds and Sayings* VI, 2.

[4]In the biblical text, Ehud hid the dagger on his thigh and thrust it into Eglon's belly.

[5]Cf. *Acts of the Saints* (September) VI:308.

And it would be dangerous to the people and its rulers if individuals on their own authority were to attempt to kill their rulers, even tyrants. For evil persons expose themselves to such dangers more often than good persons do. And evil persons usually find the rule of kings no better than the rule of tyrants. This is because, as Solomon says in Prov. 20:26, "the wise king puts the wicked to flight." Therefore, such presumption by individuals would risk greater danger to the people by losing good kings than any relief by removing tyrants.

And it seems that public authority rather than individuals' private initiative should take action against the severity of tyrants. First, indeed, if a people should have the right to provide itself with a king, the same people can justly depose the king it has installed, or curtail his power if he should abuse the power tyrannically. Nor should we think that such a people in deposing a tyrant acts unfaithfully, even if it had previously subjected itself to him in perpetuity. For the tyrant himself deserved this, since he acted unfaithfully in not governing the people as the duty of kingship requires, and subjects need not keep their pact with him. Thus the Romans deposed Tarquin the Proud, whom they had accepted as king, because of his tyranny and that of his sons, and substituted a lesser power, namely, that of consuls. So also the Roman Senate killed Domitian, who was the successor of the most gentle emperors Vespatian, his father, and Titus, his brother, when Domitian practiced tyranny. And a decree of the Senate justly and beneficially nullified every wicked deed of his. As a result, a decree of the Senate returned to Ephesus Saint John the Evangelist,[6] whom the same Domitian had exiled to the island of Patmos.

And if a higher power has the right to provide a people with its king, the people should seek relief from the wickedness of a tyrant from the higher power. Thus when the Jews lodged a complaint with Emperor Augustus against Archelaus, who had now come to the throne in Judea after the death of Herod, his father, and was imitating his father's wickedness, Augustus indeed initially diminished Archelaus' power by taking away his title and giving half of his kingdom to his two brothers. Later, when Archelaus was not restrained from tyranny in this way, Emperor Tiberius exiled him to Lyons, a city in Gaul.[7]

But if the people should be altogether unable to obtain human help against a tyrant, it should have recourse to the universal king, God, who is "a helper in times of oppression and distress."[8] For it lies in his power to

---

[6]Cf. Eusebius, *Chronicles* II (PG 19:551); Jerome, *On Illustrious Men* 9 (PL 23:625).
[7]According to Jerome, *Commentary on 7the Gospel of Matthew* II, 22 (PL 26:28).
[8]Ps. 9:9.

turn the cruel heart of a tyrant to gentleness, as Solomon says in Prov. 21:1: "The heart of the king is in the hands of God; God will turn it howsoever he wishes." For example, he turned the cruelty of the king Assuerus, who was planning the death of the Jews, to gentleness.[9] He so turned the cruel king Nebuchadnezzar to such piety that the king became a herald of divine power: "Now, therefore," he said, "I, Nebuchadnezzar, praise, exalt, and glorify the king of heaven, since all his works are true, and all his ways judgments, and he can lay low those who walk arrogantly."[10]

And he can remove those he deems unworthy of conversion from our midst or reduce them to a lower position, as Sir. 10:7 says: "God has destroyed the thrones of proud leaders and raised the meek to sit in their place." For example, he, seeing the plight of his people in Egypt and hearing its cries, cast down the tyranny of Pharoah and Pharoah's army into the sea.[11] He deposed the aforementioned Nebuchadnezzar from the royal throne because of prior arrogance, cast him out of human society, and transformed him into the likeness of a beast.[12] Nor do his hands have so short a reach that he cannot liberate his people from tyrants. For he promises his people through Isaiah in Is. 14:3 that it will be given rest "from the toil and the beatings and the harsh slavery" under which it had previously served. And he says through Ezekiel in Ez. 34:10: "I shall free my flock from their jaws," namely, the jaws of shepherds who feed themselves rather than the flock. But the people, in order to merit to gain this benefit from God, should stop sinning, since he allows the wicked to rule as a punishment of sin, as the Lord says through Hosea in Hos. 13:11: "I shall in my anger against you give you kings." And Job 34:30 says that "he causes hypocrites to rule because of the people's sins." Therefore, we should eliminate sin if we wish to eliminate the scourge of tyrants.

---

[9]Est. 15:11.   [10]Dan. 4:34.
[11]Ex. 14:23–8.   [12]Dan. 4:30.

Glossary

Action: *activity*. There are two basic kinds of activity. One kind, transitive activity, is efficient causality, that is, action that produces an effect in something else. The second kind, immanent action, perfects only the being that acts. Immanent action produces effects in living finite beings. Plants have the immanent activities of nutrition, growth, and reproduction. Animals have, in addition, the immanent activities of sense perception and sense appetites. Human beings have, in addition, the immanent activities of intellection and willing. *See* Cause.

Appetite: *the desire or striving of finite beings to actualize potentialities.* Nonliving material beings have natural appetites. Plants have, in addition, the vegetative appetites of nutrition, growth, and reproduction. Animals have, in addition, sense appetites. Human beings have, in addition, an intellectual or rational appetite, the will. *See* Concupiscible, Irascible, Will.

Cause: *something that contributes to the being or coming-to-be of something else.* The term refers primarily to an efficient cause, that is, a cause that by its activity produces an effect. For example, a builder and those who work under the builder are efficient causes of the house they construct. A final cause is the end for the sake of which an efficient cause acts. For example, a builder builds a house to provide a dwelling suitable for human habitation (objective purpose) and to make money if the house is to be sold (subjective purpose). An exemplary cause is the idea or model of a desired effect in the mind of an intellectual efficient cause that preconceives the effect. For example, a builder preconceives the form of the house the builder intends to build. Efficient, final, and exemplary causes are extrinsic to the effects they produce. In addition, form, which makes an effect to be what it is, and matter, which receives the form, are correlative intrinsic causes. For example, houses are composed of bricks and mortar (the matter), which are given a structure or shape (the form). *See* End, Form, Intention, Matter.

Charity: *the supernatural virtue whereby one is characteristically disposed to love God above all things and to love all other things for his sake. See* Virtue.

Concupiscence: *the inclinations of human beings' sense appetites toward actions contrary to the order of reason. The inclinations are not completely subject to reason.* Concupiscence is not to be identified with the concupiscible appetites as such. *See* Concupiscible, Will.

Concupiscible: *a sense appetite for something pleasant.* Love and hate, desire and aversion, joy and sorrow are movements of concupiscible appetites. *See* Appetite, Irascible.

Conscience: *the dictate of reason that one should or should not do something.* *See* Synderesis.

Emotions: *movements of sense appetites.* Emotions may be ordinate (in accord with right reason) or inordinate (contrary to right reason). Emotions involve either desire for pleasant things or repugnance regarding difficult things. *See* Concupiscible, Irascible, Moral Virtues.

End: *the object for the sake of which something acts.* The end may be intrinsic or extrinsic. The end is intrinsic if it belongs to the nature of an active thing. The end is extrinsic if it is the conscious object of a rational being's action. *See* Cause.

Essence: *that which makes things what they substantially are.* For example, the human essence makes human beings to be what they are as substances, namely, rational animals. When the essence of a being is considered as the ultimate source of the being's activities and development, it is called the being's nature. For example, human nature is the ultimate source of specifically human activities (activities of reason and activities according to reason). *See* Form, Property (2).

Form: *that which makes things to be the kind of things they are or to possess additional attributes.* For example, the human form makes human beings human, and other forms make them so tall and so heavy. *See* Essence, Matter.

Genus: *see* Species.

Habit: *the characteristic disposition or inclination to be or to act in a certain way.* Habits belong chiefly to the soul, that is, to the intellect or the will. They may be innate or acquired, natural or supernatural, good or bad. For example, the habit of logical argumentation belongs to the intellect; the habit of justice belongs to the will; the habits of the first principles of theoretical and practical reason are innate; the habit of cleanliness is acquired; the habit of courage is natural; the habit of faith is supernatural; the habit of generosity is good; the habit of stinginess is bad. Habits belong secondarily, not chiefly, to the body, as the latter is disposed or made apt to be readily at the service of the soul's activities. *See* Virtue.

Intellect: *the human faculty of understanding, judging, and reasoning.* Thomas Aquinas, following Aristotle, holds that there is an active power of the intellect that moves the passive or potential power of the intellect to understand the essence of material things, to form judgments, and to reason deductively. *See* Reason.

Intellectual Virtues: *virtues consisting of the right characteristic disposition of the intellect toward truth.* Theoretical intellectual virtues concern understanding first principles, scientific knowledge, and theoretical wisdom. Practical intellectual virtues concern practical wisdom and skills. *See* Practical Wisdom, Principle, Science, Theoretical Wisdom.

Intention: *striving for things.* Human beings, in their specifically human acts, strive for things as their reason understands the things to be good. Irrational animals strive for things as their senses perceive the things to be good. Other material things strive for things as their natures determine them to act. *See* Appetite, Cause, End.

Irascible: *a sense appetite for a useful object that can be attained only with difficulty.* The object does not seem pleasant and can be attained only by overcoming opposition. Hope and despair, fear and anger are movements of irascible appetites. *See* Appetite, Concupiscible.

Justice: *the moral virtue consisting of the right characteristic disposition of the will to render to others what is due them.* This is the special virtue of justice, and there are two particular kinds. One kind, commutative justice, concerns the duties of individuals and groups to other individuals and groups. The other kind, distributive justice, concerns the duties of the community to insure that individuals and groups receive a share of the community's goods proportional to the individuals' and groups' contributions to the community. But justice in general is moral virtue in general, insofar as all moral virtues can be directed to the common good. Thomas calls such justice legal justice because human laws prescribe the moral virtues expected of citizens. *See* Moral Virtues, Virtue.

Kingly Wisdom: *the archetype of political wisdom in governance. See* Political Wisdom, Practical Wisdom.

Law: *an order of reason, for the common good, by one with authority, and promulgated.* For Thomas Aquinas, the archetypical law is God's plan for the universe and everything he creates. Aquinas calls this plan the eternal law. Human beings, as rational creatures, can understand God's plan for them and can judge what behavior it requires of them, and they in this way participate in the eternal law. Aquinas calls this participation in the eternal law the natural law. And human beings need to establish laws for their communities. These human laws either adopt conclusions from the general precepts of the natural law (e.g., do not commit murder) or further specify the precepts (e.g., drive on the right side of the road). Aquinas calls those human laws that are proximate conclusions from the general precepts of the natural law the common law of peoples (*jus gentium*), and he calls those human laws that are more remote conclusions from, or further specifications of, the general precepts civil laws.

Matter: *the stuff or subject matter out of which things are constituted.* See Cause, Form.

Moral Virtues: *virtues consisting of the right characteristic disposition of the will toward requisite ends (for example, just, courageous, moderate deeds).* Reason directs moral virtues, theoretical reason by understanding their ends, and practical wisdom by choosing means to those ends. Moral virtues concern the mean between too much and too little. One moral virtue, justice, concerns external things. Other moral virtues concern control of emotions. *See* Emotions, Justice, Practical Wisdom.

Nature: *see* Essence.

Political Community: *the organized community wherein and whereby human beings are able fully to achieve their proper excellence or well-being.* Like Aristotle, Thomas Aquinas holds that human beings are by their nature social and political animals. Human beings need to associate with one another for self-defense and economic development, but they also and especially need to associate with one another for their full intellectual and moral development. Only an organized community of a certain size can be self-sufficient to achieve these goals. Political community thus differs from the state, which is the supreme agency responsible for organizing the community, and differs from government, which is the machinery and personnel of the state. Unlike Aristotle, however, Aquinas envisioned a supernatural end for human beings beyond their temporal well-being and, by reason of that supernatural end, the membership of Christians in another, divinely established community, the church. The relation between the natural and the supernatural ends of human beings, and the relation between the two communities promoting those ends, were important concerns of Aquinas. *See* Polity.

Political Wisdom: *the practical intellectual virtue consisting of the right characteristic disposition to reason about matters of governance.* Kingly wisdom is the archetype of political wisdom in rulers, and other kinds of rulers share in this wisdom in a lesser way. Citizens or subjects of the rulers have another kind of political wisdom, one that consists of the right characteristic disposition toward rulers' governance. *See* Kingly Wisdom, Practical Wisdom.

Polity: *the regime or constitution that gives a political community its distinctive form.* For Thomas Aquinas, polity also has the meaning of a particular regime or constitution that mixes or combines elements of a rule that is monarchic (rule by one best person), aristocratic (rule by the few best persons), and democratic (rule by the multitude). Such a regime includes only limited popular participation. *See* Political Community.

Power: *the active capacity to perform a certain kind of activity.* For example, the intellect and the will are powers of human beings.

Practical Wisdom (Prudence): *the intellectual virtue consisting of the right characteristic disposition to reason about what human beings should or should not do.* Practical wisdom concerns human action and so differs from theoretical wisdom, which concerns the ultimate causes of things irrespective of related human action. Theoretical reason understands the ends of moral virtues, and practical wisdom chooses the mean to achieve those ends. As the most important natural virtue connected with human action, practical wisdom is sometimes considered as if it were one of the moral virtues. *See* Habit, Moral Virtues, Political Wisdom, Theoretical Wisdom, Virtue.

Principle: *the universal major premise of an argument.* Principles presupposing no principle, or at least no principle other than the principle of contradiction, are called first principles. There are theoretical first principles (e.g., everything coming to be has a cause) and practical first principles (e.g., do good, avoid evil, live sociably with others).

Property (1): *any kind of material possession.*

Property (2): *a quality or characteristic that necessarily belongs to something but is neither part of the thing's essence nor part of the thing's definition.* For example, the ability of human beings to use speech to convey ideas is a characteristic proper to them but not part of their essence or definition (rational animal).

Reason: *(1) the process of drawing conclusions from principles; (2) the power to draw conclusions from principles; (3) the power of the intellect in general.* In the selections in this work, Thomas Aquinas frequently uses the term in the third sense. *See* Intellect.

Regime: *see* Polity.

Science (Aristotelian): *knowledge about things through knowledge of their causes.* Science studies the efficient, final, material, and formal causes of things. Physical, psychological, and social sciences study the secondary causes of material and human things, and philosophy (metaphysics) studies the first causes of being as such. For Aristotle, philosophy is the highest science. For Thomas Aquinas, theology, the study of God in the light of Christian revelation, is the highest science. *See* Cause, Intellect, Intellectual Virtues, Theoretical Wisdom.

Slavery: *involuntary servitude.* In medieval society, war captives became slaves, and their servitude could be terminated only by ransom or treaty. The feudal institutions of serfdom and vassalage were similar to slavery in that serfs, vassals, and their children were bound to certain lifetime duties to their lords and masters. But serfs and vassals, unlike the slaves of ancient Greece and Rome and those of the antebellum American South, had rights that their lords were in theory bound to respect.

Species: *the substantial identity of material things insofar as that identity is common to many things.* The species concept (e.g., human being) is composed of a genus concept (e.g., animal), which indicates the essence of particular material things in an incompletely determined way, and a specific difference (e.g., rational), which distinguishes different kinds of things of the same genus. The species concept, or definition, thus expresses the whole substance or essence of a particular kind of material thing.

Subject (1): *that in which something else inheres.* In the strict sense, subjects are the substances underlying accidental characteristics. For example, human beings are the subjects of their powers and acts. In a broader sense, powers can be considered the subjects of the powers' acts. For example, the intellect is the subject of intellectual acts.

Subject (2): *a human being bound to obey another human being.* For example, British citizens are British subjects, that is, bound to obey British authorities.

Synderesis: *habitual understanding of the first principles governing human action.* This is an innate disposition. Human beings are disposed by their rational nature to recognize that they should seek the good proper to their human nature and should avoid things contrary to it. The human good involves preserving one's life in reasonable ways, mating and raising offspring in reasonable ways, seeking truth, and living cooperatively with others in an organized society. *See* Habit.

Theoretical Wisdom: *the intellectual virtue consisting of the right characteristic disposition to reason about the ultimate causes of things.* See Intellectual Virtues, Practical Wisdom, Virtue.

Virtue: *human excellence.* Virtue is a perduring quality and so a characteristic disposition. Thomas Aquinas distinguishes three kinds of virtue: intellectual, moral, and theological. Intellectual virtues have intellectual activities as their object. Concerning theoretical truth, intellectual virtues comprise understanding first principles, scientific knowledge, and theoretical wisdom. Concerning practical truth, intellectual virtues comprise practical wisdom and skills. Moral virtues consist of characteristic readiness to act in practical matters as practical wisdom dictates. Practical wisdom and moral virtues may be acquired or infused. There are three infused theological virtues: faith, hope, and charity. *See* Charity, Habit, Intellectual Virtues, Moral Virtues, Practical Wisdom, Principle, Science, Theoretical Wisdom.

Will: *the human intellectual (rational) appetite, the intellectual faculty of desire.* The will necessarily desires the ultimate human perfection, happiness, but freely desires particular goods, since the latter are only partially good.

Wisdom: *see* Kingly Wisdom, Political Wisdom, Practical Wisdom, Theoretical Wisdom.

Select Bibliography

On Aristotle's philosophical system, see:

Ackrill, J. L. *Aristotle, the Philosopher.* Oxford: Oxford University Press, 1981.

Barnes, J. *Aristotle.* Oxford: Oxford University Press, 1982.

Grene, Marjorie. *A Portrait of Aristotle.* Chicago: University of Chicago Press, 1967.

Robinson, Timothy A. *Aristotle in Outline.* Indianapolis: Hackett Publishing Co., 1995.

Veatch, Henry B. *Aristotle; A Contemporary Appreciation.* Bloomington: Indiana University Press, 1974.

On Aristotle's political theory, see:

Jaffa, Harry. "Aristotle," in *History of Political Philosophy*, second edition, pp. 64–130. Edited by Leo Strauss and Joseph Cropsey. Chicago: University of Chicago Press, 1981.

On the rediscovery and reception of Aristotle in the medieval world, see:

Steenberghen, Fernand van. *Aristotle in the West: The Origins of Latin Aristotelianism.* Translated by L. Johnson. New York: Humanities Press, 1970.

For an up-to-date, scholarly chronology of the life and works of Thomas Aquinas, see:

Torrell, Jean-Pierre. *St. Thomas Aquinas.* Volume 1: *The Person and His Work.* Translated by Robert Royal. Washington: The Catholic University of America Press, 1996.

Tugwell, Simon. "Introduction to St. Thomas," in *Albert and Thomas: Selected Writings*, pp. 201–351. New York: Paulist Press, 1988.

For an accurate and well-integrated English condensation of the Summa, *see:*

Aquinas, Thomas. *Summa Theologiae: A Concise Translation.* Edited and translated by Timothy McDermott. Westminster, Md.: Christian Classics, 1989.

For a guide to the context of Aquinas' thought, see:

Pieper, Joseph. *Guide to Thomas Aquinas.* Translated by Richard and Clara Winston. New York: Pantheon, 1962.

For expositions of Aquinas' general philosophy, see:

Copleston, Frederick. *A History of Philosophy.* Volume 2, pp. 302–424. Westminster, Md.: Newman, 1950. Also available in Image Books, Doubleday. Volume 2, part 2.

Davies, Brian. *The Thought of Thomas Aquinas.* Oxford: Oxford University Press, 1992.

Gilson, Etienne. *The Christian Philosophy of St. Thomas Aquinas*. New York: Random House, 1956.

McInerny, Ralph. *A First Glance at St. Thomas Aquinas: A Handbook for Peeping Thomists.* Notre Dame, Ind.: University of Notre Dame Press, 1990.

On the ethics of Aquinas in general, see:

Aquinas, Thomas. *Commentary on the Ethics.* Translated by Charles I. Litzenger. Chicago: Regnery, 1963.

——————. *The De Malo of Thomas Aquinas.* Translated by Richard J. Regan, with introduction by Brian Davies. New York: Oxford University Press, 2001.

——————. *Virtue: Way to Happiness* [selections from the *Summa*]. Translated by Richard J. Regan. Scranton: Scranton University Press, 1999.

Elders, Leon J., and Hedwig, K., editors. *The Ethics of St. Thomas Aquinas.* Studi tomistici 25. Vatican City: Libreria Editrice Vaticana, 1984.

——————. *Lex et Libertas: Freedom and Law According to St. Thomas Aquinas.* Studi tomistici 30. Vatican City: Libreria Editrice Vaticana, 1987.

Finnis, John M. *Aquinas: Moral, Political, and Legal Theory.* Oxford: Oxford University Press, 1999.

Flannery, Kevin L. *Acts amid Precepts.* Washington: The Catholic University of America Press, 2001.

Mullady, Brian T. *The Meaning of the Term Moral in St. Thomas Aquinas.* Studi tomistici 27. Vatican City: Libreria Editrice Vaticana, 1986.

Stevens, G. "Moral Obligation in St. Thomas," in *The Modern Schoolman* 40 (1962–1963): 1–21.

On choice and human action, see:

Donagan, Alan. *Human Ends and Human Action: An Exploration in St. Thomas's Treatment.* Milwaukee: Marquette University Press, 1985.

——————. *Choice: The Essential Element in Human Action.* New York: Routledge, 1987.

Powell, Ralph. *Freely Chosen Reality.* Washington: University Press of America, 1983.

Sokolowski, Robert. *Moral Action: A Phenomenological Study.* Bloomington: Indiana University Press, 1985.

On virtue, see:

Geach, Peter. *The Virtues.* Cambridge: Cambridge University Press, 1977.

Hibbs, Thomas. *Virtue's Splendor: Wisdom, Prudence, and the Human Good.* New York: Fordham University Press, 2001.

Pieper, Joseph. *The Four Cardinal Virtues: Prudence, Fortitude, Justice, and Temperance.* New York: Harcourt, Brace, and World, 1965.

Porter, Jean. *The Recovery of Virtue: The Relevance of Aquinas for Christian Ethics.* Louisville: John Knox Press, 1990.

On practical wisdom, see:

Westberg, Daniel. *Right Practical Reason: Aristotle, Action, and Prudence in Aquinas.* Oxford: Oxford University Press, 1994.

On Thomist natural law, see:

Armstrong, Ross A. *Primary and Secondary Precepts in Thomistic Natural Law Teaching.* The Hague: Nijhoff, 1966.

Lee, Patrick. "Permanence of the Ten Commandments: St. Thomas and His Modern Commentators," in *Theological Studies* 42 (1981): 422–43.

May, William. *Becoming Human: An Introduction to Christian Ethics.* Dayton: Plaum, 1975.

Regan, Richard J. "The Human Person and Moral Norms." Chapter 1 of *The Moral Dimensions of Politics*, pp. 12–28. New York: Oxford University Press, 1986.

Reilly, James P. *St. Thomas on Law.* Etienne Gilson Series 12. Toronto: Pontifical Institute of Medieval Studies, 1990.

Rhonheimer, Martin. *Natural Law and Practical Reason: A Thomist View of Moral Autonomy.* Translated by Gerald Malsbary. New York: Fordham University Press, 1999.

Simon, Yves. *The Tradition of Natural Law: A Philosopher's Reflections.* New York: Fordham University Press, 1965.

On contemporary interpretations of natural law, see:

Finnis, John M. *Natural Law and Natural Rights.* Oxford: Clarendon Press, 1980.

——————. *Fundamentals of Ethics.* Washington: Georgetown University Press, 1983.

George, Robert P. *Natural Law Theory: Contemporary Essays.* Oxford: Oxford University Press, 1992.

Hittinger, Russell. *Critique of the New Natural Law Theory.* Notre Dame: University of Notre Dame Press, 1987.

Kaczor, Christopher. *Proportionalism and the Natural Law Tradition.* Washington: The Catholic University of America Press, 2002.

On Aquinas' political philosophy, see:

Aquinas, Thomas. "Commentary on the Politics" [selections], in *Medieval Political Philosophy*, pp. 298–334. Edited by Ralph Lerner and Muhsin Mahdi. Translated by Ernest L. Fortin and Peter D. O'Neill. New York: Free Press, 1963.

Bigongiari, Dino. "Introduction." *The Political Ideas of Saint Thomas Aquinas*, pp. vii–xxxvii. New York: Hafner, 1953.

Finnis, John M. *Aquinas: Moral, Political, and Legal Theory.* Oxford: Oxford University Press, 1999.

Fortin, Ernest L. "St. Thomas Aquinas," in *History of Political Philosophy*, second edition, pp. 223–50. Edited by Leo Strauss and Joseph Cropsey. Chicago: University of Chicago Press, 1981.

Maritain, Jacques. *Man and the State.* Chicago: University of Chicago Press, 1951.

Regan, Richard J. "Aquinas on Political Obedience and Disobedience," in *Thought* 56 (March 1981): 77–88.

――――――. "The Human Person and Organized Society: Aquinas." Chapter 2 of *The Moral Dimensions of Politics*, pp. 37–46. New York: Oxford University Press, 1986.

For a Thomist philosophy of democracy, see:

Simon, Yves. *Philosophy of Democratic Government.* Chicago: University of Chicago Press, 1961.

On recent bibliography on Aquinas, see:

Ingardia, Richard. *Thomas Aquinas: International Bibliography, 1977–1990.* Bowling Green: Philosophical Documentation Center, Bowling Green State University, 1993.

Index